William Rasch (ed.)

»Tragic Choices«

Luhmann on Law
and States of Exception

Herausgeber:
Dirk Baecker, Zeppelin University, Friedrichshafen
Cornelia Bohn, Universität Luzern
William Rasch, Indiana University, Bloomington
Urs Stäheli, Universität Basel
Rudolf Stichweh, Universität Luzern

Redaktion:
Johannes F. K. Schmidt

ISBN 978-3-8282-0457-7
ISSN 0948-423-X

© Lucius & Lucius Verlagsgesellschaft mbH, Gerokstraße 51, D-70184 Stuttgart
   Tel. (+49) (0)711/24 20 60, Fax (+49) (0)711/24 20 88
   E-Mail: lucius@luciusverlag.com. Internet: www.luciusverlag.com

Satz: Sibylle Egger, Stuttgart
Druck: Rosch-Buch, Scheßlitz

Printed in Germany

SOZIALE SYSTEME

ZEITSCHRIFT FÜR SOZIOLOGISCHE THEORIE

Jahrgang 14 (2008), Heft 1

»Tragic Choices«
Luhmann on Law and States of Exception
ed. by William Rasch

Inhalt

2

Soziale Systeme 14 (2008), Heft 1, S. 3-17

William Rasch

Introduction: The Form of the Problem

Abstract: In asking the question about indispensable norms, Luhmann does not look to give a normative answer, but rather explores what he sees as the »form of the problem.« This introduction places Luhmann's discussion of undecidability and the aporias of communication media of the various function systems within the larger »form of the problem« of modernity as Luhmann sees it, in particular the dissociation of reason and moral order. This introduction then uses this larger picture to examine the arguments of the various contributors to the volume.

I

The aim of this issue of *Soziale Systeme* is, yet again, to encourage the Anglophone world to engage with Niklas Luhmann's brand of systems theory. As in so many other ways, the United States remains obdurate, but interest in Luhmann's work, especially in the areas of political theory and law, has taken hold in the United Kingdom. To accelerate further engagement and perhaps to familiarize German-speaking readers more with British and North American scholars working in these areas, we present seven responses to two essays by Luhmann published here in English translation: »Are There Still Indispensable Norms in our Society« (hereafter: »Norms«; Luhmann 2008) and »Beyond Barbarism« (hereafter: »Barbarism«; Luhmann 2008a). As readers of these pages will see, Luhmann raises issues, using strikingly topical examples, that have become even more theoretically and emotionally fraught since their original publication in the early to mid-1990s. The question to be asked of these examples (e.g. torture or the *favelas*) is to what they point. To themselves? Or to the structure of Luhmann's social theory? When entertaining, for example, the legitimacy of torture in extreme cases, is Luhmann more interested in settling the question or in observing how best to pose the problem? Luhmann explicitly claims the latter. Indeed, the need for more complex modes of observation that ›adequately‹ capture the intricate contours of social structures and the problems that may inhere in them became Luhmann's stock answer to those who, in their insistent defense of the necessity for critical or normative theory, accuse the systems theorist of complacency and conservatism; and Luhmann does not pass the opportunity of repeating his demand for greater theoretical complexity in the texts translated here. But in the responses we solicited from scholars who work within the ambit of systems theory as well as from those who view Luhmann's contribution to social thought in a more negative light, we received both answers. To put it in a nutshell: Those who approach the problems raised by Luhmann from a perspective informed by systems theory tend to treat norms as social facts and ask of their function; others approach the discussion of norms normatively, remaining, as it were, on the level of the self-description, not the social or *wissenschaftlich* description, of norms. The latter group, in other words, seems to exemplify a more immediate concern with upholding legal and moral norms in »our society« that the former group attempts to observe and explain. Though Luhmann might have denied theoretical *Satisfaktionsfähigkeit* to the »normative« thinkers represented in this volume,[1] their enactment of the steadfast, counterfactual expectations that, according to Luhmann, necessarily characterize adherence to legal norms serves as exemplary and instructive model of the behavior under investigation. In the various responses, therefore, we have not only descriptions (of Luhmann's description) of the problem, but also explicit, normative answers to the dilemmas the examples pose. In both sets of responses, criticism of »the master« is not neglected.

Before allowing Luhmann and his interlocutors to have their say, I offer some opening reflections.

II

In »Norms«, Luhmann (2008, 18) enjoins us to imagine the following situation:

> You are a high-level law enforcement officer. In your country – it could be Germany in the not-too-distant future – there are many left- and right-wing terrorists. Every day there are murders, fire-bombings, the killing and injury of countless innocent people. You have captured the leader of such a group. Presumably, if you tortured him, you could save many lives – 10, 100, 1000 – we could vary the situation. Would you do it?

»One can vary the hypothetical case,« he adds. »The terrorists have a nuclear bomb, and it must be found and disarmed. Would you use torture?« Empirically we know the answer. Yes, almost every one of us »ordinary men« (and women) would be capable of doing it, and worse, under the (im)proper circumstances.[2] But the question is not empirical. »Would you do it?« asks for a normative answer. Still, to whom is this question addressed? To *you*? Would *you* do it? Not, at any rate, to the sociologist. »As a sociologist, one is interested in the *problem* … in the *form of the problem*.« As to any concrete answer, »One can only get it wrong. It is a matter of ›tragic choice‹.« (2008, 19) Pre-

---

1 On theoretical *Satisfaktionsfähigkeit*, see Moeller 2008.
2 Reference is to Browning 1998. See especially the references to the Zimbardo and Milgram experiments, 167-68, 171-176, 184.

cisely because the question is »ultimately undecidable,« because, as Luhmann implies, no set of rules or definitive guidelines can provide one and only one legitimate answer, the »form of the problem« can be of no direct help to one struggling with the dilemma. Understanding the problem, observing its »form,« in no way provides an unambiguous answer to the unavoidable challenge of the question, »Would you do it?« Yet, proper observation of the form of the problem must do something, otherwise why the following claim that ends his essay? »Ultimately, this situation confronts us with the question: What can we do? But before we can ask that one, there is a vital preliminary question: How can one observe and describe adequately?« (2008, 35) Why is this preliminary question vital when its answer will still leave us with ultimate undecidability? Is it both preliminary and vital because »tragic choices« and resultant undecidability *presuppose* a particular way of observing, a particular form of the problem, *Luhmann's* form of the problem?

I think it is fair to answer »yes« to that last question. This is not to say that Luhmann rigs the game, but that he works within a long-standing tradition and draws what seem to be the necessary consequences from it. The legal form of the problem of norms is but a particular manifestation of the general form of the problem (and solution) Luhmann calls modernity. We will see that to observe »adequately,« as he instructs us to, is to recognize limits, but also, in an odd, almost Nietzschean way, to embrace fate.

Readers of Luhmann will know that to observe adequately – to observe at all – we must start with a distinction. In the case of legal norms, we start with the distinction between normative and cognitive expectations. When cognitive expectations are thwarted or contradicted, we learn from our failure to understand and thus alter our communications accordingly. One can think of the idealized form of the scientific experiment (falsifiability) as one mode of cognitive expectation, or, perhaps, something like Aristotle's notion of *phronesis* in the realm of the political. In any case, the ability to learn and thus alter expectations defines the cognitive. Normative expectations, however, are stubborn. No matter how often they are disappointed, one refuses to learn otherwise and thus sticks with them through thick and thin. Here then is the form:

> Our functional definition of law leads to certain consequences concerning the concept norm (or more pedantically: the concept of the normative mode of expectations). In contrast to a large body of literature in legal theory, the concept norm is not defined by special attributes of the character of a norm but by a distinction; this distinction refers to the possibilities of responding in the case of disappointment.
>
> Expectations are either given up when they have been disappointed or they are retained. If one anticipates such a bifurcation and opts in advance for one of its strands, one predetermines one's expectations as cognitive in the first case and as normative in the second. In this way, the concept norm defines the one side of a form, which form also has another side. The

concept does not exist without that other side; it must be pitched against it while keeping options open for transition from the one side to the other. The concept norm is the result of an option that an observer has, and it occurs empirically only when this form is used for making distinctions. (Luhmann 2004, 149)

Again, readers of Luhmann will recognize the moves made in this passage. All terms are part of a two-sided form, for no term is comprehensible in isolation. Norms are defined as a particular type of expectation in contrast to another type and can be understood only with reference to its paired counterpart. The apparent psychological mode implied in the word »expectation« should not fool us, for expectations in the social realm reveal themselves only as communication, as a communicated anticipation, confirmation, satisfaction, or disappointment. What distinguishes normative expectations from cognitive ones is precisely the type of its communicated reaction. Norms, like the little train that could in the children's story, never lose heart.

A counterfactual (Luhmann's term, though one suspects a gentle poke in Habermas's ribs) normative mode of expectation does not serve to guide or dictate motivations, but rather to stabilize expectations and thus make them predictable. »Norms,« in other words, »do not promise conduct that conforms to norms but they protect all those who are expecting such conduct« (Luhmann 2004, 150). Norms *guarantee* nothing, but do give »legitimacy« to the communications of those whose actions count on the counterfactual persistence of belief in the »validity« of norms, even when they are violated with impunity. If I lend money to a friend, even in an informal manner, it is reasonable to expect repayment without appearing foolish. And if the friend should fail to repay the debt, I may never lend *him* (or, of course, *her*) money again, but I do not give up the belief in the social fact that a debt incurs an obligation. I have learned something about my friend, but have learned nothing new about the obligation to repay debts. More drastically, refusal of Israel, Europe, and North America to respond meaningfully to the ruling of the International Court of Justice condemning the construction of the wall in Palestine may lead to further knowledge about the political commitments of Israel and its powerful helpmates, but if one treats the ICJ seriously, one ought not alter one's expectations about the legitimacy of that institution or its rulings. As a norm, »justice« (which, according to its name, the Court claims to embody) prevails, even when existentially thwarted. Thus, the distance one achieves from unlinking one's faith in norms from their day-to-day, hit-or-miss, empirical efficacy produces a sense of security, of certainty – nothing more (the friend still refuses to pay; construction continues on the wall), nothing less (one continues to lend money to others; one continues one's faith in the legitimacy of the ICJ). In each case, normative expectations are maintained, no matter the empirical outcome. From this rather minimalist perspective Luhmann concludes that the *legal* norm is not a special type or quality of norm, but rather the »form of a general stabilizing function, which derives its specific legal quality only from being differentiated as and in the legal system« (Luhmann 2004, 151).

But, as Peggy Lee famously asked in song: Is that all there is? Certainly the type of »critical« thinker that Luhmann habitually disdained, the »normative« thinker who derives the function of a norm from its content and thus sees it as a tool, a form of »soft power« to be used for affecting behavior – such a thinker would not find Luhmann's description satisfying. Norms, they might insist, must be thought – well – normatively. And in a clever and typically well-crafted passage, Luhmann concedes the point:

> [I]t is normatively expected that one must expect normatively. Law is, in other words, not indifferent towards itself. Neither does it merely demand that it be obeyed. It transforms the distinction between cognitive and normative expectations into an object of normative expectations in its own right. (Luhmann 2004, 157)

This, of course, Luhmann, »as a sociologist,« does not do. His is not the self-description of the normativity of the norm, legal or otherwise. Rather, he observes the distinction he has made cognitively, from the perspective of *Wissenschaft*. Indeed, the distinction itself could be made only from that perspective; it is a cognitive distinction that purports to describe, not a normative distinction that insistently prescribes. Defining the function of norms as, essentially, a component of the rationalization of society that makes life more calculable would seem to some to be woefully insufficient; for it says nothing about the quality or normative validity of that society itself. To observe norms from a normative position would have to use something like a normative / deviant distinction, a specifically evaluative distinction that upholds the upholding of norms and that could, presumably, judge the deficiencies of society with a view toward correcting them. But such an assertion, according to Luhmann, would not be theoretical (*wissenschaftlich*), at least not social-theoretical, and thus not adequate to the society it describes – in short, not *satisfaktionsfähig*, not worthy of an intellectual dual, but also not very satisfying as a position from which one might start to understand the peculiarities of our age, »our society.« *That* position has to be the position of society itself.

Here then we run up against the form of the problem, the vital knowledge of which, according to Luhmann, should be more important than the answer to the secondary question: Would you do it? The form of the problem looks something like the following: Even ostensibly symmetrical distinctions cannot help but skew symmetry into its opposite. More specifically: Even ostensibly symmetrical distinctions made from the point of view of knowledge cannot help but privilege its own position, explicitly or implicitly. There is not only no unity of the difference that distinctions make, a point Luhmann repeats incessantly; there is also no agreement on distinctions themselves, how they are made, who ought to make them, and thus ultimately what they display. Only from the position of science (*Wissenschaft*) is the cognitive / normative distinction »self-evident.« With regard to expectations, this distinction may be construed to represent two separate but equal systems (»science« and »law«), but is itself cognitive and therefore »scientific.« The distinction makes a claim to knowledge – to description, explanation, understanding; to science (*Wissenschaft*), theory, reason – about the world (including itself), and thus creates a universe (of, for instance, »expectations«) in which cognitive and non-cognitive varieties of communications exist. The world that is so created is, however, a »cognitive« world (a world that theory is able and called upon to describe) and thus draws the distinction cognitively. Thus one side of the distinction describes itself and its others in its own terms. The model of such an operation is none other than the age-old distinction between Greeks and Barbarians. The Greeks can observe Barbarians only as non-Greek; conversely can see themselves as a unity only by locating their barbarian others *within* their world but not *of* it. Similarly, in the world that theory describes – and, for Luhmann, theory is Luhmann's theory, systems theory – theory is always Greek. All else stammers an incomprehensible or at best antiquated language.

None of this is a critique of Luhmann but rather, it seems to me, an inevitability – not just an inevitability of systems theory but of »modern«, »post-metaphysical«, »subjective« reason. The world Luhmann describes – or, more accurately – the world we see Luhmann describing is the world we see ourselves inhabiting, even if we protest our enforced tenancy and prepare elaborate plans for escape. When we moved from substance to function in our understanding of the universe (to pick in near-arbitrary fashion Cassirer's (1953) account that can stand in for a myriad of other intellectual-historical examples, one that reflects Luhmann's own use of terms), we gave up the last vestiges of imagining a classically and thus morally structured order of the universe. One may decry the specter of a historicist, relativist, perspectivist, pluralist, and finally functionalist universe all one wishes; one may point to the difficulty logical reason may have in forming a consistent, non-contradictory, paradox-free image of such a universe; but the suspicion remains that one can deny such »nihilist« modes of description *only* by way of what Weber called a »sacrifice of the intellect« (Weber 2004, 31). Lamentations of near Biblical proportions – from Leo Strauss, from Husserl and Heidegger, from the current Pope, and not least from Habermas, whose *Philosophical Discourse of Modernity* is one long excoriation of the Great Betrayal of Reason perpetrated by Nietzsche, Adorno, Heidegger, and Habermas's French contemporaries – all point to the degeneracy of modern reason, its devolution into scientific rationality.[3] Once upon a time, so the story goes, reason stabilized human counterfactual expectations by upholding the metaphysical fundament that undergirded our world. Even with the loss of its

3 Relevant texts include, among many others, Strauss 1953; Husserl 1970; Heidegger 1977; Benedikt XVI 2007; Habermas 1987.

metaphysical foundations, so the story continues, a self-validating, procedural rationality is available (thanks to Habermas) to serve as the functional equivalent of god, nature, and whatever else once stood as unmoved mover of all rational and moral inquiry. And the moral of the story is: To deny reason this quality, is to declare that all is lost.

Luhmann abides by this historical trajectory but rejects the fable-like ending. Here is (one of) Luhmann's version(s) of the story, a kind of update of, and comment on, Weber's account (Weber 2004, 14-18). Only Europe, Luhmann writes, »has brought forth worldwide social descriptions« (Luhmann 1998, 22); but this ability is only possible due to »the dissolution of a rationality continuum that had connected the observer in the world with the world« (23). For articulations of this continuum, reference could be made to Greek reason with its invention of the concept of nature; to medieval reason, which forges the link between the divine spark of human rationality and God (Jerusalem) or nature (Athens) to form a single moral order; and finally to »[t]ranscendental philosophy« and the »figure of the autonomous subject«, which »may have been Europe's final attempt to achieve ... an order of knowledge that obligates cognitively, ethically, and aesthetically« (1998, 37-38). Indeed, the so-called rationality continuum, the great chain of being, is all about the unity of the True, the Good, and the Beautiful, a unity that Kant knew no longer existed, yet wished to will back into being, at least as a conditional (»as if«) imperative. Since Luhmann sees himself as a sociologist and not an intellectual historian, he must associate this semantic »erosion« with »a radical structural transformation of society since the late Middle Ages« (22). Belief in the unity of the eternal verities that the rationality continuum guarantees requires a society in which privileged centers – Luhmann habitually refers to stratified hierarchies, at the pinnacle of which lie aristocratic courts and/or urban centers – become the nodes of decision that are able to distinguish true from false descriptions of the cosmos. One need only think of the medieval Catholic Church as the institutional embodiment of substantive reason and natural law.[4] And for its part, a stratified society requires a metaphysical notion of cosmic order to serve as its source of legitimacy. Hierarchies can be non-arbitrary only in a non-arbitrarily ordered universe.

What caused this neat, tightly coupled, mutually reinforcing social and intellectual order to fail? The sociological answer: functional differentiation. How did functional differentiation come about? The sociological answer: evolution.

---

4 »In addition to divine revelation itself, an authentic and authoritative interpreter of both divine revelation and the natural moral law, the Church, is likewise morally necessary to safeguard and inculcate moral truths and values, to supply with sureness explicit and implicit moral principles to concrete, complex, and changing circumstances of human life and activity, and to settle moral difficulties and doubts that harass even the most learned ... It is indeed undeniable that the great development, refinement, and certainty of rational ethics in Christian circles owe very much to the extrinsic aids afforded by divine revelation and Christ's Church« (Hanley 1998, xxxvi).

As with all socio-historical trajectories and causal schemes, Luhmann's sketch is fine in broad strokes, but may lose clarity when examined in detail. This, however, should not overly concern us. Whether we believe that today's general incredulity regarding the rationality continuum is the result of structural change or merely a fall from grace, this fallen state remains the one we inhabit and the one that gives shape to the form of the problem we are pursuing.

The European rationality continuum – more conventionally called substantive or objective reason – relied upon both a metaphysical (God, nature) and a social-structural (e.g. the Church) ground that blocked endless regress and self-reflection. Yet, corrosive reflexivity always accompanied self-confident reason, as Sophism in Greece, as nominalism and voluntarism in the Middle Ages, and as modernity's enlightenment of enlightenment, best (but certainly not exclusively) represented by Nietzsche. The serpent has always already been there, apple at the ready. Reason invents nature to serve as critical ground from which one could authoritatively attack the authority of convention; but what prevents the same critical impulse from seeing that nature is no ground, just another floating island awaiting its own deconstruction? God, first reduced to omnipotent but arbitrary will and then mere contingency, suffers the same fate. And finally reason itself is subjected to its own exacting mode of interrogation. What Kant exposed (and tried to cover up again); the scab that Nietzsche mordantly picked at; what Weber clarified as the reemergence of warring gods; and what much of the 20th century tried feverishly to immunize itself against is reason's original sin, its quest for knowledge of itself. Reason, then, is modernity's paradise lost. And the serpent always has the last word:

> Is it possible in this world of magic and irony, imagination and mathematics, schizophrenia and individualization to seek rationality through an observation-of-the-self-as-observer? Certainly not if we think we can describe the world as it really is and then communicate to others how they ought to think and act. No distinctions-logical concept of rationality would ever lead back to this position of unity and authority. Reason – never again! (Luhmann 1998, 34-5)

Nie wieder Vernunft! Instead: distinctions, both socially (functional differentiation) and cognitively (observation of observation). This is the fallen state from which we will never recover; this is the state from which – and *only* from which – theory can perform its observations.

So: Would you do it? Theory can help us realize that theory can*not* help us prestidigitate an answer and make it look necessary, determined, and incontrovertible. In the absence of a final ground, we are left to our own devices. This, after all, is the definition of undecidability – namely, the ineluctable necessity of coming to a decision, not arbitrarily, but without determinate criteria or guidelines that would absolve us of the responsibility for the decisions we come to. Neither can theory answer the titular question: Are there still indispensable norms in our society? If we say that modern, complex, functionally differentiated society – and perhaps all forms of society – needs at least a modicum of rationalization and predictability and therefore needs to have expectations stabilized, then we can say that norms as the counterfactual stabilization of expectations are necessary. But to say norms are necessary (from such a functionalist perspective) is not to say that any *particular* norm is necessary. Let us remind ourselves: functionalism is all about functional equivalency. It is as if norms comprised a gaseous cloud which was crucial for life on earth. The cloud is indispensable, but is each and every molecule indispensable? To find out we would have to isolate and subject each to specially devised tests, just like the test Luhmann devises with regard to torture. If, however, all we can say is that as a conglomerate norms are indispensable, we have no guidelines to determine whether norm A, B, or C is in itself necessary. Social theory – »science« – reaches its limit. Luhmann, »as a sociologist,« provides no answer, no outcome of his own molecular experiment, except the outcome that says theory can provide no definitive criteria for an answer.

III

Perhaps the »form of the problem« of Luhmann's theory could be phrased best in the Möbius-like words of Michael King (2006, 52):

> [Luhmann's] message is ... that there are other possibilities, other ways for society to organize itself, other ways of conceptualising society and its problems ... [T]he downside of Luhmann's message is that continuing to believe that solutions are just around the corner and can be achieved through more effective social regulation or control is paradoxically likely to decrease the chance that these possibilities, these new ways of conceptualizing society, will eventually become visible ... Luhmann's *usefulness*, therefore, might well lie precisely in the *uselessness* of his theory as a blueprint for the improvement of social systems and those who try and make his theory useful in this way may well be contributing to the theory's ultimate *uselessness*.

This sounds almost like the classical German *Bildungs*-ideal: Learn Greek (and Greek antiquity) not for the practical knowledge thus gained but for the conceptual exercise of imaging things other than the way they are and the formal exercise of learning to learn. Nevertheless, Chris Thornhill (2008), in his article included in this volume, detects a potential normative thrust to Luhmann's version of »Greek.« Referring to Luhmann's work as perhaps the first thoroughly *social* theory of norms, Thornhill views the notion of »adequacy« to be of use. By construing social semantics as only marginally related to social structure and viewing semantics, therefore, as the repository of norms, social theory may help determine which norms of the prevailing repertoire best serve the continuing of modern society. The imperative might then be phrased something like: Act such that your decisions are in accord with the preservation of functional differentiation. This may smack some as an odd sort of normativity since it stands in the service of »power« (»capitalism,« »globalization,« etc.) and not in the service of »truth,« and the imperative does seem to echo the 1950s triumphalism of the Weberian modernization thesis in which the gradual universalizing of functional differentiation would eventually cure all of society's historically inherited ills; but Luhmann was surely no blind optimist, and the triumphalist mode of rhetoric was equally foreign to him. The imperative is consonant with an »indispensable« Luhmannian postulate, namely that society can only be observed and described from within society and not from outside the city walls. Still, Thornhill's contention gives substance to what is clearly Luhmann's semi-acknowledged normative stance, namely the command »Thou shalt not de-differentiate,« until, of course, »catastrophe« reveals a new form of social organization.

Thornhill's panoramic essay does more than just tease out the normative implications inherent in Luhmann's social theory. It also gives a good account of what it means to treat norms as social facts. And it nicely explains the function of legal and political rights as a means for depoliticizing more and more aspects of society. If Luhmann's political and legal theory can be said to resemble some of the more pronounced aspects of neo-liberalism (in, for instance, his critiques of the welfare state), then Luhmann's view on rights (as explicated by Thornhill) might also confirm Carl Schmitt's fears about the juridification and de-politicization of society. As Niels Werber has noticed before (Werber 1995) and revisits in this volume (2008), Luhmann walks up to the edge of a political theory of the exception (or emergency), but each time he does he evades addressing the issue head on. Werber's piece is an extended meditation on the exceptional torture scenario and its not so distant cousins. Werber too comes to some troubling conclusions about systems theory's own tragic choices between normative and tactical, pragmatic decision-making. If systems theory precludes the type of normative procedures dictated by traditional and modern natural law doctrines, say, or Habermas's version of rational grounding, the type of »maneuvering without principles« that results might be equally damaging to the function of modern social systems and their codes. »Tragic choice« is not just the convenient label applied to abstract thought experiments, but also to the reality of a normality that at any time can be challenged at its core, a normality that Luhmann can defend, it seems, by assuming its dogged endurance. Thinking the exception is quite literally thinking the unthinkable.

Thornhill reminds us that Luhmann not only saw norms as social facts but also that the »normative reality of law … duplicates itself, reflexively, in the normative reality of the theory of law, and both the norms of law and norms of law's theory are then conjoined to constitute the elements of society's factual normativity« (2008, 47). John Paterson (2008) gives us then a direct investigation of the »form of the problem« as it is reflected in law's theory. Luhmann acknowledged that the legal system of modern society has two competing self-descriptions, legal positivism and *Vernunftrecht* (rational principles), a descendent of natural law (Luhmann 2004, 448). Paterson (using John Finnis and Ronald Dworkin as his chief examples) nicely shows how each runs up against the same aporia, no matter how finely each argues its case. Furthermore, Paterson discusses interesting recent judgments in British Common Law to point to similar entanglements, concluding, not with regret, but with the realization that judgment entails responsibility that cannot be relegated solely to procedures or fundamentally established norms.

Two of our contributors, however, William Scheuerman (2008) and Costas Douzinas (2008), wish to make the case for the indispensability of proclaiming single, indispensable norms (in this case, the ban on torture) from within normative theory, located roughly within politics and law. Both refer to natural law, Scheuerman in passing, Douzinas in a particularly Derridian way. Scheuerman operates in the field staked out by debates between idealists and realists in international relations and law. While he understands that the extreme versions of each side of the debate ignore value conflicts and »tragic choices« by insisting on the purity of moral norms or *Realpolitik*, Scheuerman nevertheless insists that norms do more than stabilize expectations, they shape them and thus actively direct behavior. On the one hand, this seems obvious, but taken in its strongest form, which I believe Scheuerman does, it states that moral and legal norms have the power to oppose and vanquish political force, which makes the counterfactual assertion of threatened norms by way of principled argumentation all the more urgent. In asking whether there are aspects of the natural law tradition that might be salvageable, he seems to agree with Thornhill that it is possible to unlink semantics from structure and view semantics as the repository of norms that may be called upon at different times and in different circumstances. However, Thornhill's view of the latent normative potential of Luhmann's theory would radically differ from Scheuerman's, as it would from the type of normative urgency espoused by Douzinas as well. Douzinas views natural law as an empty »shell« that retains its original form of opposition (nature vs. convention) even as it loses all elements of its former substance. Nature, he writes, is »philosophy's tool« that, as an »evaluative standard ... emancipates reason from the tutelage of power and gives rise to natural right.« (2008, 120) Like Scheuerman, Douzinas would resist the »nihilist« trajectory of reason I outlined above and identified with Luhmann's notion of the »form of the problem«, the »form« that bedevils us in the exceptional scenarios we construct and which we face. It is clear that for Douzinas the empty shell of natural law stands in close proximity to Derrida's notion of justice, and both – the shell of natural law and justice as deconstruction – could, it seems to me, quite easily be covered by Luhmann's notion of justice as contingency, the distance from positive law that shows that things (laws) could be other than they are. Douzinas, however, wishes to give directionality to contingency, wishes to speak of the justice to come and the magnetic horizon toward which all our thoughts and, we hope, history itself are drawn. Positing natural law as an empty signifier, but gracing it with the pathos of emancipation, is meant to limit contingency's contingency, for contingency left to its own devices is quite literally a roll of the dice.

Hans-Georg Moeller (2008) returns to the question of theory's adequacy by focusing on Luhmann's critique of the humanism inherent in the enunciation of human rights. Explicitly arguing against a leftist discourse of *human* emancipation, Luhmann, Moeller argues, sees rights as a form of *social* inclusion. Again, there are hints in Luhmann of modernization triumphalism, but the real challenge to Luhmann's notion of world society and the possibilities (along with problems) that it may bring came from Luhmann's epiphany, as it were, that not just modernity but society itself seemed to have its limits at the entrance to the *favelas*. The super-coding inclusion/exclusion that Luhmann surmises may overarch the serial inclusions and exclusions managed by social differentiation might best be marked by Ernesto Laclau's notion of heterogeneity. For Laclau, the possibility of forming political »hegemonies« (such as popular movements) requires antagonism (friend/enemy, oppressor/oppressed, or, more benignly, government/opposition) within a shared representational space. Likened, however, to Hegel's notion of »peoples without history«, heterogeneity is an »outside« that »does not have access to the space of representation« and thus is simply a »leaving aside«. Like the »residue left in a tube after a chemical experiment,« Laclau explains, »[t]he break involved in this kind of exclusion is more radical than the one that is inherent in the antagonistic one: while antagonism still presupposes some sort of discursive inscription, the kind of outside that I am now discussing presupposes exteriority not just to something within a space of representation, but to the space of representation as such« (Laclau 2005, 140).[5] Laclau's heterogeneity might well apply not just to the barbarians outside the gates of our shining cities, but to the peoples without personhood, the bodies who are held in our camps, both the ones we know about and the ones we do not. How does systems theory confront bodies that lie outside the social, that is, outside the space of representation? Andreas Philippopoulus-Mihalopoulus (2008) attempts to answer that question in the only article in this issue that directly confronts Luhmann's »Beyond Barbarism«. Thus, Philippopoulus-Mihalopoulus addresses not exclusion itself, but Luhmann's theory construction, postulating a necessary »space of absence« within the theory's social architecture to allow for the »trace«, the possibility of »seeing« the peo-

---

5 One might take Laclau's analysis further and ask whether Luhmann's inclusion/exclusion super-coding is a logically necessary and constitutive element in the formation of modernity; whether, in other words, the pure, homogenized (even if neatly differentiated) space imagined as world society is even possible without an excluded outside. Such a question might bring us back once again to Schmitt and the logical necessity of exclusion for the smooth functioning of Europe (now: Europeanized world society). For more on heterogeneity see Laclau 2005, 139-156.

ples without history who otherwise, apparently, strike us dumb whenever we approach the edge of the »known« world at the gates of the *favelas*.

IV

»As a sociologist« Luhmann need not answer the question – »Would you do it?« As citizens we must. But can we? I close with another scenario, one Luhmann did not live long enough to formulate.

> Imagine: You are the citizen of a country that claims to be democratic – that is, that claims its actions represent the will of »the people« – and has an electoral form of politics. Collectively binding decisions are legitimated every bit as much by »no« votes as by »yes« votes. Opposition, in other words, is part of the form of the political system. This country, of which you are both a citizen and an embodiment of »the people«, has now formally (by law) declared that a former normative expectation – that the torture of prisoners was constitutionally prohibited – has been declared no longer normative. The new norm reads something like: »Torture [now cowardly phrased as »enhanced interrogation techniques«] is permitted under certain circumstances, to be determined exclusively by the executive branch of government and its agencies.« What would you do?

Note that what is postulated is not a state of exception, but legal normality; and note that the question has changed. Not: Would you do it? You are not asked to commit the act in question. A cadre of professionals, especially trained for that purpose, has already been pressed into service and is »doing it.« Rather: What would you do? How would you react to a legislative change performed in your name that asks you to dispense with a normative expectation you had previously been taught was indispensable? Would you adamantly continue to communicate the normative expectation that you hold to have been violated? Or do you react cognitively and understand that the rules of the game have changed? What does it mean to react cognitively, to change your former normative expectation to a cognitive one? Let us suppose that you still oppose the legalization of torture. (One assumes that one can learn from the violation of an expectation without necessarily accepting the consequences of that violation. One can learn, for example, that the International Court of Justice is a sham without ceasing to be concerned about the construction of the wall.) Is your reaction and are your resultant actions different, depending on the mode of expectation you hold? It must be remembered that within the political system of your state, you are not absolved of responsibility for the change, no matter what you may personally say or think. With your indispensable »no«,[6] your support of the opposition (in, say, an election held 2004), made the political

---

6 Parody of Habermas is intential.

and legal decision every bit as legitimate as he or she who voted with the government. What purpose do you now serve by upholding the old norm rather than adapting to the new one? Or conversely, what purpose do you serve by recognizing the change even when not agreeing with it? Are lamentations to the normative heavens and invocations of a better, more just future in order? Is, in other words, faith in Tinkerbell or other goddesses of wishful thinking still productive? Conversely, is organized political protest – knowing that protest also legitimates what it protests against – the way to go? Or does one violently take to the streets with »Up against the wall, motherfucker!« nostalgically on one's lips, not stopping to reflect that »against the wall« (or »under the water«) is precisely the sentiment one is reacting to? To the »system« in question, does it make a damn bit of difference what you do, think, or say?

What does systems theory, what does any theory say to a difference that makes no difference?

References

Benedikt XVI (2007): Gott und die Vernunft: Auf zum Dialog der Kulturen. Augsburg: Sankt Ulrich Verlag.

Browning, Christopher R. (1998): Ordinary Men: Reserve Police Batallion 101 and the Final Solution in Poland. New York: Harper.

Cassirer, Ernst (1953): Substance and Function and Einstein's Theory of Relativity. Both Books Bound as One. Trans. William Curtis Swabey and Marie Collins Swabey. New York: Dover.

Douzinas, Costas (2008): Torture and Systems Theory. Soziale Systeme 14, 110-125 (in this volume).

Habermas, Jürgen (1987): The Philosophical Discourse of Modernity: Twelve Lectures. Trans. Frederick G. Lawrence. Cambridge, Mass.: MIT.

Hanley, Thomas R. (1998): Translator's Preface. Pp. xxxiii-xxxviii in: Heinrich A. Rommen. The Natural Law: A Study in Legal and Social History and Philosophy. Trans. Thomas R. Hanley O.S.B. Ph.D. Indianapolis: Liberty Fund.

Heidegger, Martin (1977): The Question Concerning Technology and Other Essays. Trans. William Lovitt. New York: Harper.

Husserl, Edmund (1970): The Crisis of European Sciences and Transcendental Phenomenology. Trans. David Carr. Evanston: Northwestern UP.

King, Michael (2006): What's the Use of Luhmann's Theory? Pp. 37-52 in: Michael King / Chris Thornhill (eds.), Luhmann on Law and Politics: Critical Appraisals and Applications. Oxford: Hart.

Laclau, Ernesto (2005): On Populist Reason. London: Verso.

Luhmann, Niklas (1998): Observations on Modernity. Stanford: Stanford UP.

Luhmann, Niklas (2004): Law as a Social System. Trans. Klaus A. Ziegert. Oxford: Oxford UP.

Luhmann, Niklas (2008): Are There Still Indispensable Norms in Our Society? Soziale Systeme 14, 18-37 (in this volume).

Luhmann, Niklas (2008a): Beyond Barbarism. Soziale Systeme 14, 38-46 (in this volume).

Moeller, Hans-Georg (2008): »Human Rights Fundamentalism«. The Late Luhmann on Human Rights. Soziale Systeme 14, 126-141 (in this volume).

Paterson, John (2008): The Fact of Values. Soziale Systeme 14, 68-82 (in this volume).

Philippopoulos-Mihalopoulos, Andreas (2008): On Absence: Society's Return to Barbarians. Soziale Systeme 14, 142-156 (in this volume).

Scheuerman , William E. (2008): »Against Normative Tone-Deafness«. Soziale Systeme 14, 102-109 (in this volume).

Strauss, Leo (1953): Natural Right and History. Chicago: Chicago UP.

Thornhill, Chris (2008): On norms as social facts: A view from historical political science. Soziale Systeme 14, 47-67 (in this volume).

Weber, Max (2004): Science as a Vocation. Pp. 1-31 in: David Owen/Tracy B. Strong (ed.), The Vocation Lectures. Ed. Trans. Rodney Livingstone. Indianapolis: Hackett.

Werber, Niels (1995): Von Feinden und Barbaren. Carl Schmitt und Niklas Luhmann. Merkur. Deutsche Zeitschrift für europäisches Denken 9, 949-957.

Werber, Niels (2008): A Test of Conscience. Without Indispensable Norms: Niklas Luhmann's War on Terror. Soziale Systeme 14, 83-101 (in this volume).

Prof. William Rasch
Department of Germanic Studies, Indiana University
Ballantine Hall 644, Bloomington, IN 47405-7103
wrasch@indiana.edu

Soziale Systeme 14 (2008), Heft 1, S. 18-37

Niklas Luhmann

Are There Still Indispensable Norms in Our Society?[1]

Abstract: In his Heidelberg University lecture of 1992, the author uses an all-too pre-scient torture scenario to exam the function and putative indispensability of norms in modern society. In the exceptional case, recourse to the »normativity of norms« or to »values« proves to be untenable because all norms and values reveal themselves to be undecidable. Viewed from within the legal systems, the validity of norms remain unquestioned, but viewed from »society« (by, say, the sociologist), norms are seen as social facts and thus open to discussion. The author works his way through many permutations of the torture question (»Would you do it?«) not to give us a norma-tive answer to the problem, but to exemplify the seeming impossibility of reasonably expecting that any given legal norm is normatively indispensable.

I

Following good legal custom, presenting a case might help attune us to the topic of this talk. Imagine: You are a high-level law-enforcement officer. In your country – it could be Germany in the not-too-distant future – there are many left- and right-wing terrorists – every day there are murders, fire-bombings, the killing and injury of countless innocent people. You have captured the leader of such a group. Presumably, if you tortured him, you could save many lives – 10, 100, 1000 – we can vary the situation. Would you do it?

In Germany the matter seems simple. One consults constitutional law. Article 1 (Human Dignity) provides for no exception.[2] Indeed, the layman is at first astounded that the norm is formulated as fact. Is it therefore possible for tor-ture not to violate human dignity? The jurist will let him know better. So far, so good. If not in terms of justice, then at least in terms of the legality.

For common law, which doesn't operate in such legal-positivist terms, there is an extensive discussion that is relevant here. The question is whether or not every legal question can be decided on the basis of weighing the conse-quences. If so, one could influence the decision by manipulating the evaluation of consequences. Or whether or not there are indispensable rights that are to be observed regardless of any of the decision's consequences.[3] It is striking that

---

1 Translated by Todd Cesaratto. The translation follows the German original: Niklas Luhmann, Gibt es in unserer Gesellschaft noch unverzichtbare Normen? Heidelberg: C.F. Müller, 1993.
2 Also see Hassemer 1988.
3 Foremost on this see Dworkin 1978.

the discussion is about *rights,* and not, for instance, as Pufendorf, Kant and above all Jewish law would suggest, about *duties.*[4] The emphasis on rights may be a liberal inheritance, but it has the advantage that one can use it in a legal-technical sense to allot authority in a case. Not to mention that globally the discussion is about human rights and not about human duties. Still this question does not help us to decide, because we still always have a prior decision to make: Are there rights fully independent of consequences?

To complicate the decision and make it ultimately undecidable, one can vary the hypothetical case. The terrorists have a nuclear bomb, and it must be found and disarmed. Would you use torture?

It does not lie in the sociologist's competence either to make a decision or even simply to recommend a certain decision (»after weighing all factors« as jurists say). As a sociologist, one is interested in the *problem;* or, as one could say, owing to particular theoretical guidelines, in the *form of the problem.* One can only get it wrong. It is a matter of »tragic choice«.[5] While in the normal case, jurists have no doubt that they are just when they distinguish between just and unjust and decide accordingly (however that may be justified), one could pose this case conversely: one is unjust when one distinguishes between just and unjust. The usual solution to the paradox of the self-reference of the just/unjust code – which consists in doubling its positive value and explaining the distinction itself as lawful – does not work. Or it works only if one applies the same operation of solving the paradox to the negative value. As in early Greek tragedies, the assertion of justice is for its part unjust. The code itself must first be generated, first institutionalized, free of paradox. Athene intervenes, establishes the Areopagite Council and retains for herself the right to decide »hard cases« (as Americans would say in their inimitable fashion).

Since our law lacks a religious legitimation, this expedient does not enter into consideration for us. We also no longer preside over the institution of »Divine Judgments«, by means of which such »hard cases« were once decided.[6] Thanks to *Gödel* we now know that we must »gödelize« such problems of system-inherent paradoxicality and require external references to do so. At the same time, however, the development of semiology since *Saussure* has taught us that such external references do not exist; rather a system remains dependent upon self-implemented distinctions.

To be sure, with these considerations we have not gained a decision, but rather the insight that the problem is a matter of high theoretical caliber. Here it is above all advisable to avoid every moral judgment (and that also means every ethical construction of the problem) because that could only lead to morally

---

4 Compare Horowitz 1973, 7f.
5 Such is the formulation of economists. See Calabresi/Bobbitt 1978.
6 See Bottéro 1981. Compare also Alafenish 1982.

discrediting one or the other option[7] and expelling the law's devil with morality's *Beelzebub*. Instead of this, I suggest resorting to a sociological analysis, thus exploiting the distance between sociologists and the legal system. It should be clear in advance that the jurist may expect no recommendation for a decision. However, a certain semantic reorganization of knowledge might be helpful, at least regarding the effort to reach a proper formulation of the problem for modern society.

For it could well be that a long tradition burdens us with an error in controlling the way problems are posed. Perhaps we are still expecting, but probably without much hope for success, a correspondence between decision and principle, a redemptive, conclusive formula, a system in the sense of *Kant's* or a general law, valid a priori.[8] However, the final ground of all deciding lies not in a principle but in a paradox.

II

The sociologist's distance does not begin with the question of deciding whether or not there are indispensable norms in modern society. Rather, and in a quite general manner, the notion of the normative itself undergoes estrangement. With the concept of the norm, jurists (and the same could be said, mutatis mutandis, for ethicists) presuppose a particular manner of existence that since the 19th century has been termed »validity« and distinguished from factual existence. They work with this presupposition because, for the legal system, it is a matter of ordering facts according to norms and deciding whether behavior corresponds to the norm or violates it. Therefore the legal system seeks the foundation for its own method of observing the world in the *distinction* between norms and facts. In contrast, sociology is free to deal with norms as facts as well – obviously as facts of a particular kind. A possible construction is to understand norms as formulas for *contra-factual expectations*, for expectations of behavior, that is, that do not allow themselves to be irritated by factual behavior, but which are adhered to even when they are frustrated.[9] The guiding distinction here is not fact / norm but learning / not-learning. The usual manner of speaking, which is calibrated to »ought« and talks of »validity«, is then conceived if as an expression for the right to refuse learning and the right to maintain expectations, even when they are frustrated. But this manner of speaking always deals with factually occurring, determinable expectations; therefore

---

7   On this some caveats worthy of consideration in Jewish law – but then again, on the basis of religious legitimation. Compare Cover 1983.
8   In reference to tradion, see for instance Girolamo Cardano (1663, 277): »Unum bonum est, plura verò malum« [there is only one good, but truly there are many bad things]. Compare also the guarantee from above directed against Aristotelians: »non ergo tendunt in unum se ab uno procedunt« (279) [therefore they do not tend toward one but proceed from one].
9   See Luhmann 1983, 40f. Also Luhmann 1993.

with expectations in the social system of society, with facts of a case that one can grasp through empirically recognizable communications. Thus determining whether or not the communication of »indispensable norms« finds success in a society – and what tests (Scenario: Terrorists have an atom bomb!) the acceptance of such a norm can handle – also becomes a matter of facts.

In a somewhat different terminology, one can describe the cultural invention of normativity as a *doubling of reality* – just as one can distinguish between a game and life or, according to the evolution of language, between a language's signs and what they signify. Something similar applies to the assumption of a religious meaning behind the phenomenal world or for the art system's distinction between fictional reality and real reality – no matter how one then imagines the coupling and the possibilities of transgressing borders in such cases. There is no doubt that linguistic communication really happens, even when it »is« not what it »signifies«. There is also no doubt that behavior in accordance with norms really is expected, even if – especially if – it must be distinguished from anticipated behavior and may not be confused with it. Only with the help of such doubling of reality can one gain the possibility of cultivating a more precise conception of real reality, of hard factual reality – precisely because one can distinguish it and observe it from the other side of the distinction. Cultural-historically it will not be wrong here to think immediately of the semantics of religious transcendence; and one also sees that both law and art develop in a gradual process of differentiation, and then generate their own forms of comparison and also their own descriptions of real reality.[10] The hardening of reality is first possible through fictionality. The nominalist individualism of facts (*Ockham* and successors) creates its own fundament in a language theory that suits it. Induction problematizes itself and legitimates its reality deficit through mere »habits« (*Hume*) and today through statistical analyses that describes no single concrete situation.[11] And this applies to contemporary positive law as well.

As opposed to societies that start with a religious positing of the world, modern societies cannot integrate these descriptions of reality, which rely on a doubling, into a transcendental principle. In this respect (as in others), the transcendental subject has failed. Our society describes itself »poly-contextually«,[12] that is, with the help of a plurality of distinctions, whereby the distinctions with which an observer designates his objects serve simultaneously to distinguish him from his objects, thus setting him in an »unmarked space«,[13] from which he can observe something – but not his observing.

In reflecting on the theme of the indispensability of certain norms, these considerations offer the freedom of describing how the legal system describes this

---

10 For early European poetics, compare for instance Schlaffer 1990.
11 On this see Spencer Brown 1957.
12 This is Gotthard Günther's Terminology. See for example Günther 1979.
13 According to Spencer Brown 1979.

problem, and thereby, from a sociological prospective, of discovering non-arbi-trary facts. Thereby we depart from the mode – which is also more typical of sociology – of investigating the »institutionalizability« of norms. Ultimately it becomes a matter of asking whether and in which regard normative expecta-tions are normatively expected, and above all whether and how far these nor-mative expectations of normative expectations may be assumed without further information.[14] In this way, one would indeed arrive at an empirical analysis of normalization's social chances of success, but not at the problem that is here interesting, namely whether and with which semantic means the legal system can establish the *indispensability* of norms.

III

If one inquires into the legal-theoretical or legal-philosophical attempts at identifying and establishing indispensable norms, one's attention will likely be drawn, even today, to natural law. That »the eternal return« of natural law has already been the topic of discussion should indeed give us pause,[15] and *Noberto Bobbio* has therefore inferred from this an insufficient maturity.[16] But since the concept belongs to the few who have remained in the discussion, and since safeguards against political atrocities are always expected from natural law, testing it springs immediately to mind. In so doing one indeed stumbles across some of the tradition's peculiarities that are hardly present in today's discussion. This holds for both the Aristotelian concept of nature as well as for the few references from the tradition of Roman civil law.

For *Aristotle*, nature was distinct from technique, from fabricated products, and was determined by this distinction. Among other things, entities that could observe themselves – that is, people –were counted among nature, as well as cities and other social bodies. Accordingly if one asks how one's own or for-eign nature is to be observed, one meets with the following instruction: The observer should attend to the perfect state and not the corrupt one.[17] Accord-ing to this, nature can evidently assume a natural and an unnatural state. Thus nature presents itself to the observer, who must differentiate accordingly, as an inherently paradoxical state of existence. The paradox is resolved through the assumption of a self-normalization of nature in the direction of its own perfec-tion. Nature is conceived to be teleologically ordered, and *Aristotle* assumes that in most cases nature achieves that toward which it exerts itself. One has

14 On this see the always worth reading Allport 1933.
15 Thus according to the much cited publication of Rommen 1947.
16 See Bobbio 1972, 159ff. (190).
17 Thus Politeia 1254a 36-37 (formulated with skopeîn, thus observe!). Compare also Thomas of Aquinas, *Summa Theologiae* IIae, IIae, q. 57 a.2 ad primum: »Natura autem hominis est muta-bilis. Et ideo id quod naturale est homini potest aliquando deficere.« [The nature of man is mutable, and therefore that which is natural to man can at some time fail.]

to deal only with the deficient remains. The home's economic order and the city's political order, among other things, see to this. This concept of nature is no longer common today, nor would the assumed congruent relation between normality and normativity be very convincing anymore either.

It is difficult to discern exactly how large a roll the concept of nature played in the texts handed down from Roman civil law. However one finds a very similar state of affairs. In an Ulpian passage, which was often used in the Middle Ages, natural law is differentiated from *ius gentium* (law of the people) and civil law, but is in no way viewed as superior law. Rather, natural law is distinguished through the fact that it governs all living entities, thus humans and animals.[18] As a result one must conceive of the civilizing process as a *deviation from natural law*. Marriage constricts the natural reproductive drive.[19] Property constricts equal access to all goods (supposed as originally common property). And institutions such as slavery, serfdom or contractual wage labor constrict what must be presupposed as natural freedom. Consequently, medieval civil and canon law construe the legal condition as a deviation from natural law, although, at the same time, they use – and again we stumble upon a hidden, canceled paradoxicality – concepts like *communitas, universitas, civitas* as designations for natural bodies.[20]

The problem does not change fundamentally in the 17th century when social contract (*pactum unionis*) doctrine becomes operative. The contract only sets the constitutive paradox more sharply in relief. The origin lies now in the presumption of individually manageable freedom; but that also means (and this is uncontested until late into the 18th century) that the ability to renounce freedom on the basis of well-considered grounds belongs to freedom. Later paradoxicality will be built into and resolved in the concept of freedom through a distinction precisely targeted at freedom, that is, through the distinction between *libertas* and *licentia*.[21]

In this version natural law's historical semantics could accompany the feudal order and its disintegration, the newly developing territorial state, and the transition to an absolutist understanding of statehood; and even enlightened absolutism, even the transition to the constitutional state in the liberal mold availed

---

18 See D 1.1.1.3: »Ius naturale est, quod natura omnia animalia docuit.« [the law is natural in that nature teaches all creatures.] Incidentally it is considerable that nature teaches itself. Natural law must thus be neither taught, nor learned, nor studied. Study relates to texts, not nature!

19 Highly engaged with this is Weigand 1967.

20 And on this there is another fitting, also much-cited Gaius-text from D.4.5.8. that states that a change in currently valid law does not extinguish natural law, »quia civilis ratio naturalia iura corrumpere non potest.« [Because civil reason cannot corrupt natural laws.] As always the legal decisions indeed fit each other, but not the mnemonics and founding formulas that the Middle Ages then draw from the texts.

21 In addition, this distinction – since it makes the concept of freedom usable through the unfolding of paradoxes – can serve both more conservative as well as revolutionary ends; it is simply a matter of excluding arbitrariness from the concept. See for example Wolff 1740, Pars I, §§ 150f. (reprint Hildesheim 1972, 90f.). See also Price 1776, 12ff.

itself of the idea of natural law.[22] In contrast to all that was conjectured and postulated after 1945, the semantics of natural law remain captivating precisely because of its capacity for political assimilation. The idea of human rights and their inalienability first enters the discussion toward the end of the 18th century. This holds for states that still know slavery, persecution of religious opponents, massive expropriation of property from »royalists«, as well as immense profit speculation (but as a sign of modernity), namely the North American States. All of this speaks for the fact that natural law remains only as an empty shell of a word, applicable in flowery phrases – which now requires being made into positive law constitutionally.[23] In any event nothing results from the historically deducible meaning of natural law that could answer our question as to the validity of indispensable norms in today's society.

IV

How could it have been assumed at all that from within its own nature *any* norm contain *in itself* the assurance for unassailable, indispensable validity? In the old world this had been guaranteed through the myths of origin – for their part, resolutions of the paradoxicality of a beginning without a »before«. Since the early modern age the metaphor of the »source of law« (hardly used in antiquity) assumes this function.[24] The paradox of decision hides behind the notion of an origin without precedent, which constructs an alternative in which the decision does not occur.[25] How is such an assumption plausible? Evidently not by inquiring further back into the origin of the origin or the foundation of foundation. The metaphor is used as a halt to reflection; it has the function of making the decider of the decision invisible. If it is plausible, then its plausibility stems from other reasons.

As a sociologist, one may suppose that unfolding of paradoxes of this type or another – that is, the substitution of distinctions with fixed identities – owe their plausibility to their social-structural adequacy. This demands analyses by way of the sociology of knowledge. For this we no longer use the Marx-Mannheim diction that resorts to class or position and thus ultimately to (conscious or unconscious) actor-specific interests. We replace this by presuming a connection between a society's semantics and the currently prevailing form of system-differentiation.[26]

---

22 For more recent times and for the transition into the 19th century, compare Klippel 1976.
23 Or, as Klippel (1976) shows – natural law is only pursued when a political constitution is unattainable.
24 In lieu of still-lacking thorough research following the model of intellectual history, compare Sève 1982. There is also ample material by Vallet de Goytisolo 1982.
25 On this see Shackle 1979.
26 By way of introduction, see Luhmann 1980.

It is not hard to show that the semantics of natural law (insofar as one accepts the preceding depiction) correlate with the immanent imperative of a noble society, thus with the imperative of stratified differentiation, and through this obtain its power to convince. That a society with higher organizational demands must be founded upon a deviation from natural law represents precisely the noble stratum's requirements for differentiation. Family genealogy must be secured through lineage, thus through marriage, whatever else the natural reproductive drive achieves in terms of pathologies. The nobility must be able to name property its own and defend it, whatever other requirements accrue.[27] Stratified social systems compel inequality of rank and resource distribution and they see in this an essential (indispensable!) condition of social organization. That work must be done and thus freedom limited also belongs to this. It is only much later that this arrangement can be supported by an adequate appeal to earning and spending money, that is, by wage labor.

It may be remarkable that this order must be declared a *deviation* from natural law. However, that evidently suffices for depicting its relationship to nature – as eternally given in a cosmos of essences or as created by God – and for providing specific justifications for respective deviations. The de-paradoxicalization of paradoxicality is plausible in the extant order, for which no alternatives are in sight.

The same applies to the Aristotelian concept of nature. It can be directly copied into the nobility's self-depiction. Nobility demands that one is well-born and sound (*arete, virtus*), thus a nature that is not already in and of itself what it is, rather something that requires attention and care. An immense literature, which blossoms again in noble circles of the 16th and 17th century, discusses the weighing of these criteria.[28] Doctrines of education emphasize that adolescence in particular is endangered by passion and temptation. But this refers to children of noble birth, circumstance and advantage. In any event, it is clear to jurists that a farmer cannot become noble through twice as much virtue.[29] Ennoblement or the certification of old nobility is required for that. The ambivalence of the concept of nature proves itself, one could say, in a discussion that does not lack clearness and criteria for managing problems – as long as society is differentiated through the form of stratification.

---

27 This must not necessarily be, and normally is not, secured via individual property in a juridical sense. It does not at any point presuppose a clear distinction between criminal law and civil law for the ordering of ruling and protective authority. It is the money economy that first compels, above all for the safeguard of credit, individual rights of provision; thus it is a disintegration of the feudal order. On this and the consequences of the first English inflation circa 1200, see Palmer 1985b and 1985b.

28 From the extensive secondary literature, compare Donati 1988; Jouanna 1981; Schalk 1986.

29 One reads, »Rusticus, licet probus, dives & valens, tamen non dicitur nobilis« [a farmer can be virtuous, wealthy, and stout, but he is never called noble] in Bartolus, *de Dignitatibus fol 45 v and ad 52*, quoted according to the Omnia edition, quae extant, Opera Venetiis 1602, vol. VIII. In reality the relations were by no means so unambiguous, especially when it was a matter tax exemption.

Today, society is construed differently, and that has far-reaching consequences extending into all details of social semantics. The primary form of societal differentiation has been shifted from stratification to functional differentiation. That pertains above all to the societal position of the individual. For until late in the 19th century, the emphasis on the individuality of individuals was that semantic mechanism with which the old order of societal division was undermined. The societal position of individuals no longer results from their lineage but from their careers, which of course are helped or hindered by lineage to varying degrees. But lineage (and eventually race and gender) acts on a complicated integration mechanism, which has a primarily temporal structure, so that attained positions are prerequisites for the attainment of further positions. Every step depends on a contingent (for example, economically sensitive) collaboration of self-selection and hetero selection.

This corresponds to a time orientation in which past and future are no longer always already bound to assigned necessities / impossibilities through essential forms, but rather must be coupled through decisions. That also implies that one attributes things, which are no longer alterable, to decisions and plans decisions in terms of series of decisions that are dependent but not yet determinable. Hence, time is no longer experienced in the difference between *aeternitus / tempus* (eternity / time), so that there can also no longer be time-invariant norms. Rather, the dominating time distinction is that between past and future, and only the border, separating both sides of this time form, counts as the present, which, however, can no longer be situated in the form. Therefore, the social orientation must also be adjusted to insecurity and risk, to »in the next moment things are different.«[30] It depends on developing social forms of accommodation that tolerate such instability and thereby maturate. This also applies to the projection of norms with which one attempts to bind future expectations to the schema conformist / deviant and therewith distribute positions as favorable / unfavorable – with the proviso that the decision will eventually change.

The reason for such a degree of individualization and temporalization lies in functional system differentiation. This differentiation does not allow concrete individuals to assign themselves to a given functional system and only to that one system, so that one individual »exists« only legally, another just educationally, the next one only economically and still another just politically. Rather, societal inclusion must be kept open and all individuals must be granted access to all functional systems. For precisely this reason, freedom and equality are made abstract norms, so that the degree of inequality and freedom's limitation results from the regulation of inclusion in functional systems. The reason for choosing this form of normativity rests in the fact that the future is unpredictable and hence one must reckon with the as-yet-unknown outcomes of actions.

30 On this, see Luhmann 1991.

Therefore there can be no societal hierarchy of subsystems and their relation to each other, thus no representation of society in society. Rather the influence of the subsystems on each other, which is much more intense than in the older order, changes from situation to situation and cannot be steered through society. This is the case for sequential as well as simultaneous events, so that the inner-societal environment becomes uncontrollable for systems.

If this analysis applies even crudely, it must have consequences for the theme of the indispensability of one or several fundamental norms. It would certainly be premature to conclude that these consequences lead to »decisionism,« relativism, or the basic arbitrariness of »anything goes.« Those are mere devaluations that impose themselves when one doesn't wish to forgo the old world's certainties of orientation. On the contrary, one will have to assume that such a structure of contingent operations – a structure that is organized recursively, non-hierarchically, but rather hetero-archically – generates »Eigenvalues« and projects »inviolate levels« that correspond to their organizational archetype.[31] The only question is: in which forms?

V

If one pays attention to what modern society itself recommends, the motto is: values. The concept of values has a long, multi-track history, which, however, produces nothing for our question. That applies to the nobility's concept of valor as well as to the economic distinction between value and price. Already in the 18th century one finds a casually applied, unspecified value concept. However, this concept first wins a top-ranking semantic position in the course of the 19th century. And that is a first indication of the adoption of a specifically modern semantics.

The concept certainly owes this appreciation in value to philosophy – partly to the philosophical distinction between being and validity, partly to neo-Kantianism, partly to phenomenology, in any case to an unquenchable thirst for aprioris. Meanwhile, value as a concept concept has fallen out of philosophical fashion. In contrast, it seems to be essential for the formulation of party programs and the juridical desicions of the Federal Constitutional Court. When it comes to formulations, value replaces the orientation according to a real analysis of societal circumstances that confront politics and the orientation according to classical forms of juridical dogmatism (approximately: subjective rights). The concept marks exactly what we are seeking: maximum relevance with normative content. Thus one would like to know more specifically to what

---

31 On »Eigenvalues« in connection with this logical-mathematical concept, see von Foerster 1981, as well as other contributions in the cited volume. On »inviolate levels« as forms of the development of self-referential paradoxicality, see Hofstadter 1979, specifically 686f.

– besides itself – the concept refers. For sociology this has to mean: to what type of reality.

The use of value judgments in the course of communicative conduct makes conspicuous that these judgments are not asserted as theses, but run in tandem as implications. Values »are valid« in an imputational manner of communication. One assumes that consensus exists regarding value assessments, that advance understandings can be used. When talk is of smoking, one assumes that it is harmful to the health, and that all participants value the positive value, health, and not the negative value, disease. Or: Life is preferred and not death, peace and not war, freedom and not bondage, democracy and not tyranny, and so forth. The question, »Why?« is omitted, because in communication, making something explicitly thematic is always understood in such a way that acceptance or rejection of the imposed meaning comes into consideration. The mere insinuation of this would miss value's validity and be misunderstood, or at any rate understood as a provocation.

Values, then, are valid without justification – as the observation of communication, as it actually occurs, shows. But then it is not possible to request justification for values. In practice, values serve to halt reflection. When that does not work, smaller systems differentiate themselves in which it does work. From the perspective of normal communication, as inspired by television, such deviations then appear radical, fundamental, esoteric. They are dealt with through a distancing semantics; although, in terms of genesis and validity, the same mode is in effect as in the realm of universally accepted values. Even differentiations and alienations, even controversies and conflicts do not call into question the semantics of values as *form*. This might also serve as an indicator for an »inviolate level« – a deep location that replaces nature and reason for the anchoring of norms.

Like stars in the heavens there are countless values. Therefore basic values are needed for emphasis. Here traditional concepts like freedom, equality, justice, peace, security, dignity, welfare and solidarity are used to designate special status.[32] With that the order of value references reinforces itself once more. But even when it is a matter of easily quotable values, nothing changes in terms of the implicated mode of validity. Nor can one pose the question during ongoing communication – especially not then – whether these values are accepted or rejected.

In this form, having values is easy. If certain values become questionable, new »inviolate levels« will form. But there's a catch to the matter: Nothing follows

32 Traditional concepts – in the process taking into account that all these concepts change their meaning and in part their linguistic form during the transition from stratified to functionally differentiated society. Already *Pufendorf*, in terms of dignity, shifted from *dignitas* to *dignatio*. In the 17th century, *securitas* sheds the old religious connotations for a measured self-security. Freedom is made singular in the 18th century. Solidarity appears for the first time in the 19th century, and along with it, a reference to the consequences of functional differentiation (at first: industrialization) is already signaled.

from values to aid in the adjudication of value conflicts. There is, as is often said, no firm hierarchical (transitive) order of such a type that certain values are always preferable to certain other ones, for instance, that freedom is more important than security in every case, peace always more important than freedom, justice always more important than peace, etc. The question of preference is only decided in advance when a value refers to its opposite (peace is better than war), but not when it refers to the contradictory demands of various distinctions between value and non-value. Different values do not exclude each other reciprocally, hence they always allow for the addition of new values. They remain available to all of us, therefore, as orientating points of view within the system. Value theorists base their hope for stability on this. Collisions of value are reduced to individual cases. But it is precisely in these individual cases that values must demonstrate their practical relevance. They lose their prescription value right at the moment it is needed. And the opposite is also true. Because decisions are always and only due when values pose conflicting demands (because if not, the decision would already be decided)[33], the decisions themselves remain unregulated.

For purposes of comparison, it might be of use to see how this problem of collision is solved at the level of the law's typical conditional programs. Either this occurs through rules of cancellation – new law breaks old law or (when it is a matter of constitutional law) vice versa – or the collision is brought into the schema of rule and exception. One proves the rule, as the saying goes, by conceding the exception. In this way law generates growth, differentiation, commensurability to cases in forms that can be handed down as such. All this however cannot be transposed to the level of values. In the case of a collision, one value does not delete another. Nor is a gain in complexity produced in the form of stable (and expandable) rule-exception regulations. Value collisions can only be decided ad hoc, because one requires evidence derived from the situation in order to justify the consideration of values, which applies a fortiori if more than two values are in play. The more values, the more chaos at the level of the decision.

Here again we have a possible paradox. One can also put it into a modal-theoritical version. Values are *necessary* in order to give decisions recourse to indisputability. Decisions however bring this *necessity* into the form of *contingency*. The necessity of adhering to values becomes for its part a contingent evaluation – when it comes to deciding – which can turn out differently depending on value constellations, the site of decision, and influences on the course of decision. Jurisprudence and legal dogmatics speak of »consideration of values«,[34] but that is a formula that has unity only insofar as it does not reveal to which results it leads. Thus (as is typical for the unfolding of paradoxes) the formula

---

33 One can add: »Only those questions that are in principle undecidable, *we* can decide,« with von Foerster 1992, 14.
34 For many examples, compare Pawlowski 1991, 378ff. and elsewhere.

does not say that it does not say what it does not say. Obviously this is not a mistake to be rebuked, but a transitory semantics that enables the cultivation of precedent decisions, which can be subsequently attended to with the proven technique of juridically analyzing the grounds of decision, or further developed in a process of distinguishing and overruling.

As far as it depends on values and decisions, society operates under the condition of *self-generated uncertainty*.[35] It first creates the »frame«[36] that establishes that what is to emerge as a decision is not yet established. One will have to grow accustomed to the consequences this has for social interaction, for the constant updating of modified understandings, and for a corresponding culture of self-representation.

One may doubt whether or not something like a concept of jurisprudence in the classical style will ever arise from this. Perhaps the development is going more in the direction of precedents, typical of common law, coupled with a correspondingly complex demand for proficiency in decision-making and a less conceptual style of argumentation. This is already a widespread practice in continental law with regard to rationales for authorizing appeals. Neither the arbitrariness of decision nor external influences on legal practice can be inferred in any way from the law's paradoxical founding. If anything, one needs to take the poorly synchronized self-formation of the legal system into account. But then that would be a typically predictable trait of a functionally differentiated social system. Slower and faster changes occur simultaneously in functional systems and synchronization becomes ever more difficult.

In this way, more than is officially acknowledged, the problem of the indispensability of specifiable norms or an inventory of such norms has dissolved. The substitute solution, that is already practiced, provides only for a paradox capable of developing as a formula for unity. Looking backward one can construct the history of the problem as if this would have always been the case. But that is a history written for our time. In today's society, it may depend on the insight that the problem does not lie in the difference between loyalty to principles and arbitrariness. Principles must be generalized in such a way that they signify nothing anymore. But on the other hand, arbitrariness – viewed factually – does not occur in social reality. Therefore the question can only be, whether or not maintaining the legal system's autonomy, self-determination and operative closure will also work in the future.[37] There is, then, no question that this system can structure its own autonomy, develop the paradox of its own distinctions' unity (even that between just and unjust) and come to terms with the necessity of contingency. The indispensability of norms – that is the autopoiesis of the system.

35 As in a somewhat differently specified context, Ladeur 1992.
36 »Frame« in the sense of Erving Goffmann 1974.
37 On this conceptuality, see Luhmann 1992, as well as the subsequent discussion. More comprehensively, see Luhmann 1993.

VI

But even then the problem of the tragic choices still remains, the problem, that is, of the right to violate the law.* From *Kant* to *Habermas* one can observe a quest for solutions that approximate the concept of system autonomy. For *Kant* »eternal peace« can only be guaranteed through states that grant citizens legal protection.[38] *Habermas* adds this desideratum the affected persons' democratic participation in constitutional procedures to.[39] Both suggestions are modern insofar as they avoid a dogmatic (metaphysical, religious, indisputable) anticipation of correct decisions that would sort the rams from the sheep in advance. But both suggestions are also characterized by other-worldliness and ignorance of the law. Neither *Kant* nor *Habermas* poses himself the problem of the right to break the law. For both the problem's solution lies in arrangements that enable access to the insights of reason. For its part reason is handled like a tribunal or like a source of insight that, under conditions of uncoerced communication, enables precisely that which it presupposes, namely, understanding without coercion. However, if negation actually exists, then there is not only positive self-reference, but negative self-reference as well. The state of today's world guides the gaze more to the problem of a decision between justice and injustice that is made not in accordance with the law – for example, as mentioned at the beginning, the case of torture, or cases of international intervention, or cases of the retroactive condemnation of »crimes« that were covered by positive law (but ostensibly not through »supra-positive« law) at the time of their commission.

It follows that in spite of a global society that communicates worldwide and has extensive interdependences in all functional sectors, the postulates of functional autonomy – the constitutional state [*Rechtsstaat*] and democracy – can only count as implemented in a few regions.[40] Implemented, that is, in the sense that violations can be handled as isolated cases, which can be processed using procedures belonging to the system they have violated. Globally this is more the exception than the rule – and this is so despite the fact that an alternative concept is nowhere in sight. A general diagnosis would therefore have to state that world society has adapted itself to the functional differentiation of systems, but in many functional domains (including economics, politics and law) such an evolutionarily improbable form of differentiation cannot assert itself – but neither can any other!

---

* Editor's note: Luhmann refers here to conflicts between the law and other social values. For example, conflicts between law and religious conviction or personal ethics, between existing law and political actions (e.g., civil disobedience) designed to modify the law or specific political structures, and, in its most extreme case, so-called emergency powers used by the executive branch to preserve the state (it's constitution) from extinction.

38 On Kant's Traktat »Zum ewigen Frieden«, see Tesón 1991, who elaborates Kant's viewpoints.

39 For example, Habermas 1992.

40 On this see Neves 1992.

This situation seems to correspond to the widespread appearance of »tragic choices«: economic development only through exclusion of large segments of the population; democracy only through presidial despotism and the like; guarantee of rights only through the right to break the law. If one confines the investigation to the legal system provided one brackets, among other issues, the much more complicated problem of an all-appropriate ethics), then one finds examples for our problem of the just-unjust system code's paradoxicality that have been made juridical with thorough success – one famous case and one less famous, yet highly pertinent.

The classical case is the case of derogation, the illegal breaching of the law by the holder of the highest political power.[41] In the Middle Ages this right to violate the law was seen as a component of an all-encompassing *iurisdictio*, and thus was moved into proximity with the regulation of exceptions – for the preservation of privileges, for instance. The early modern era saw in this a problem of »reason of state«. The Venetian state murders, for example, were thus justified (public interest of the commonwealth comes before private rights!).[42] Admittedly, only with a sigh and only in the case of emergency did one demand that this occur. On this basis, then, the notion of an eminent law (ius eminens) in states of emergency had become accepted parallel to the development of a right to expropriation of property against compensation based on eminent domain (dominium eminens). In the 18th century, this falls under the repertoire of the sovereign's normal legal authority[43] and finally under the matters that a constitution should regulate.

A second, less well-known legal development follows from the premise that the exercise of rights cannot be against the law. »Qui suo iure utitur neminem laedit.« (He who acts according to his own rights hurts no one.) But then one would have to forbid everything that could possibly injure others. The hard alternative »either legal or illegal,« which is and remains sensible as system code, would then take effect at the program level. In order to prevent this, legal figures were invented that stipulate that one can be held liable (strict liability) for, say, damages resulting from a perfectly unobjectionable (legal, guiltless) use of the law.[44] Presupposed as a concomitant institution is insurability and

41 For older literature, see Bonucci 1906. Also compare de Mattei 1953; 1969.
42 For example, compare Giovanni Maria Memmo 1563, 12: »Et Meglio e, che un Cittadino privato patisca a torto, che permettendogli, si tanta licenza, & autorità, egli ci faccia lecito a una Repubblica fare ogni opera, quantunque ingiusta, derivando da quella una tanta utilità, quanta e la libertà publica.« [And it is better that private citizen suffers a wrong, than to allow onself so much license and authority, and to legally oppress one's public liberty for the conservation of that which is legal in a republic even though injustice comes from this one such use, as well as public liberty.]
43 Compare for instance Weitzel 1749.
44 The trend-setting German monograph is Esser 1941. For the just-unjust code problematic, also see Merkel 1895. Common law's method of argumentation – which, departing from the concept of hazardous items, led to the concept of comparable results – is well traced by Levi 1948. More than anything, the enormous claim amounts and limits of insurability, which in turn allow total innocents to suffer as a result of economic effects, have provoked the more recent discussion in the United States. Just see Priest 1990.

the possibility for the offsetting of costs through pricing-raising, and then once more: equal treatment of market competitors.

One needs only to use one's power of imagination a little to see that our case of torture has a similar structure. One could therefore also think here of a similar juridical solution – regardless of all legalistic considerations based on Article 1 of the German Federal Constitution. For example: Allowance of torture through internationally supervised courts, closed-circuit surveillance of the scene in Geneva or Luxemburg, long-distance supervision via telecommunications, transferring the just / unjust distinction on to the victim's option of being either hero or traitor. Taken altogether, not very satisfying solutions. But it is equally unsatisfying to do nothing at all and thereby sacrifice innocent-bystanders to the fanaticism of terrorists.

VII

Viewed globally one can currently observe a growing attentiveness to the problem of human rights. Indeed the old- and new-European style of justification was hardly able to convince by way of nature or reason. Neither are rights such as »freedom« and »equality« well suited to function as human rights. In and of themselves, they are constructed paradoxically. They include their opposite and therefore must always be modifiable via law or contract. A disposition regarding this cannot be centralized. What one can observe is however a very primal way of generating norms on the basis of scandalous incidents to which the mass media gives global coverage. Whether there are texts that forbid such acts – or whether there are people who determine and ratify these texts and people who do not – hardly plays a role in the matter. One is not instructed to compare legal texts and conduct in order to read from this whether or not something violates the law or not. On a much more immediate level, scandal itself can generate a norm (that was not previously formulated at all) in cases like forced deportation and resettlement, the traceless disappearance of persons accompanied by state obstruction, illegal incarceration and torture, as well as political murder of every type. One who reacts indignantly and expresses counterfactual expectations in such cases does not have to reckon with dissent – almost as though the meaning of the norm was vouched for by sacred powers. The generation of norms follows the Durkheim model, it avails itself of public outrage (colère publique).[45] A juridical bestowal of form, a regulation in accordance with international law, can only attach itself to this but not act as source of law.

The dominant tendency, particularly since the end of World War Two and the decolonization of the globe, is to expand human rights – as well as broaden

---

45 See on this Emile Durkheim 1973. In particular see chapter II, 35ff.

their content and demand global observance. Corresponding to the development of the welfare state, the concept of protection within the realm of human rights has been completed – if not replaced – through a concept of public support. One places together needs and interests of »the« human, which are putatively foundational, and demands redress.[46] This corresponds exactly with the value concept, as dealt with above, and presents to all those engaged with it, either professionally or casually, a good starting point for communication. The question, »How are value conflicts resolved?« can thus be put on hold for the time being. Politically the notion of human rights is a foundation for poorer countries' demands on richer countries. At the same time, there comes a frightening magnitude of injuries to the minimum requirements for human dignity. From here, the inflation of the idea and terminology might lead to the widespread impression that human rights are disregarded anyway (one also speaks of ideals), and that in this question, everyone is sitting in a glass house. Therefore it is advisable to limit the discussion of human rights to the problems of injury to human dignity.[47] When this no longer occurs, one can inquire further with typical juridical caution.

Correspondingly one must distinguish among causes: »exemplary experience of injustice«[48] is one thing, horror and (helpless) outrage is another. In any event, it cannot be a matter of some type of global-style social work when a norm that evades all conflicts of interest is sought. That this is not an objection to social work or developmental aid should be self-explanatory. But with regard to political opportunity and limited economic possibilities, the problem is a matter of a different caliber. Of injuries to human rights, experienced globally in a unified manner, one can speak only of unambiguously unacceptable occurrences, when the weighing of pros and cons is no longer an option, and at best an understanding for tragic choices may still be expected. Injustice, in any case.

In this situation one could replace the semantics of human *rights* with one of human *duties*. That would mean holding state governments responsible, at least in the sense of keeping order within their territory. And it would correspond to a mounting tendency that also structures the global societal system more strongly for politics, and that understands the state organization not only as an expression of the will of the »people« but also, and perhaps first and foremost, as the international address for questions about the provision of order.

46 Just see Brugger 1989; 1992 – indeed with reference to the dangers of »inflating« (1992, 31) and ideologizing (1992, 30), which however are hardly to be avoided in this concept. In relation to the *juridical* applicability of *anthropological* justifications, Riedel (1986, 205ff., 346ff.) expresses skepticism.
47 Thus also see Bielefeldt 1988.
48 Thus see Brugger 1989, 562, and 1992, 21f. on the distinction between »exemplary experience of injustice« and »elementary experience of suffering«, and with a different catalogue of criteria. As to the latter sense, I understand the formulation of Heiner Bielefeldt (1988, 430): concrete, historical experiences of injustice. But the formulation should be sharpened in order to distinguish the scandalous from justified discontent over a given situation.

But then one would also have to consider what would be surrendered by this change of terminology. Talk of subjective rights had been a program for the unfolding of paradoxes. It was a matter of lending *objective* validity to *subjective* rights – of socially recognizing individuality and, through this, making the individual's unsociability the basis for regulating the legal system of society. Notwithstanding all the legal-theoretical controversies that might indicate the illogicality of this thought, it has proved its value in legal practice. Precisely this figure has proven to be the basic principle covering all possible claims up to the claim that law and politics are to be formed in accordance with the individual's own opinion. This may or may not be tolerated according to political requirements of scale, but when it leads to conflict between individuals, the state (as far as there still is one) will not be able to look on inactively just because it finds that both sides are right. It may also come to a loss of plausibility for the program of unfolding the paradoxes of subjective rights – but not necessarily to an abandonment of the legal-technical figure. The program, however, certainly leads to questions about the relevance of the figure when the problem of the indispensability of certain systems-vital norms is posed.

In effect this analysis changes the way in which the indispensability of norms becomes a problem. Realistically viewed, it is not a matter of conclusive formulas for an edifice of norms, nor of principles, nor of a basic norm, nor even of a highest value that encompasses and trumps all others. But it is also not a matter of postponing decision until uncoerced discourses have led to a reasonable result that will produce consensus among all sagacious individuals who only require certain procedural guarantees for this. Viewed cognitively, it concerns paradoxes – the self-blockage of knowledge that is not resolvable logically, but only creatively. And normatively viewed, it is about scandals with norm-generating potential. A high degree of contemporary relevance inheres in this problem given global-societal realities and the creeping intellectual defeatism that reacts to the problem. Ultimately, the question this situation confronts us with is: What can we do? But before we can ask this, there is a vital preliminary question: How can one observe and describe adequately?

References

Alafenish, Salem (1982): Der Stellenwert der Feuerprobe im Gewohnheitsrecht der Beduinen des Negev. Pp. 143-158 in: Fred Scholz / Jörg Janzen (eds.), Nomadismus, ein Entwicklungsproblem? Berlin: Reimer.

Allport, Floyd Henry (1933): Institutional Behavior: Essays Toward a Re-interpreting of Contemporary Social Organization. Chapel Hill, NC: University of North Carolina Press.

Bielefeldt, Heiner (1988): Die Menschenrechte als Chance in der pluralistischen Weltgesellschaft. Zeitschrift für Rechtspolitik 21, 423-431.

Bobbio, Noberto (1972): Giusnaturalismo e positivismo giuridico, 2nd ed. Milano: Ed. di Communità.

Bonucci, Alessandro (1906): La derogabilità del diritto naturale nella scolastica. Perugia.

Bottéro, Jean (1981): L'ordalie en Mésopotamie ancienne. Annali della Scuola Normale Superiore di Pisa, Classe di Lettere e Filosofia ser. III, Bd. XI, 1005-1067.

Brugger, Winfried (1989): Menschenrechte im modernen Staat. Archiv des öffentlichen Rechts 114, 537-588.

Brugger, Winfried (1992): Stufen der Begründung von Menschenrechten. Der Staat 31, 19-38.

Calabresi, Guido / Bobbitt, Philip (1978): Tragic Choices. New York: Norton.

Cardano, Girolamo (1663): De uno. Pp. 277-283 in: Caroli Sponii (ed.), Opera Omnia 1. Lyon (Reprint Stuttgart / Bad Cannstatt 1966).

Cover, Robert M. (1983): The Supreme Court, 1982 Term. Foreword: Nomos and Narrative. Harvard Law Review 97, 4-68.

de Mattei, Rodolfo (1953): Il problma del deroga e la ›Ragion di Stato‹. Pp. 49-60 in: Enrico Castelli, (ed.), Cristianesimo e Ragion di Stato. Roma: Fratelli Bocca.

de Mattei, Rodolfo (1969): Dal Premachiavellismo al Antimachiavellismo europeo del Cinquecento. Firenze: G.C. Sansoni.

Donati, Claudio (1988): L'idea di Nobilità in Italia: Secoli XIV-XVIII. Rome: Laterza.

Durkheim, Emile (1973): De la division du travail social, reprint of the 2nd Ed. Paris: Presses universitaires de France (The Division of Labour in Society. Basingstoke: Macmillan, 1984).

Dworkin, Ronald (1978): Taking Rights Seriously. Cambridge: Harvard University Press.

Esser, Josef (1941): Grundlagen und Entwicklung der Gefährdungshaftung: Beiträge zur Reform des Haftpflichtrechts und zu seiner Wiedereinordnung in die Gedanken des allgemeinen Privatrechts. München: Beck.

Goffmann, Erving (1974): Frame Analysis: An Essay on the Origin of Experience. Cambridge, Mass: Harvard University Press.

Günther, Gotthard (1979): Life as Polycontexturality: Pp. 283-306 in G. Günther, Beiträge zur Grundlegung einer operationsfähigen Dialektik, Vol. 2. Hamburg: Meiner Felix Verlag.

Habermas, Jürgen (1992): Faktizität und Geltung: Beiträge zur Diskurstheorie des Rechts und des demokratischen Rechtsstaats. Frankfurt a.M.: Suhrkamp (Between Facts and Norms: Contributions to a Discourse Theory of Law and Democracy. Cambridge, Mass.: MIT Press, 1996).

Hassemer, Winfried (1988): Unverfügbares im Strafprozeß. Pp. 183-204 in: Arthur Kaufmann / Ernst J. Mestmäcker / Hans F. Zacher (eds.), Rechtsstaat und Menschenwürde. Festschrift für Werner Maihofer zum 70. Geburtstag. Frankfurt a.M.: Vittorio Klostermann.

Hofstadter, Douglas R. (1979): Gödel, Escher, Bach: An Eternal Golden Braid. New York: Basic Books.

Horowitz, George (1973): The Spirit of Jewish Law. New York: Central Book Co.

Jouanna, Arlette (1981): L'idée de race en France au XVIe siécle et au début du XVIIe, 2. Ed., 2 Vols. Montpellier: Presses de l'Imprimerie de Recherche – Université Paul Valéry.

Klippel, Diethelm (1976): Politische Freiheit and Freiheitsrechte im deutschen Naturrecht des 18. Jahrhunderts. Paderborn: Schöningh.

Ladeur, Karl-Heinz (1992): Postmoderne Rechtstheorie: Selbstreferenz –Selbstorganisation – Prozeduralisierung. Berlin: Duncker & Humblot.

Luhmann, Niklas (1980):, Gesellschaftliche Struktur und semantische Tradition. Pp. 9-71 in: N. Luhmann, Gesellschaftstruktur und Semantik, Vol. 1. Frankfurt a.M.: Suhrkamp.

Luhmann, Niklas (1983): Rechtssoziologie, 2nd ed. Opladen: Westdt. Verlag (A Sociological Theory of Law. London: Routledge, 1985).

Luhmann, Niklas (1991); Soziologie des Risikos. Berlin: de Gruyter (Risk: A Sociological Theory. Berlin: de Gruyter, 1993).

Luhmann, Niklas (1992): Operational Closure and Structural Coupling: The Differentiation of the Legal System. Cardozo Law Review 13, 1419-1441.

Luhmann, Niklas (1993): Das Recht der Gesellschaft. Frankfurt a.M.: Suhrkamp (Law as a Social System. Oxford: Oxford University Press, 2004).

Levi, Edward H. (1948): An Introduction to Legal Reasoning. University of Chicago Law Review 15, 501-573.

Memmo, Giovanni Maria (1563): Dialogo … nel quale dopo ›alcune filosofiche dispute, si forma un perfetto Principe, & una perfetta Republica, e parimente un Senatore, un Cittadino, un Soldato, & Mercatore. Vinegia.

Merkel, Rudolf (1895): Die Kollision rechtmäßiger Interessen und die Schadenersatzpflicht bei rechtmäßigem Handeln. Straßburg: K.J. Trübner.

Neves, Marcelo (1992): Verfassung und Positivität des Rechts in der peripheren Moderne: Eine theoretische Betrachtung und eine Interpretation des Falls Brasilien. Berlin: Duncker & Humblot.

Palmer, Robert C. (1985a): The Origins of Property in England. Law and History Review 3, 1-50.

Palmer, Robert C. (1985b): The Economic and Cultural Impact of the Origins of Property 1180-1220. Law and History Review 3, 375-396.

Pawlowski, Hans-Martin (1991): Methodenlehre für Juristen: Theorie der Norm und des Gesetzes, 2nd Ed. Heidelberg: C.F. Müller.

Price, Richard (1776): Observations on the Nature of Civil Liberty, The Principles of Government and the Justice and Policy of the War with America, 2nd ed. London: Printed for Edward and Charles Dilly, and Thomas Cadell.

Priest, George L. (1990): The New Legal Structure of Risk Control. Daedalus 119, 4, 207-227.

Riedel, Eibe H. (1986): Theorie des Menschenrechtsstandards: Funktion, Wirkungsweise und Begründung wirtschaftlicher und sozialer Menschenrechte mit exemplarischer Darstellung der Rechte auf Eigentum und Arbeit in verschiedenen Rechtsordnungen. Berlin: Duncker & Humblot.

Rommen, Heinrich (1947): Die ewige Wiederkehr des Naturrechts, 2nd ed. München: Kösel.

Schlaffer, Heinz (1990): Poesie und Wissen: Die Entstehung des ästhetischen Bewußtseins und der philologischen Erkenntnis. Frankfurt a.M.: Suhrkamp.

Schalk, Ellery (1986): From Valor to Pedigree: Ideas of Nobility in France in the Sixteenth and Seventeenth Centuries. Princeton: Princeton University Press.

Sève, René (1982): Brèves réflexions sur le Droit et ses metaphors. Archive de philosophie du droit 27, 259-262.

Spencer Brown, George (1957): Probability and Scientific Interference. London: Longmans, Green & Co.

Shackle, G.L.S. (1979): Imagination, Formalism, and Choice. Pp. 19-31 in: Mario J. Rizzo (ed.), Time, Uncertainty, and Disequilibrium: Exploration of Austrian Themes. Lexington, Mass: Lexington Books.

Spencer Brown, George (1979): Laws of Form. Reprint. New York: Julian Press.

Tesón, Fernando R. (1991): The Kantian Theory of International Law. Columbia Law Review 92, 53-102.

Vallet de Goytisolo, Juan B. (1982): Estudio sobre fuentes del dereche y método jurídico. Madrid: Montecorvo.

von Foerster, Heinz (1981): Objects, Tokens for (Eigen-) Behaviors. Pp. 273-285 in: H.v. Foerster, Observing Systems. Seaside, California: Intersystems Publications.

von Foerster, Heinz (1992): Ethics and Second-Order Cybernetics. Cybernetics and Human Knowing I, 9-19.

Weigand, Rudolf (1967): Die Naturrechtslehre der Legisten und Dekretisten von Irnerius bis Accursius und von Gratian bis Johannes Teutonicus. München: Hueber.

Weitzel, Carl (1749): Von der Macht weltlicher Regenten wider göttliche (sic) Rechte Gesetze zu geben. Frankfurt a.M./Leipzig.

Wolff, Christian (1740): Jus naturae methodo scientifica pertractatum. Frankfurt a.M./Leipzig (reprint Hildesheim 1972).

Soziale Systeme 14 (2008), Heft 1, S. 38-46   © Lucius & Lucius, Stuttgart

Niklas Luhmann

Beyond Barbarism[1]

Abstract: The author treats the question of »barbarism« in the modern world as a question of the relationship between semantics and social structure. The antique Greek distinction between »Hellenes« and »Barbarians« represents the general, asymmetrical schema of »inclusion« and »exclusion« that is characteristic societies marked by stratification. Modern, functional differentiated society eliminates this distinction in the name of a full inclusion of all. Yet this total inclusion reveals itself to be the mere self-description of modernity, for in truth complete exclusion from all function systems of society exist without disrupting the stability of society as a whole. The author concludes that a type of inclusion/exclusion super-coding may become the operating distinction of world society in this century.

In view of the changing meaning of important cosmological, social, and political concepts in the second half of the eighteenth century, the question whether old »word-shells« should still be used or rather discarded frequently arises. We do not have this problem when the words »abarbarians,« »barbaric«, »barbarism« are concerned. These words are today only used to express disgust and to supply one's disgust with an aura of objectivity. One can do without them; for this, there are countless other possibilities.

There are, however, also modern concepts of barbarism. One can think of, for instance, the distinction between »savages« and »barbarians« in Schiller's »Letters on the Aesthetic Education of Man«: The savages perceive the world sensually, and therefore experience it as a variety of the diverse. The barbarians, on the other hand, have subscribed to reason. They are those who grant absolute primacy to the unity of reason over the variety and individuality of all the phenomena. Barbarians are those who have only one iron left in the fireplace. They cultivate, so to speak, a monoculture of reason. It may be politically convenient to continue this conception of barbarism – but it is not advisable, because nowadays one would no longer associate it with Robbespiere – but with Habermas. Robbespiere had a guillotine at hand. The modern adherents of reason are,

---

1 Translated by Hans-Georg Moeller. The translation first appeared in Hans-Georg Moeller (2006): Luhmann Explained: From Souls to Systems. Chicago/LaSalle, IL: Open Court, Pp. 261-272. Reprinted by permission of Open Court Publishing Company, a division of Carus Publishing Company, Peru, IL, copyright © 2006 by Carus Publishing Company. The translation follows the German original: Niklas Luhmann (1995): Jenseits von Barbarei. Pp. 138-150 in: N. Luhmann, Gesellschaftsstruktur und Semantik. Studien zur Wissenssoziologie der modernen Gesellschaft, Vol. 4. Frankfurt a.M.: Suhrkamp.

pleasantly, distinguished by taking provocative and appellative speech as already being politics and are content with this.

Moreover, by continuing that use of language one would lose the possibility of comparing ancient conceptional dispositions with modern ones. If one has such comparative intentions, it is out of question to conceive of barbarism as a historical universal category. One would no longer have the possibility of doing what is attempted in the following: to investigate the *problem* that came to expression with the distinction between barbarians and Hellenes – a problem which under the conditions of present-day social structures is likely to take on a very different shape from Greek antiquity. A supposition obtrudes that this new shape may be the distinction between inclusion and exclusion.

II

In order to reflect on conceptual dispositions in the old world one can relate to Kosselleck's analysis of asymmetric antonyms[2] or to Louis Dumont's *englobement du contraire*.[3] In this light, the distinction between barbarians and Hellenes is one among many. Such distinctions resulted from the attempt to continue a hierarchical world-architecture in the face of increasing complexity. The world is more perfect if it contains not only angels, but also stones, not only men, but also women, not only Hellenes, but also barbarians. Formally this is about oppositions; or more abstractly, about distinctions by which the higher evaluation of the one side does not only underscore the contradistinction of the two elements, but also the fact that they belong to a hierarchical order. The »better« side has therefore a double function in a horizontal and a vertical direction. It represents the hierarchy within the distinction, and this in turn justifies its superiority.

It is important to note that oppositions of this kind are not understood as antagonisms. They are only classifications according to a specific order of species and genus as they were already conceived by Plato and logically elaborated by Aristotle. What matters is to exclude one side of the distinction from the other, one species from the other, one determination from its opposite. Accordingly the barbarians cannot be Hellenes, and the Hellenes cannot be barbarians. This suffices as a logical guarantee for order. If opposition would be understood as antagonism, as an invitation to conflict, then a stable order would be impossible and modern conditions would be anticipated – for instance, the Hobbesian constellation of individuals that only allowed for a self-transcending (later it will be said: dialectical) solution, or the later attempts at a totalitarian logic that intended to humanize all humans.[4] Only modern society will, beyond barbarism, conceive of such instabilities and try to cope with them.

2 See Kosselleck 1975, 65-104.
3 See Dumant 1963.
4 On this issue see Herbst's (1976, 69ff.) typology of logic.

The stability of the semantic type of asymmetrical oppositions and the variety of its applications allows for the assumption that it had socio-structural correlates that supplied it, despite all its ambiguity, with sufficient plausibility. We can reduce these correlates, by drastic simplification, to three aspects:

(1) These societies are regional societies, but increasing border-crossing contacts force them to develop a consciousness of multiple ethnicities and to provide rules for contacts with different ethnicities, although these rules and designations are not recognized as universal, but as society-specific. No one would have expected the barbarians to describe themselves as barbarians. Corresponding problems finally arise even within the city, as it is evidenced by the formation of a *ius gentium* in Rome.

(2) These societies are *de facto* aristocratic societies, although the importance of birth (descendance) and bureaucratic positions vary greatly. In Greece, an aristocrat, even when refraining from taking on »political« positions, is still of significant inter-Hellenian importance in the areas of diplomacy, sports, as well as a *theoros* who trustfully reports on foreign affairs. The description of society therefore has to take into account the differences of social status. And this means mainly: human beings cannot be socially excluded simply because they lack social rank, liberty and *dignitas*. To realize the hierarchy all ranks are necessary. And this has:

(3) consequences for the regulation of inclusion and exclusion. Inclusion is essentially up to the family homes, and thus exclusion also becomes more or less automatically its business, from the killing or exposition of infants, to the expulsion of juveniles, who then have to somehow make a bare living; for instance as criminals, beggars, legionaries, or (in England) in the Navy. Since the middle ages, corporations were added as absorbing institutions, in the form of guilds, the church, orders, monasteries, and universities, for instance. But of course, these do not serve the lowest strata, especially not the peasants.

III

This connection between the semantics of asymmetrical oppositions and structural conditions of plausibility loses its meaning with the transition to modernity, and in the beginning practically without any substitution. If in Naples even today people are identified as *saraceni* and accordingly treated without any responsibilities then this can only be characterized as a regional peculiarity.

This change can roughly be conceived of as the transition from a social order of stratification to a society differentiated into function systems. This transition at first de-legitimizes social stratification. Stratification becomes a mere byproduct of the function systems, especially of the economy and education system. Besides, a regional convergence of the boundaries of function systems can no longer be assumed. The borders between states are not borders of the economy system, the systems of science and mass media are anyways conceived globally. Since the second half of the 19th century a world-time exists that allows for everything that happens to happen simultaneously, no matter if it is, regionally viewed, morning or evening. Communication that transcends regional borders loses its exceptional status. National events are internationally observed. It is still disputed if the result should be called »world society« (*Weltgesellschaft*) or »global system«, because no sufficient social theory is yet available. Certainly, classifications of identity in the pattern of »we and all the others« lose their meaning. Classifications, for instance »Serbs and Croats,« may still come up, but they represent, at most, a temporal emphasis of specific distinctions in relation to equally possible others.

Along with these structural changes of the primary type of differentiation, the family loses its function to regulate inclusion and exclusion. Families become private families, which, among other things, means that they no longer determine the lifestyle of their members and no longer operate under public supervision, but instead are supposed to accept individual life-form choices with sympathy and support. Moreover, the absorption-system of the old-style corporations no longer exists, instead there are modern organizations based on membership decisions, that is to say on the inclusion of a few members and the exclusion of all others.

As opposed to those organizations, the social system and its function systems are laid out to include the entirety of the population. There are no obvious grounds on which one can be excluded from the use of money, from being a legal subject, from having citizenship, from education, or from marriage – or obvious grounds on which all this could be made contingent upon system-internal licenses or special conditions. Given the principal full inclusion of everybody, the function systems themselves decide how far someone gets: if he/she is legally right or wrong, if his/her knowledge is accepted as true or not, if he/she is successful in gaining reputation in the system of the mass media (that is to say: in attracting public attention), how much money he/she can spend, etc. This sovereignty, regarding the degree of inclusion, guarantees as such the differentiation of the function systems and is symbolically celebrated by being expressed as the freedom and equality of all individuals, which only means that the function systems assume that the population is a homogenous environment and that they can differentiate exclusively on the basis of their own criteria.

Obviously it makes no sense to describe the relations between function systems in the terms of asymmetric oppositions, as if science could classify all non-scientific communication as barbaric. Not even religion designates other function systems as pagan; its worries are more focused on competition within its own function system than on legal, political, or economic events as such.[5] The inter-

---

5   »In Toscana ci sono piu maghi che preti«– thus expressed the bishops in charge their alarm

system relations combine, in the terminology of »pattern variables« (Parsons), universalism and specification, namely encompassing competence – but only for their own function.[6]

IV

Thus, barbarism has disappeared – at least if one understands it to be a form that has another side on which there is *ethos, philia*, beauty of lifestyle, and, especially, a tight connection of these qualities. This, however, does not necessarily imply that modern society can be content with itself. Already the idea (that emerged from Europe, and that Husserl had sketched in his renown Vienna Lectures in May 1935)[7] that the life-form of the rationally enlightened, socially responsible man who only worships reason represents the *telos* of mankind ought to be terrifying. This would amount, as stated above, to a totalitarian logic that could no longer recognize any »outside«, and that would therefore lack another side which it needs merely on mathematical grounds in order to be a form and to offer possibilities of observation.[8] The consequences begin to take shape in a period of transition that registers changes and their thorough effects, but does not yet possess a social theory that is adequate to the new social conditions. Three aspects are to be especially highlighted: (1) the transformation of earlier exclusions into inclusions, (2) the formulation of philosophical theories that no longer recognize an »outside« (while at the same time concepts such as »environment« are entered into language as neologisms), and (3) the invention of »culture«. All this seems to contribute to suck the barbarians into society.

Deviant behavior is now no longer a reason for exclusion, but rather a reason for special treatment of inclusion. Given the enormous increase of delinquents (that is to say, in the first place, the enormous increase of penal law), there are still penitentiary colonies; but at the same time prisons are built in accordance with new architectonics.[9] Joblessness, begging, etc., is not defined as fate or a plague, but answered with educational programs, labor houses, industrial pedagogies, etc. Generally speaking, pedagogy switches from households to schools. Hopeless cases are »psychiatrized«, i.e., they are conceived of as illnesses or problems that society has to take care of, and that have to be solved with exceptional rights and duties within special institutions. All this was introduced with the new novel,

according to a report of the newspaper *La Republica* from April 23, 1994, while the announcements of the Roman Catholic Church in regard to the simultaneous turbulences sounded rather restrained.

6 By the way: nothing else says, if closely read, Hegel's notorious thesis of the »end of art«. Modern art may now take up *everything* as a theme, but only in so far as it can do this *as art*. Cf. Plumpe 1993, 302ff.

7 See the printed version under the title »Die Krisis des europäischen Menschentums und die Philosophie« (Husserl 1954).

8 This relates to George Spencer Brown 1979. See also Baecker 1993.

9 Cf. specifically on this issue Bender 1987.

the novel about the individual who showed in *Robinson Crusoe* and *Moll Flanders* how isolation leads to reflection, and how reflection leads to a change in behavior. The individuals lend hope to society, and they do this by being set free from previous restraints, i.e. by being »emancipated« and by being brought to self-discipline. But will they do what is expected? And according to which criteria?

Soon after this, great philosophy catches up by formulating a world without an »outside« for the subject or the spirit. Kant's reduction of the external world to the unknowable thing in itself shows the direction. Schelling's dissolving of all distinctions, including that of inside and outside, into »indifference« (symbolized either by art or religion) is another case. And there is finally Hegel's theory of absolute spirit or Husserl's ontological *epoche*. Can this be interpreted as a new cosmology for a society without exclusion?[10]

In the same context the invention of »culture« takes place. One can speak of »invention« because the modern concept of culture only emerges in the second half of the 18th century and has no predecessor in old-European semantics. Culture is initially simply a doubling of all artifacts, including texts. Besides their immediate usage, artifacts gain a second meaning as documents of a culture. Pots are on the one side pots, but on the other side they are also signs of a specific culture that distinguishes itself by its kind of pots from another culture. And what is true for pots is also true for religions. Along with the new semantics of culture the old concept of nation that was related to heritage changes too. Comparisons between nations were already common at earlier times (for instance in the context of different criteria for aristocracy), but now they take on the form of cultural comparisons. Nations have the practical communicative advantage of having proper names, so one can avoid the embarrassment of having to explain what exactly one is talking about.

The interest in culture is therefore rooted in an interest in comparisons – be they national or historical comparisons. In the perspective of comparison, nothing can be left aside. Or more precisely: what is included and what is excluded is regulated by the point of comparison, i. e. by the comparison itself, and not by innate qualities. Once more: replacement of exclusion by mobile, flexible, differentiable inclusion.

Comparisons are, expressed in the terminology that was fashionable in the 18th century, »interesting«. But that which is interesting can always be, as Friedrich Schlegel notes, more interesting. The interest in comparisons tends to expand itself, and the concept of culture is so conceived that it does not offer any resistance to comparisons. Neither in history nor in ethnology is something found that could not be compared or that would be uninteresting on principle. The

---

10 Without exclusion: this is, by the way, not the case for the philosophy of the late Husserl. Because »the Eskimos or the Indians of the fairs, or the gypsies who constantly vagabond around Europe« (1954, 318f.) do not take part in the spiritual entelechy of the European mankind.

regulatory criterion is exclusively the specification and abstraction of the aspects of comparison.

And to whose disposition are these? Firstly: modern Europe, the contemporary Zeitgeist. Now, one witnesses a peculiar return of asymmetric oppositions. The point of view of the comparison describes its findings under the aspect of culture while the cultures who are so compared are mostly unaware that they are cultures. One may read Novalis' »Christendom; or: Europe« or Schiller's »On Naïve and Sentimental Poetry«. The middle ages had not reflected on themselves as a successful spiritual totality; only so could they be one. The naïve poets did not know that the immediacy of their relation to reality was naïve. This was only told to them by the distinctions of modernity, to the effect that modernity with its culture of reflexivity became both presumptuous and melancholic. It began to suffer from itself, and to bet on the future.

The connection between these semantic dispositions of modernity becomes evident when it is observed by the guiding difference of inclusion and exclusion. The existence of hell is denied – but then better and worse places in heaven must be distinguished. One recognizes problematic cases, and has to help out with therapy, social work or developmental aid. The logic of functional differentiation excludes social exclusion, but then it has to allow distinctions within the function systems according to their criteria. But is this logic sustainable? How can there be inclusion if there is no exclusion?

V

To the surprise of the well-meaning it has to be ascertained that exclusion still exists, and it exists on a massive scale and in such forms of misery that are beyond description. Anybody who dares a visit to the *favelas* of South American cities and escapes alive can talk about this. But even a visit to the settlements that were left behind after the closing of the coal mines in Wales can assure one of it. To this effect, no empirical research is needed. Who trusts his eyes can see it, and can see it so impressively that all explanations at hand will fail.

We know: there is talk about exploitation, or about social suppression, or about *marginalidad*, about an increase of the contradiction between center and periphery. But all these are theories that are still governed by the desire for all-inclusion and therefore are looking for addressees to blame: capitalism, the ruling alliance of financial and industry capital with the armed forces or with the powerful families of the country. But if one takes a closer look, one does not find anything that could be exploited or suppressed. One finds existences reduced to the bodily in their self-perception and other-perception, attempting to get to the next day. In order to survive they have to have capabilities of perceiving dangers and of making available what is most needed – or resignation and indifference with regard to all »bourgeois« values: including order, cleanliness, and self-respect. And if one adds up what one sees one can conceive of the idea that this may be the guiding difference of the next century: inclusion and exclusion.

The search for addressees to blame and the search for points of attack to bring about changes towards all-inclusion still calculates on the basis of a primary stratified society. In proportion to the degree by which this assumption becomes inadequate and is passed on as a mere ideal, and by which phenomena can no longer be well traced back to the activities of certain ruling circles, the search for a different explanation becomes more worthwhile. At this point, one can make use of the theory of functional differentiation in so far as it is distinguished from the classical theory of labor division (increase of profits with unavoidable costs).

Functional differentiation cannot, as opposed to what the self-descriptions of the systems are claiming, realize the postulated full-inclusion. Function systems, when operating rationally, exclude persons or marginalize them so drastically that this has consequences in regard to getting access to other function systems. No education, no work, no income, no regular marriages, children with no birth certificate, no passport, no participation in politics, no access to legal advice, to the police or to the courts – the list can be extended and it concerns, dependent on the circumstances, all marginalizations up to total exclusion. No one will say that it has to be this way according to some kind of Malthusian population law. It is, however, sufficient to see that it is so and how such an amplifying effect is produced at the margins of function systems. Perhaps religion could offer an exceptional opportunity? But if one inspects more closely the countless new cults of the modern world, based on states of trance as medium, no distinction of black and white magic, healing as a promise without differentiation of medical and other life-problems, then one understands the hesitation of the Catholic church to espouse religiosity of this type in the churches.

Facts of this kind turn the common theory of integration held by many sociologists upside down. Modern society is indeed highly integrated, but only in its area of exclusion, as negative integration, and above all – without consensus. In the realm of inclusion, however, the normal conditions of stability reign: loose coupling, relatively high capability of coping with errors, careers as the mode of integration of individuals and society, multiple contexts of observational perspectives, and better or worse conditions of life with a high degree of acceptance of individualized communication.

Still, the corresponding disintegration of inclusion can also be reflected upon, and this is what present-day theoreticians of modernity are currently focusing on. The integration of the individual and society no longer finds its principles in common consensus; it switched from provenance (and thus determined: from *ethos*) to career, that is to say to processed contingency. Moreover, the mutual-increase connection between culture (*Bildung*) and freedom predicted by neo-humanists did not come true, but has rather been dissolved. In modern supply-society, freedom is not restricted by coercion, but rather structured by supply in such a way that the enacting of freedom can no longer be attributed as the self-realization of the individual. One buys for a good price, watches the advertised films, chooses a religion or not as one likes – just like the others. Even God is a supply-God. He offers, and the model is of course Pascal's wager, his love so impressively and so independent of moral judgments that the refusal would be meaningless or, theologically speaking, fulfills the definition of sin. This demonstrates that culture and social conditions have made the enacting of freedom so asymmetrical that the individual is only left with meaningless decisions – or with protests that do not change anything.

This was, of course, never different. But in modern society this hits the vital element of the self-description of the system as »humane.«

With a certain nostalgia we can now think back to the barbarians or to the other ethnicities, the pagans, the savages. They were left with their own social order. We did not have anything to do with it. We were free to convert them or to enslave them, or to cheat them when exchanging goods. And it were our concepts, European concepts, when we spoke of *humanitas*, of *ius gentium*, of humankind or of human rights. All this is no longer adequate in the situation modern society finds itself in – not to speak of concepts such as *societas civilis* or *communitas* that we are getting from our basements like *Sauerkraut* to enjoy them reheated.[11]

If this diagnosis is only roughly correct, society can neither expect advice nor help from sociology. But it could make sense to search for theories that do more justice to the facts than the optimistic-critical traditional ways of thought within our discipline – justice to those facts with which society constructs itself.

References

Baecker, Dirk (ed.) (1993): Kalkül der Form. Frankfurt a.M.
Bender, John (1987): Imagining the Penitentiary: Fiction and the Architecture of Mind in Eighteenth-Century England. Chicago.
Dumant, Louis (1963): Essais sur l'individualism. Paris.
Herbst, Philip G. (1976): Alternatives to Hierarchies. Leiden.
Husserl, Edmund (1954): Die Krisis des europäischen Menschentums und die Philosophie. Pp. 314-348 in: E. Husserl, Husserliana, Vol. 6. The Hague.
Koselleck, Reinhart (1975): Zur historisch-politischen Semantik asymmetrischer Gegenbegriffe. Pp. 65-104 in: Harald Weinrich (ed.), Positionen der Negativität. Poetik und Hermeneutik, Vol. 6. München.
Plumpe, Gerhard (1993): Ästhetische Kommunikation der Moderne, Vol. 1. Opladen.
Spencer Brown, George (1979): Laws of Form. New York (reprint).

11 In the oral presentation, I had referred at this juncture to the *Witwe Bolte*. This aroused displeasure. Perhaps I came too close to the matter. (The *Witwe Bolte* – a widow named »Bolte«– is a prominent personae in 19th century German popular literature. She appears in the satirical children's book *Max und Moritz* by Wilhelm Busch. Max and Moritz, two juvenile »villains,« steal *Witwe Bolte*'s chickens from the hearth while she is getting sauerkraut from the basement. Later in the story, the miller grounds Max and Moritz to grist because of all the mischief they did. It should also be noted that Luhmann refers to the oral presentation of the paper at the *Institut für Sozialforschung* in Hamburg which is a »hotbed« of German Critical Theory and leftist thinking – Luhmann, however, was still able to leave the location unharmed; translator's comment.)

Soziale Systeme 14 (2008), Heft 1, S. 47-67

Chris Thornhill

On Norms as Social Facts:
A View from Historical Political Science

Abstract: This essay addresses the concept of norms and the connection between norms, social structure and politics in the works of Niklas Luhmann. Two theses are put forward in this regard. First, it is argued that, in its political implications, Luhmann's theory of society has a clear normative – or socio-normative – content. His theory implies that governmental systems, whose constitution is adapted to the pluralistically differentiated form of modern society or at least does not jeopardize or impede the evolutionary process of social differentiation, have a higher probability of legitimation (or self-legitimation) than governmental systems that fail to observe or even undermine the differentiation of the distinct function systems of society. Second, it is argued that for Luhmann the question of norms or values can never be explicitly raised. Modern societies are *polynormative* societies. Norms are in embedded in social structure in highly variable manner, and they cannot be simply disentangled from this semantic structure or transformed into objects of debate by acts of theoretical questioning. In modern society, therefore, the normative function of norms depends on the fact that through their silence they promote the differentiation of society and obstruct the possible convergence of society around normative or politically emphatic contests. Luhmann's question, whether indispensable norms exist, can thus not be adjudicated, or in fact even meaningfully posed. It imputes a politically centred or even exceptionalist form to society, which it can no longer factually assume.

Luhmann's (2008) analysis of norms suggests that norms are not prescriptively situated against factual social reality. Instead, he argues, norms can be observed »as facts« (20), and each society relies on the construction of norms as facts to organize and stabilize its communications. In particular, it is fundamental to the law of society that it produces norms and that it gives to society an apparatus that stabilizes expectations over time and consolidates the expectation-structures on which a society depends for its future orientation. Moreover, it is also fundamental to the law of society that it articulates itself in theories of law, and that these theories allow society to generate new principles – that is, new norms – to reflect on and to analyze itself, and its law. The normative reality of law, in other words, duplicates itself, reflexively, in the normative reality of the theory of law, and both the norms of law and the norms of law's theory are then conjoined to constitute the elements of society's factual normativity. For Luhmann, neither the norms of law nor the norms of law's theory are external to society or to law: they are internal communications or factual meta-reflections of society's need for a legal (normative) order in which to communicate about its communications. To be sure, Luhmann sees norms as facts of a particular kind. He designates them as »contra-factual expectations« (20), as facts, that is, that cannot originate in any material reality, but through which a communicative system (in particular, law) produces its own internally cohesive reality as »doubling of reality« (21), and so articulates and underwrites the expectations that are specific to that system. Nonetheless, norms have the specific factual function that they create a relatively organized set of references to stabilize society's future communications, and that they provide reflexive devices in which a society can articulate and externalize possible or necessary forms forth its self-construction. It is in this quality that norms are social facts.

Luhmann's theory of norms undermines three standard ways of thinking about norms. First, this theory undermines the view underlying classical normative philosophy, which claims that norms are deductive principles, whose content can be contested and determined by human rationalities, and to which, when they are (or when it is conceded that they are) adequately demonstrated, social reality can be held to account.[1] Second, this theory undermines more established positions in the sociology of norms. It opposes sociological views on norms that identify the emergence of norms as the outcome of probable patterns of social behaviour, oriented around typical processes of social (or anthropological) formation (see Popitz 1980). Moreover, although he follows elements of the more classical functionalist theory of norms, Luhmann also opposes the view expressed by Talcott Parsons and other US-American sociologists that norms are institutionalized expectations, sustained by a discrete cultural system, that confront and are internalized by social agents as co-ordinating and socializing aspects of a society's structure.[2] Third, then, Luhmann's theory also undermines more recent attempts to combine normative and sociological analysis, which examine societies as reliant on publicly generalized norms for their integrative stability and designate rationalized norms as the necessary substrates of legitimate political orders and of relatively stable socio-factual existence (see Habermas 1992, 569). It is against views in the third category that Luhmann turns perhaps most manifestly. For Luhmann, there is never any *between* in the relation of facts and norms; there is no dichotomy between *Faktizität* and *Geltung;* and the attempt to devise procedures of normative deduction that both reflect socially embedded rationalities and contain postulates possessing some degree of invariability against social forms is at once substantively self-

---

1   For Luhmann's critique of normative political philosophy as insufficiently complex, see: Luhmann 1970, 159.
2   See Parsons's (1967, 7-8) reading of Durkheim, which stresses the role of ›patterns of normative culture‹ as social facts internalized by particular social agents, which build social structure and stabilize the social system as a whole. See also Merton's (1957, 166) theory of ›cultural structure‹ as an aggregate of general values that promote conformity to institutionalized norms. See also Nisbet's (1970, 223-225) view of norms as internal elements of culture.

deluding and methodologically unnecessary. For Luhmann, norms are facts, and norms cannot disarticulate themselves from facts in order to provide a gener-alizable construction of themselves as other than facts. Moreover, it is also worth emphasizing (and here he turns against earlier normative sociologies)[3] that Luhmann sees norms as eminently *social* facts: that is, they are the facts of society's (not humanity's) self-construction, and they must be observed and examined (not deduced) as terms that refract the evolutionary exigencies of society (not humanity). Norms are the factual form into which a society brings its exchanges in order to articulate them as stable, plausible and necessary. Any suggestion of a possible antinomy between facts and norms, in consequence, is a false antinomy.

On this basis, Luhmann's work might be viewed as the first completely and resolutely sociological theory of norms and normative necessities. His theory identifies societies as – by necessity – possessing »non-arbitrary« (2008, 22) normative forms: that is, he argues that norms are fundamental to the structure of society, and they cannot be simply imposed on a society or arbitrarily revised. At the same time, however, his theory determines normative forms, not as outcomes of deduction or behavioural association, but as factual elements of society's self-reflection. The necessity of norms as facts, therefore, results from the fact that societies, and particularly the legal and the political systems in society, *need norms* and, under certain conditions, quite specific norms, in order sustainably to articulate and externalize their most adequate form. Indeed, as they are required to elaborate their foundations in ever more complex and more contingent environments, modern societies create and encounter an escalating requirement for more and for increasingly refined and rapidly iterable constructs in which they are able, from within themselves, to describe and render plausible their functions: they thus obtain a hypertrophic need for norms. It might in fact be taken as a universal *fact* that as the pluralism of society's environments increases, so too, commensurately, does the volume of norms necessitated by a society in order to adapt to its own pluralistic shape. Norms, however, do not result from any rationality that is anything other than *social* or that is founded in anything other than society's contingent and auto-communicated reality. They have no basis in any rationality that can be aligned to the Leibnizian definition of human reason as a monad or the Kantian definition of reason as the form of subjective synthesis: that is, in both instances, as a perennial and essentially self-identical form that contains the principles of all knowledge, or at least all authorizable knowledge, for all things, for all places and for all time. For this reason, then, it is fundamentally misguided to assume that norms constitute an immovable ethical foundation for society; that – in their *necessity* – they place prescriptive or perennial checks on the positivity – or the *contingency* – of law; or that they facilitate the ascription of ethical pre-

---

3 See note 2 above.

ference to some social exchanges over others. The contrary is in fact the case. Norms are necessary as facts that externalize the internal self-explanations of society's systems; norms allow society's systems to store an account or a number of accounts of themselves through which they can construct themselves relatively cohesively against dramatically evolving external realities; as such, norms underlie the wider evolution of society as an acentric, multi-rational, fully positivized and self-valorizing and, in consequence, necessarily heteroarchical totality of differentiated communications. Norms, thus, are facts of society, for which society has a specific necessity, and only theory that takes society, or the auto-communicative reality of society that is *the social*, as its primary unit of analysis is able to understand norms and their necessity.

Of particular relevance to the analysis of norms is Luhmann's concept of *semantics*. With this concept, Luhmann suggests that, at different points in their evolution, societies rely on different semantic structures in order to form a basis of demonstrable knowledge to which they can refer in their selections, decisions and their ongoing adaptation (Luhmann 1980, 49-50). It is through semantics that societies organize and solidify the temporal-sequential structure of their communications: semantics allow societies to generate and to preserve, as their own conceptual histories, functionally specified reservoirs of evidentially sustainable knowledge, and they allow them to store the self-constructions of different social systems in a temporally ordered body of terms and categories, around which further social communications can then simplify and plausibilize themselves. Semantics, in other words, are the conceptual repositories in which societies bring their distinct communications into security, and into which they transfer their communications about themselves into a differentiated systematic or evidential form to consolidate a corpus of plausibilizing constructs in order (as far as possible) adaptively to pre-empt and so to *securitize* the process of their evolution (1980, 55). For Luhmann, in consequence, there is a deep relation between norms and semantics, and he argues that the normative bedrock of society – that is, the terms around which a society articulates the preconditions of its ongoing security – is grounded in semantics. Norms are not stored in a society as dominant manifestations of consensus, convention, socializing prescription, or shared belief in collective goals: they are stored as semantics, or as values, and the function of these semantics is specifically not to act as orientations toward society's common goal-attainment, but to maintain a hyper-fictionalized or »self-generated« (Luhmann 2008, 30) foundation for society in its contingency. It is in this respect, then, that Luhmann introduces the concept of *paradoxes*: he explains that the organizing principles in the semantics of society's self-construction have only *paradoxical* grounds for their evidence and plausibility, and they are validated and sustained only through their ability, however fictitiously, at once to distinguish and to unify communications pertaining to one specific realm of social exchange. In linking norms to semantics and semantics to paradoxes, therefore, Luhmann's work casts an ironic reflex both on the rationalist metaphysics of post-Cartesian philosophy,[4] which assume that norms derive from and are authorized by perennial rationalities, and on the norm–structure relation underlying much of traditional Western sociology.[5] His attitudes to both these theoretical legacies in fact converge in the same position: namely, in his claim that norms are society's norms; that they express their foundation, not through adjudicable evidence, but through reference to paradoxes; and that they are stored, and made available to society, as semantics.

It is in this correlation between norms, semantics and paradoxes, additionally, that Luhmann raises his most far-reaching questions for more conventional political analysis and political theory. Luhmann indicates that theories of politics are themselves part of society's semantics, or of society's semantic memory, and they have no normative distinction against the realities which they describe and over which they pronounce.[6] Political theories have the factual function for a society that they enunciate paradoxes (Hobbes, for example, proposed the paradox of the social contract; Locke offered the paradox of natural law and natural rights; Montesquieu added to this the paradox of the constitutional state; Sieyès augmented these reserves by formulating the paradox of the sovereign nation capable of parliamentary representation) in order to cover, authenticate and organize society's norms. As articulated doctrines, then, these theories allow societies, or systems within societies, to integrate and memorize the motives for their normative authorization and organization, and societies can recurrently take recourse to these memories to support their self-descriptions and their normative self-articulations. A contemporary society wishing to obtain legitimacy for its politics by recruiting political support for some degree of welfare provision, for instance, might refer to Rawls; similarly, a society intending to obtain legitimacy for its politics by instituting a big-tent approach to governmental policy might refer to Habermas. However, Luhmann is clear that these theories have no supra-contingent authority against the facts (norms) about which they communicate: they are in fact embedded in these facts (norms), and they allow these facts (norms) to adapt and to continue to exist as facts (norms). Concepts postulated by political theory might be the meta-descriptions that a society, auto-

---

4 For Luhmann's critique of post-Cartesian metaphysics, see Luhmann 1967, 106.
5 See note 2 above again. For earlier accounts of relations between norms and structure, see Durkheim, 1960, 29; Weber 1921, 15-16.
6 It has become habitual to use supposedly social-scientific principles in the historical reconstruction of political theory. Some interpreters have observed the elements of theory as exceeding the intentions of their authors and as reflecting a ›political language‹ in which a society, at one historical moment, communicates about itself (Pocock 1972, 35). Other interpreters have argued that theoretical concepts act as ›indicators of socio-political transformation‹, disclosing underlying structural changes in society (see Koselleck 1979, 23). The conceptual-historical argument implicit in Luhmann's work, however, is that the formation of political concepts has no independence of socio-functional processes and should therefore be viewed in exclusively sociological terms. Other approaches to conceptual history are thus, on this view, not adequate to the theoretical preconditions of the social sciences.

genetically, produces and memorizes for the simplification of its paradoxes, and around which, for as long as they can be sustained, it permits its differentiated functions to reflect and construct themselves.[7] Yet the theories that underscore the presuppositions of politics and law are nothing more than society's own theory: they are factual aspects of the inner-societal process in which social systems (and especially law and politics, from which other systems habitually borrow their self-constructions) allow new articulations of their contingent foundations to emerge and to be reflected. These theories, then, can be fully comprehended, not by normative, but only by sociological theory (Luhmann 1980, 63): theory is only theory as the form in which society tests and externalizes its self-constructions, and as such it can only be comprehended by theory that recognizes this unity of facts and norms and that identifies theory (and itself) as factual/normative communication.

The sociology of theory and the factual memory of society

If Luhmann's work provides the first fully sociological account of norms, therefore, it also provides the first fully sociological theory of theory, which he views as fully integrated into the factual/normative self-construction of society. In this respect, however, although he stands against all conventional premises of theoretical political analysis, Luhmann's thought permits – or at least facilitates – two significant new departures in theoretical reflection on politics. First, it might be argued that Luhmann's work marks a crucial opening for a historical sociology of political theory, and it invites socio-theoretical inquiry to reconstruct theory, in its entire history, as an integrated element of society's semantic self-consolidation. Indeed, Luhmann is quite clear that the classics of political theory, from Aquinas, to Hobbes, to Locke, to Rousseau, to Kant, to Hegel, might be viewed as society's auto-communicative descriptions of the functions that stabilize the semantic substructure of its law and its politics (see Luhmann 1984; Luhmann 2000, 319-371). In addition to this, however, Luhmann's work also clears the ground for an entirely new lineage in political reflection, and it offers an opportunity for a sociological re-orientation of political theory towards a standpoint that at once accepts the functional unity of theory (norms) and society (factual) but that also re-imagines theory's normative status and normative properties on this foundation. In other words, Luhmann's work creates an opening for theory that, on one hand, follows his claim that norms are simply observable as social facts, but that also, on the other hand, follows his theory of semantics in recognizing that some factual norms have a specific adequacy to (or indispensability for) a modern society,

---

7 For an excellent examination of political theory as the memory of the political, see Bußhoff 2003, 10, 18, 33.

and that some factual norms offer greater support than others in conceptualizing and underwriting the necessary and formative functions of a modern society. On this basis, in fact, Luhmann's thought might be seen to provide a horizon for developing a *socio-normative* political theory.[8]

A socio-normative political theory, following Luhmann, might thus be a political theory that acknowledges the factual contingency of society's norms, but that recognizes that some norms, in certain societal conjunctures, are *necessary* for society, and they thus require specific preservation (both by theory and by society). In this respect, a socio-normative theory might appoint itself as an observer of the norms in which a society constructs itself; it might reflect that (at one juncture in society's evolution) society obtains a more effective self-construction in some norms than in others; and it might provide explanations of the benefits that accrue (for society) from certain norms. A socio-normative theory, therefore, might conclude that the unity of theoretical norms and social facts does not mean that society cannot express a preference for some norms (or facts) over others, and it might assert that, precisely because norms are facts, some facts and norms act appropriately in underscoring society's adequate form whilst others do not. Theory, in consequence, might be motivated by Luhmann to step outside the conventional (i.e. metaphysical) facts / norms dichotomy, yet also, in so doing, it might preserve some (albeit reduced) normative function for itself. This theoretical potential of Luhmann's theory seems to have been largely ignored, although Luhmann himself was not silent about the socio-normative implications of his research, and, in the course of his work, he clearly identified some of society's paradoxical constructs as preferable to others and he saw some of society's norm-founding self-descriptions as specifically adequate to the tasks allotted to theory by society.[9] This is why, critically, Luhmann repeatedly expressed irritation about the role of the welfare state in modern Western democracies. He viewed the welfare state as a self-description for law and politics that over-extends the normative/legitimatory construct of rights to include distributive rights of material equality and programmatic rights of societal regulation, and thus as a construct that exorbitantly expands the plausible paradoxicality of both politics and law and holds law and politics accountable to unreliably expansive normative expectations (see Luhmann 1981, 48). This is why, affirmatively, Luhmann argued that the constitutional state merits ›highest admiration‹ as a normative paradox that assists society in providing an adequately stabilizing description for its political communications (Luhmann 1984, 113). In »Are there still indispensable norms in our society«, moreover, Luhmann also implies that, if human rights are understood as semantic constructs, by means of which the justice of law and the legitimacy of politics can, as contingent facts, reflect and generalize themselves, the con-

---

8 For my attempt to apply Luhmann's theory in this way, see Thornhill 2008.
9 This normative dimension in Luhmann's theory is habitually, although rather absurdly, denied by some commentators. Egregious in this regard is Brodocz 1999, 338.

cept of human rights as a social necessity can also be affirmed as an eminently successful (and thus largely indispensable) »basic principle« (2008, 35) for concentrating the positivity of these two systems.

Reading between the lines of Luhmann's theory, therefore, it is possible to reconstruct his work as suggesting that some principles in society obtain what might be called a *functional normativity*. This status might attach to those theoretical norms and paradoxes that specifically uphold the differentiated form of society as a whole and that prevent the convergence – or the *de-differentiation* – of society around expansive or trans-systemic regulatory duties or totalizing accounts of its orientation or direction. Theory that is encouraged by Luhmann's theory to think socio-normatively might thus observe that at certain points in a society's ongoing evolution some theoretical constructs directly serve (and so are thus perhaps indispensable for) the pluralistic shape of society, so that society's theory and society's practice fortuitously coincide, and theory might offer a cautious endorsement or preference for certain theoretical paradigms on that basis. Such theory, in particular, might follow Luhmann in concluding that, amongst all society's paradoxes, the paradox of the constitution, of constitutional rights, and of the rights-holding person have the important distinction that they provide both a sustainable conceptual (normative) and a sustainable functional (factual) underpinning for a modern differentiated society, and that, in both these respects, they produce a plausible and workable account of the sources of the norms that underscore both politics and law under conditions of social differentiation (see also Luhmann 1965, 135).

In any case, Luhmann's sociology directly provokes political theory to think about norms, and the normative status of theory, in two distinct dimensions. First, it challenges political theory to understand norms as inner-societal self-descriptions of society's function systems. Second, it challenges political theory to measure the plausibility of norms (and of theories giving rise to norms) by examining the extent to which norms and normative theories, objectively and observably, sustain the preconditions of society's differentiated form and preclude the collapsing of society into pre-pluralistic self-constructions and render unlikely the coalescence of different subsystems of society around obstructive objectives or self-images. This model of socio-normative theory, it might be argued, is the last sustainable place for theory that commits itself as normative yet that also identifies itself as determinately social-scientific (that is, as theory whose object can be accounted for as *social*). Indeed, there remains a suspicion that, in the contemporary social sciences, theories that fail to reflect on the enriching and disarming implications of Luhmann's ideas on facts and norms and theory fall short of the theoretical actuality that is required of social-scientific research, and they can perhaps not be described as belonging to the *social sciences* at all. It might thus be argued, following Luhmann, that theory that does not reflect on its normative content (and its own status as society's norm-producer) as an element of a wider dynamic of social self-reflection cannot provide fully conclusive accounts of its normative structure, and it relies upon unaccountable metaphysical/anthropological preconditions in order hypostatically to uphold its normative observations. It is only through hypostasis, in fact, that theory is commonly able to designate some of society's norms as indispensable and others as not.

The transformation of society's norms

Despite these innovative resonances of his theory, however, it is also in the issue of theory building and normativity that Luhmann's work is most susceptible to questioning, and it contains aporia that are directly relevant to the overlying concern of the article examined here: *Are there still indispensable norms in our society?* Indeed, it might be suggested that Luhmann's preparedness to pose this question is itself a symptom of an unresolved tension in his theory or even of an inability of his theory (perhaps momentary, in this essay alone) to meet the stringent demands for conceptual complexity and hyper-contingency that it imposes upon itself.

To elucidate this observation, it is necessary to inquire again into Luhmann's theory of theory, and its relation to norms, semantics and paradoxes. At one level, as discussed, Luhmann argues that theories are societal self-reflections, and they produce paradoxes and give rise to norms which permit social function systems, in whatever degree of contingency, semantically to integrate stabilizing self-descriptions. In this account, Luhmann necessarily views theories, norms and paradoxes as transitory and subject to alteration and displacement. However, he also indicates that the process through which the paradoxical sources of social communication might be modified or revised can only ever be structurally indeterminate, highly contingent and multi-causal. As discussed, to be sure, theories might be seen to obtain a particular sustainability if they articulate preconditions for the differentiation of society as a whole, and they might be modified or supplanted, or they might even become *redundant,* if they manifestly impede the process of society's differentiation. Paradoxes, therefore, might be displaced where they outlive their semantic utility or where alternative constructs evolve that capture the unity and distinction of socially required functions more effectively or more plausibly. Under such conditions, paradoxes might lapse or they might be transfigured in favour of new constructs that are better equipped to sustain the contingency of norms at a level of societal adequacy.[10] Underlying this theory of semantics, however, especially if it is understood as tied to the concept of the paradox, is the sense that there is no necessary cause of theory or theoretical adjustment; there is no *structural* or

---

10 On the paradox as effecting a displacement of a system's self-description, see Luhmann 1993, 294.

material substrate for theory's paradoxes; and, owing to its multi-causality, it is essential to theory that it offers a multiplicity of concepts in which a society might – variably – opt to explain its functions. Indeed, if paradox and semantics are correlated as the organizing matrix in which a society memorizes a volume of paradigms for examining the form in which, in its increasing complexity, it might normatively structure its communications and project these communications adaptively into the future, it is implicit that a society is likely to contain many interdependently contingent paradoxes in its normative fabric, and that a society will explain some of its exchanges through reference to one paradox, some in reference to another, and some in reference to many paradoxes at the same time.[11] If this interpretation is correct, it is also implicit in this theory that a complex society is likely to store many highly variable norms, even in the same communicative system, and that these norms might resist their polarization around simple oppositions, contradictions and decisive adjudications. In this construction, then, the evolution of society's theory might be viewed, archaeologically, as forming a reservoir of increasingly augmented theoretical options and of incrementally varied and contingent self-explanations in society, and this reservoir allows a society at any time to disengage from its structure (i.e. its semantics) a variety of terms to explain its communications. In this account, in fact, it is also implicit that theoretical semantics, though presupposing some form of social structure, also act to build and to replace any pre-existing or more integral social structure, so that a modern society relies on dense theoretical memories concretized communicatively as semantics, and it is these semantics, not any stratified or rigidified structure, that provide the background co-ordinates for further communications (including actions) in society.[12] This, in fact, is the underlying reason why modern societies contain highly ramified and flexibly contingent options for adaptation and self-positivization. This of course does not imply that there are no external reasons why theories, and their normative substance, change. However, it does imply, in quasi-Hegelian fashion, that theories and norms are seldom fully discredited or rendered dispensable: instead, they are integrated, as sublated elements, into the conceptual/historical or semantic structure (if not the higher rationality) of society (see Hegel 1969, 33). This, in turn, also implies that a mono-paradoxical perspective is not adequate for understanding society's semantics or for examining the norms that inhere in these semantics. Society's semantics contain many paradoxical forms, and they are rarely susceptible to addressing the binary question of whether one norm excludes one other norm or whether one norm is dispensable whilst alternative norms are not.

---

11 On the proliferation of paradoxes at the entry to modern society, see Luhmann 1980a, 228-229.
12 See Hellmann 2005, 33-34. For a different view, which emphasizes both the disjuncture and the unitary foundation of social structure and semantics, see Stäheli 1998.

At a different level, however, Luhmann also tempers this outlook by indicating that norms, ar.d the paradoxes that found them, are subject to revision and overthrow because of broader changes in objectively determinable social structure. As a consequence of this, he also suggests that certain types of social structure are articulated with and made explicit in certain normative conceptions (2008, 22f). He argues, for instance, that the principle of natural law as the foundation of society's law and politics might be adequate to hierarchical societies that, for structural reasons, need to uphold a self-description as both quasi-natural and as relatively static.[13] The principle of natural law, however, becomes precarious in highly differentiated societies in which the law has an intensified requirement for positivity and needs to make itself accessible for many exchanges across a number of social systems. In such societies, law needs to mobilize highly fluid and iterable accounts of its validity and cannot allow itself to be constrained by externally derived principles or by principles that couple law with other social systems. Luhmann thus concludes that the dominant paradoxes of early European modernity, such as ius-naturalism and social contractarianism, have *necessarily* become redundant, and they have been replaced by paradoxes that are better empowered to facilitate integrally positivized communications and to sustain a higher degree of societal complexity. These paradoxes now include constructs of individuality, subjectivity, subjective rights, freedom, and even democratic entitlement. In this analysis, consequently, Luhmann identifies a sequence of what might be termed *semantic caesura* underlying the structural formation of modern society. These caesura are coupled with shifts in social structure, and they mark the transition between different époques of structural elaboration and different époques of paradoxical concept building. For this reason, he intimates, some paradoxes and some norms might, under certain conditions of structural change, become manifestly dispensable. As a consequence of this, then, societies might also register debate over norms, or over the suspension of norms, as fully resonant expressions of structural process, and a society might confront a controversy over norms or the suspension of norms as a deeply implicated debate about its structure.

The first element of Luhmann's theory, accentuating society's polysemous semantics, forms a key methodological intervention in the contemporary social sciences, and it dramatically differentiates Luhmann's theory from more standard sociological theorists of norms, who argue that norms express a dominant set of structural exigencies. This element contains the following implications. First, it allows for an understanding of the theoretical concepts underpinning social norms as gradually evolving and incrementally formative of society's capacities for adapting to and generating complexity. Second, it permits the insight that norm-giving theoretical constructs are only subject to partial dis-

---

13 Here Luhmann moves closer to the claim, conventional in the sociology of knowledge, that dominant cognitive principles allow societies to duplicate or project themselves as second nature (see Lukács 1968, 281).

placement, and might in fact be subsumed into, and so enrich, those constructs that supplant them. Third, it accounts for paradoxical constructs as components in a structurally necessary memory of society, and it intimates that the normative residues or recollections of a society are indispensable for the flexibility and adaptability of that society. In consequence of this, it might be observed that norms, as factual elements of structure, cannot simply disappear or lose all applicability; even where they yield to new constructs, they are memorized as principles in which a society has tested out and consolidated its functions at particular junctures in its evolution. Therefore, rather than fading into obsolescence, they are required, as co-implied social facts, as the foundations for society's evolving complexification. It is to this multi-normative facticity, in fact, that modern societies owe their existence as distinctively modern: it is to this that they owe their constitutive propensity for sustaining conditions of great pluralism, for sidestepping unified or central confrontation, and for evading convergence around dramatized or exclusionary self-reflections. This perspective, naturally, still permits normative societal analysis on the pattern outlined above, as it still supports the observation that some norms obstruct and some norms promote society's differentiation and pluralization. However, it also augments the flexibility of this argument by observing that society's pluralization is itself reliant on the fact that societies store many paradoxes and many norms (facts), and that one precondition of its pluralism is the fact that a society cannot obtain a position of self-abstraction that might allow it to observe or confront itself in a direct decision about the status of its different norms. In a society in which semantics fuses with and alters structure, in other words, norms cannot disjoin themselves from facts in a fashion that might allow a society normatively to appraise itself and fundamentally and perennially to arbitrate over its norms.

The second element of Luhmann's theory, however, is more essentially monistic. Indeed, in implying that there exists a direct correlation between society's semantics and the evolved form of social structure, this theoretical element rather impoverishes both the conceptual value and the historical plausibility of the theory of semantic memory and conceptual displacement that is contained in the first element. This is not the place to write an extensive riposte to the historical dimensions of Luhmann's theory of social structure and societal transformation. Suffice it to say here, in this respect, that Luhmann's postulate of a link between natural-law constructs and the stratification of social structure, and his resultant claim that in the eighteenth century European societies differentiated by strata were replaced by societies differentiated by function, leading to an upheaval in the semantic order of these societies, does not stand up to historical scrutiny.[14] The emergence of ius-natural legal argument, even argument borrowing ius-natural ideas from religion, was in fact a cru-

14 For more extensive context, see Luhmann 1980, 27.

cial moment in the far earlier formation of European societies, and at a much earlier historical juncture these societies obtained from natural law a body of terms that helped them to generalize power across widening social spaces and to consolidate their differentiated functional components across the regional and patrimonial boundaries that they still incorporated. The emergence of stratified territorial power was thus already an advanced stage in a process in which law and politics, using natural-law principles, had abstracted themselves from the densely personalized and interpenetrated nexus of functions characterizing pre-modern societies.[15] Indeed, social stratification in post-feudal society might be seen as necessarily correlated with a simultaneous process of *sectoral differentiation,* which anticipated and ultimately precipitated the functional differentiation that Luhmann identifies as the insignia of societies in the state of modernity. Natural law, therefore, far from naturalizing a rigidly hierarchical social order, might be seen as a corpus of paradoxical terms that originally allowed law and power to internalize fluid self-references and so to overarch the localized forms of social exchange in feudalism. This in itself renders Luhmann's imputed correlativity of semantics and social structure rather questionable, and it is at least arguable, on this basis, that semantic forms had detached themselves from any consolidated social structure long before Luhmann is prepared to suggest.

In addition to this, however, it might also be argued that the imputation of a direct and constitutive link between social structure and society's semantics critically debilitates Luhmann's examination of the ways in which societies can (and must) accommodate manifold constructs to support their norms. As discussed, the first element of his theory suggests that societies are endowed with variable and deeply pluralized semantic memories, and because of this they can store endlessly complex self-descriptions. This allows the following inferences: societies have no dominant norm-giving rationality by which to determine their norms; societies cannot produce structurally dominant or quasi-totalized accounts of their normative foundations; there is no rationality in a society that is exclusively reflective of the level of societal evolution or the modes of stratification that this entails; societies cannot be expected either to culminate in mono-valent declarations of their normative forms or to confront themselves in categorical self-analysis over the suspension or preservation of these forms. The second element suggests, in contrast, that societies tend to organize themselves around dominant or structurally necessary semantics (see Stäheli 2002, 255), and that at any evolutionary juncture a society's legal or political systems might articulate and insist on their legitimacy (and allow their legitimacy to be contested) in *distinctively plausible* and so quasi-exclusionary expressions, the suspension of which is reported through all society, potentially, as a structural trauma. Following this second theory of structure, in short, for every norm

---

15 For a very early example of this, see Lupoi 2000, 250.

there is an exception; one norm necessarily encounters other norms as its conceptual antitheses; and the suspension of one norm in favour of another signifies an enduring decision *either* for *or* against a particular normative or structural orientation. This latter claim sits uneasily with the implications of the first theoretical position, and in fact it removes some of its explanatory value.[16]

Despite the rather monistic character of the second of these theoretical elements, however, it is this element that persists in the question – *Are there still indispensable norms in our society?* Luhmann, of course, removes himself from any established position in political ethics: he evidently emphasizes the need for theory to ›observe‹ the manifold function of norms and to describe the many moral faces of society. Nonetheless, both this question, and, residually, Luhmann's answer to it, still imply that norms can be perceived as societal refractions, around which a society – or one salient aspect of a society's communications – converges, in which a society can form a binary judgement about itself and its norms (that is, as dispensable/not dispensable), and in which a society might confront alarming or exceptionally destabilizing images of itself. This suggests that society's norms are liable to frontal and exclusionary exposure to counter-norms, that norms can be substantively undermined or even structurally dislodged by momentary confrontation with such counter-norms or by examples of their own suspension, and that society as a whole can condense itself exceptionally into acts of self-observation that take the form of a conflict over norms. Because norms are determinately articulated with social structure, a society is able to obtain a privileged and generally sustaining account of itself in particular norms and it experiences debility in or contest over these norms in a ›globally‹ exceptional fashion. In other words, although Luhmann's entire work limits the exclusionary or totalizing dimension to modern society, his question here suggests that the legal or political systems of this society can be brought by a conflict over norms into a condition of *semantic exceptionality*, in which an inability to provide universal and airtight paradoxes to authorize their functions resonates as endemically problematic for all society.

From a perspective in political science that is methodologically sympathetic to Luhmann's view of theory as a factual/normative aspect of social semantics, a heuristic preference might be expressed for the first element of Luhmann's theory. Indeed, Luhmann's general theory of society allows us precisely to observe that most societies, through the course of their historical evolution, organize their law and their politics (and in fact all their societal exchanges) in multi-paradoxical and multi-normative fashion. Rather than generating exclusive normative abstractions for their structures, societies are more likely

---

16 In the postulated link between structure and stratification, Luhmann looks back to older literature (see especially Parsons 1976). In Parsons's functionalist account of structure, the distinction between structure and medium is crucial. For the distinction between *power*, as a generalized symbolic medium, and *authority*, as a normatively regulated ›quality of a status in a social structure‹, see Parsons 1969, 325.

to sediment a memory of the different paradoxes, the different norms, and the different theories in which they have rationalized or tested their legitimatory resources. As they evolve, then, societies acquire a theoretical history, in which they internalize a mass of semantic norms and paradoxes to explain their orientations and decisions (see Greven 1999, 14), and these cannot easily be mobilized against each other, or even construed as isolated conceptual antinomies. As a consequence of this, then, societies only rarely (if at all) construct their self-explanation in a form that is susceptible to binary or exclusionary confrontation. In fact, it might be observed as a specific feature of modern societies that they cannot experience themselves or their communications in a state of exceptionality to their norms; that they cannot form total verdicts about their norms; that they cannot fully identify some norms as universally dispensable and others as not; that they possess mechanisms to ensure that their founding norms are never extracted from their locality, multiplicity and polysemous interdependence in order to declare themselves in binary or exclusive constructions. As a result of these attributes, modern societies are able to sustain law and politics in a form that allows them to adapt smoothly to evolutionary realities and that involves a minimum of perturbation and a maximum of relative liberty for those social agents who are subject to law and politics. The avoidance of exceptionalism and acute self-confrontation, therefore, is one constitutive precondition of modern society.

Luhmann, clearly, was well aware of these attributes of modern society. In observing that norms are facts, he expressed the view that a society contains many norms as facts, and these can only be articulated as dramatic antipodes where they are mobilized by highly selective theoretical acts and thus (improbably and simplistically) split into a dichotomous facts-norms relation.[17] He also observed, moreover, that modern societies show their adaptability most effectively in the fact that they can avoid allowing their self-explanations to culminate in non-reconcilable postulates over norms and values.[18] For this reason, however, Luhmann's question here – *Are there still indispensable norms in our society?* – insinuates a barely accountable and unnecessary totalism into his sociological inquiry. If societies store many norms as facts, we might ask: Why do we need to inquire whether any of these norms can confront each other in categorically exclusionary fashion, or whether the suspension of one norm could force all society reliably to declare that some of its norms are indispensable or that some are not?

---

17 Laws and politics can thus, for Luhmann, not be legitimized by any normative claims articulated *ab extra*: Luhmann 1981a, 69.
18 Luhmann described a ›good politics‹ as one whose ›capacity for realization‹ does not require the concentration of society around volatile or deeply experienced political contests. This is quoted from Wirtz 1999, 175-176. On Luhmann and Schmitt, see Thornhill 2007.

Non-exceptional societies

It has recently become habitual to talk of a new exceptionalism in contemporary law and contemporary politics and to argue that we exist in a time in which, especially in the international arena, political actors routinely ignore and suspend legal norms, so that the moral fabric of Western societies is threatened with fragmentation and simplification. This argument is usually flanked by the assertion that modern societies are now subject to an intensified political density, and that the normative mesh regulating social and political actions can easily fray under the pressure of this politicization.[19] From the view outlined here, however, it appears more plausible to argue that the opposite is the case. Modern societies now possess only the most vestigial capacity for total self-construction and exceptional self-confrontation, and they incorporate a highly varied store of normative facts: indeed, it is precisely the fact, not that they are normatively exceptional, but that they store multi-normative resources, that allows modern societies on occasions to act outside their most conventionalized self-descriptions and to authorize their functions through principles that appear to contradict their more manifest or even apparently non-derogable normative reserves. This semantic flexibility confers a high degree of latitude on some societies in respect of their supposed founding norms or values, and this may easily be confused with exceptionalism or totalism. However, if a modern society appears to act in exception to or in suspension of its commonly sanctioned norms, this does not raise a once-and-for-all question about the dispensability or indispensability of these norms. It testifies, rather, to the fact that modern societies can make recourse to many norms; that they cannot easily abstract a perspective to view one norm as either inside or outside a wider normative fabric; and that they, or some of their communications, can act outside their instituted norms without forcing all society's communications to be politicized in a decision about their supreme structural preconditions. Luhmann's theory of society, despite the guiding question in this essay, provides extensive analysis of reasons for and consequences of this loss of exceptionality.

This argument can be pursued further, in fact, and it might be concluded that modern societies conform to an evolutionary logic of *de-politicization*, which has fundamentally to do with their multi-paradoxical normativity. That is to say that modern societies obtain their modernity by virtue of the fact that they abstract and limit their political power; that they avoid totalizing the principles by which they construct and legitimize politics and political norms; and that they use their primary self-descriptions in order specifically to evade the need for a high level of social politicization, particularly in respect of single issues or simple controversies. Most particularly, it might be argued that modern society's formation as relatively depoliticized is linked to the fact that the leading

19 See, for example, Huysmans 2006; Sand n.d.

or – at least – most widespread semantic in modern law and modern politics is, as Luhmann (2008) identifies, the semantic of *rights*. It is often argued that rights result either from the political voluntarism of social collectives or particular social actors outside law and politics.[20] Similarly, it is often argued that rights enshrine norms that form either categorically rational or ethically non-sacrificable foundations for all legal and political activities in a society. However, it can be observed, as Luhmann in fact suggests, that these assumptions are merely the paradox of rights, and that rights factually evolve as salient elements in the legitimatory grammar of modern societies because rights offer specific sources of political alleviation to societies: most particularly, societies need and implement rights because rights help them to *depoliticize themselves* and to reduce the volume of social themes that they are forced to hold at a level of intensified politicization. If rights are the most generalized semantic of most modern societies, therefore, they owe this generality (not dominance), not to the fact that they provide a preeminent and politically irreducible articulation of society's structural legitimatory principles, but rather to the fact that modern societies have a deep-lying need for apolicity. The reflected presence of rights (or of the human subject as a necessary holder of rights) within the law and within politics (usually codified in a constitution) is a reference that helps law and politics to operate in society and to universalize accounts of their validity without necessitating anything more than a minimal enactment of categorical principles and without coercing society into any convergent contest over its necessary norms. In fact, it can be easily observed that, if law and power reflect themselves as legitimate by externalizing (or constitutionalizing) the source of their validity in *the person as a holder of rights* (i.e. as a holder of rights of freedom of movement, freedom of labour, freedom of contract, freedom of religious observance, rights of limited political inclusion, and – perhaps – some rights of material dignity), this self-reflection acts to remove the potential for convergent political emphasis from law and politics in two quite distinct ways. First, this self-reflection permits law and politics to store within themselves and recursively to articulate a convenient simplifying paradox for their communications: modern law and modern politics both conserve an idea of the citizen as rights-holder as an instrument that accompanies, eases and *de-controversializes* their positive dissemination through society. Indeed, this self-reflection allows law and politics to uphold a legitimatory image of themselves (usually in a constitution) that is relatively withdrawn from the cycles of social politicization and that can be presupposed as a reliably stable and even apolitical moment within society's legal and political exchanges.[21] Second, more generally, this

---

20 This is the case in Ishay 2004, 318-319.
21 Note Luhmann's frontal hostility to Carl Schmitt on the question of the constitution. Schmitt sees a constitution as a declaration of structurally decisive political principles (see Schmitt 1928, 87). Luhmann views it as a static, partial and apolitical element in the state and in the law (see Luhmann 1973, 12).

self-reflection also allows law and politics to provide a functionally constrained account of the limits of their communications and thus also to pursue a far-reaching de-politicization of society in its entirety (see again Luhmann 1965, 135). The self-reflection of law and politics as determined by rights means that law and politics can explain and delineate themselves as spheres of communication that obtain legitimacy specifically because they are not required to colonize those areas of society in which rights of freedom might be exercised (i.e. the economy, education, the media, religion), and because, in consequence, they are not expected to describe and legitimate themselves by overarching all other realms of social exchange. This self-reflection, in consequence, means that law and politics can obtain legitimacy without transmitting their agency across societal boundaries, without burdening themselves with hypertrophic regulatory requirements, without provoking obdurate resistances through society, and without coercing society to converge around unitary (and thus universally conflictual) legal or political accounts of its structure. Moreover, the self-reflection of law and politics as determined by rights means that, as they presuppose the citizen, consistently, as both the legitimatory source and the addressee of their law and power, and as they, in their own communications, generalize and translocate the form of the citizen across regional and temporal boundaries in a society, the legal and political systems of society can, *from within themselves*, pre-construct the general conditions under which their law and their power are applied and received through society. In doing this, they ensure that their interfaces with other spheres of social communication are generally predictable, only unusually open to political contest, and thus normally *unemphatic* (see Clam 2006, 152).

Rights, therefore, surely act as the preponderant semantics of modern society. The reason for this, however, is precisely not that they allow society's construction of itself to culminate in one dominant set of norms or self-definitions. Instead of this, rights have this status because they form a protective membrane around society's other, more submerged semantics, and they ensure that the structurally memorized semantics of a society must only very rarely be disclosed or opened to contests and confrontations that a society as a whole might register as unbalancing. Rights, in other words, are the factual precondition for the effective immunity of society's normative semantics: they are the prominent (not dominant) semantic in a modern society because they fulfil the conditions of depoliticization under which this society retains its semantic flexibility and its modernity and they mollify and disperse the tendencies to exceptionalist self-construction that a society contains. The suspension of norms that are founded in rights, therefore, may indeed – over a longer temporal sequence – prove deleterious for a society. The ongoing suspension or negation of rights-based norms, if this is repeated or perpetuated, might surely reduce the store of paradoxes over which a society disposes and it might expose society to the emergence of more entrenched and centrally registered conflicts and to longer-term destabilization. However, to assume that one breach of a society's rights regime must immediately call forth in society a structurally decisive verdict over its norms and their dispensability is rather to misidentify the essentially immunizing function of rights.

On these grounds, then, theory that internalizes and reflects on Luhmann's dismantlement of the facts–norms dichotomy might draw a final factual or socio-normative conclusion from his work, and it might allow the factuality of norms in the form of rights to constitute a new foundation for critical (and even normative) political analysis. Primarily, it might argue that, as the semantic pre-eminence of rights results from their facility in allowing social depoliticization and in immunizing society's many norm-giving paradoxes against open, simplifying or exceptional contest, theory is entitled to advise societies that their stability is most secure if they institute and preserve stable rights-regimes. Indeed, theory is entitled to suggest that the evolutionary pattern of self-depoliticization through rights is the most adequate pattern for sustainable modern societies, and that societies that opt abidingly to erode certain basic preconditions in respect of rights are liable, through an excessive saturation with social power, to malfunction and to forfeit the normative preconditions of their pluralism. This is not because rights, as the essentially modern source of norms, are anything more than facts. However, rights are the facts through which modern societies preserve their semantic flexibility and avoid the threat of structural-political exceptionality, and societies that do not have these facts are always susceptible to highly simplificatory processes of self-confrontation and differentiatory regression. On these grounds, therefore, it might be possible to argue that the norms sanctioned by rights are indispensable. Yet this is only the case because these rights make it possible for societies, by and large, to evade the need to simplify their communicative forms to such a degree that they have to pose and adjudicate questions of normative indispensability.

References

Brodocz, André (1999): Die politische Theorie autopoietischer Systeme. Pp. 337-360 in: André Brodocz/Gary Schaal (eds.), Politische Theorien der Gegenwart. Eine Einführung. Opladen: Leske + Budrich.

Bußhoff, Heinrich (2003): Das Politische der Politik. Politik als Mechanismus zur Politisierung des Politischen. Baden-Baden: Nomos.

Clam, Jean (2006): What is modern Power? Pp. 145-162 in: Michael King/Chris Thornhill (eds.), Luhmann on Law and Politics. Critical Appraisals and Applications. Oxford: Hart Publishing.

Durkheim, Émile (1960): De la Division du Travail Sociale, 7th edition. Paris: Presses Universitaires de la France.

Greven, Michael Th. (1999): Die Politische Gesellschaft. Kontingenz und Dezision als Probleme des Regierens und der Demokratie. Opladen: Leske + Budrich.

Habermas, Jürgen (1992): Faktizität und Geltung. Beiträge zur Diskurstheorie des Rechts und des demokratischen Rechtsstaats. Frankfurt a.M.: Suhrkamp.

Hegel, G.W.F. (1969): Phänomenologie des Geistes. Werke, vol. III (edited by E. Moldenhauer/K.M. Michel). Frankfurt a.M.: Suhrkamp.

Huysmans, Jeff (2006): International politics of insecurity: Normativity, inwardness and the exception. Security Dialogue, 37, 1, 11-29.

Hellmann, Kai-Uwe (2005): Spezifik und Autonomie des politischen Systems. Analyse und Kritik der politischen Soziologie Niklas Luhmanns. Pp. 13-51 in: Günter Runkel/Günter Burkart (eds.), Funktionssysteme der Gesellschaft. Beiträge zur Systemtheorie Niklas Luhmanns. Wiesbaden: VS.

Ishay, Micheline R. (2004): The History of Human Rights. From Ancient Times to the Globalization Era. Berkeley/London: University of California Press.

Koselleck, Reinhart (1979): Begriffsgeschichte und Sozialgeschichte. Pp. 19-36 in: R. Koselleck (ed.), Historische Semantik und Begriffsgeschichte. Stuttgart: Klett-Cotta.

Luhmann, Niklas (1965): Grundrechte als Institution. Ein Beitrag zur politischen Soziologie. Berlin: Ducker & Humblot.

Luhmann, Niklas (1967): Soziologische Aufklärung. Soziale Welt 18, 2/3, 97-123.

Luhmann, Niklas (1970): Soziologie des politischen Systems. Pp. 154-177 in: N. Luhmann, Soziologische Aufklärung. Aufsätze zur Theorie sozialer Systeme. Köln: Westdt. Verlag.

Luhmann, Niklas (1973): Politische Verfassungen im Kontext des Gesellschaftssystems, I. Der Staat 12, 1, 1-22.

Luhmann, Niklas (1980): Gesellschaftliche Struktur und semantische Tradition. Pp. 9-71 in: N. Luhmann, Gesellschaftsstruktur und Semantik: Studien zur Wissenssoziologie der modernen Gesellschaft, vol. 1. Frankfurt a.M.: Suhrkamp.

Luhmann, Niklas (1980a): Frühneuzeitliche Anthropologie: Theorietechnische Lösungen für ein Evolutionsproblem der Gesellschaft. Pp. 162-234 in: N. Luhmann, Gesellschaftsstruktur und Semantik: Studien zur Wissenssoziologie der modernen Gesellschaft, vol. 1. Frankfurt a.M.: Suhrkamp.

Luhmann, Niklas (1981): Politische Theorie im Wohlfahrtsstaat. Wien: Olzog.

Luhmann, Niklas (1981a): Selbstlegitimation des Staates. Pp. 65-83 in: Norbert Achterberg/Werner Krawietz (eds.), Legitimation des modernen Staates. Archiv für Rechts- und Sozialphilosophie, Beiheft 15. Wiesbaden: Westdt. Verlag.

Luhmann, Niklas (1984): Staat und Politik. Zur Semantik der Selbstbeschreibung politischer Systeme. Pp. 99-125 in: Udo Bermbach (ed.), Politische Theoriengeschichte. Probleme einer Teildisziplin der Politischen Wissenschaft. Politische Vierteljahresschrift, Sonderheft 15. Opladen: Westdt. Verlag.

Luhmann, Niklas (1993): Die Paradoxie des Entscheidens. Verwaltungsarchiv 84, 287-310.

Luhmann, Niklas (2000): Die Politik der Gesellschaft. Frankfurt a.M.: Suhrkamp.

Luhmann, Niklas (2008): Are There Still Indispensable Norms in Our Society? Soziale Systeme 14, 18-37 (in this volume).

Lukács, Georg (1968): Geschichte und Klassenbewußtsein. Neuwied: Luchterhand.

Lupoi, Maurizio (2000): The Origins of the European Legal Order. Cambridge: Cambridge University Press.

Merton, Robert (1957): Social Theory and Social Structure, revised edition. Glencoe, Illinois: Free Press.

Nisbet, Robert A. (1970): The Social Bond. An Introduction to the Study of Society. New York: Knopf.

Parsons, Talcott (1967): Sociological Theory and Modern Society. New York: Free Press.

Parsons, Talcott (1969): The Political Aspect of Social Structure and Process. Pp. 317-351 in: T. Parsons, Politics and Social Structure. New York: The Free Press.

Parsons, Talcott (1976): Social Structure and the Symbolic Media of Interchange. Pp. 94-120, in: Peter M. Blau (ed.), Approaches to the Study of Social Structure. London: Open Books.

Pocock, J. G. A. (1972): Politics, Language and Time. Essays on Political Thought and History. London: Methuen.

Popitz, Heinrich (1980): Die normative Konstruktion von Gesellschaft. Tübingen: Mohr.

Sand, Inger-Johanne (n.d.): Law and politics in a time of war, multi-culturalism and global change: Communicative complexity, fragmentation or loss of context. Unpublished paper.

Schmitt, Carl (1928): Verfassungslehre. Berlin: Duncker & Humblot.

Stäheli, Urs (1998): Die Nachträglichkeit der Semantik. Zum Verhältnis von Sozialstruktur und Semantik. Soziale Systeme 4, 2, 315-339.

Stäheli, Urs (2002): Sinnzusammenbrüche. Eine dekonstruktive Lektüre von Niklas Luhmanns Systemtheorie. Weilerswist: Delbrück.

Thornhill, Chris (2007): Niklas Luhmann, Carl Schmitt and the Modern Form of the Political. European Journal of Social Theory 10, 4, 499-522.

Thornhill, Chris (2008): Towards a Historical Sociology of Constitutional Legitimacy. Theory and Society 37, 2, 161-197.

Weber, Max (1921): Wirtschaft und Gesellschaft. Grundriß der verstehenden Soziologie, 5th edition, edited by Johannes Winckelmann. Tübingen: J.C.B. Mohr.

Wirtz, Thomas (1999): Entscheidung. Niklas Luhmann und Carl Schmitt. Pp. 175-197 in: Albrecht Koschorke / Cornelia Vismann (eds.), Widerstände der Systemtheorie. Kulturtheoretische Analysen zum Werk von Niklas Luhmann. Berlin: Akademie Verlag.

Prof. Chris Thornhill
Department of Politics, University of Glasgow
Adam Smith Building, Glasgow G12 8RT
c.thornhill@lbss.gla.ac.uk

Soziale Systeme 14 (2008), Heft 1, S. 68-82   © *Lucius & Lucius, Stuttgart*

John Paterson

The Fact of Values

Abstract: Building upon Luhmann's observations on the problems raised for law by indispensable norms and especially by conflicts between two or more of them, this paper considers some of legal theory's attempted solutions before considering some recent thinking on these issues from the common law courts. Insofar as neither theory nor practice appears able to overcome the difficulties Luhmann highlights, conclusions are drawn which suggest that, far from being a matter for regret, Luhmann's analysis clarifies the practical limitations on what may be expected in respect of values and identifies the point at which those concerned with their protection should focus their attention.

Introduction

Niklas Luhmann's question – »are there still indispensable norms in our society?« (2008) – may at first sight appear to be one that would not long detain legal theorists. The principal camps within jurisprudence, the natural lawyers and the positivists, may still have some disagreements as they wrestle with the question »what is *law*?«,[1] but even the hardest positivists would not deny that it makes sense to speak of indispensable norms within *society*. Luhmann's article as a whole, however, raises issues about fundamental values that *are* of direct relevance to law. Very strikingly, moreover, he raises those issues in such a way that both naturalists and positivists find themselves confronted with problems that they will struggle to surmount. For Luhmann applies his theoretical approach to the legal system and to its efforts to resolve the most challenging problems it is asked to deal with and in so doing reveals difficulties of an order that traditional jurisprudence normally manages to avoid. More specifically, he focuses attention on law's foundational paradox and considers how conflicts of values can be resolved in ways that satisfy the rhetoric of legal rights and judicial decision-making without problematical confrontations with that paradox. Approaching things in this way, however, reveals the extent to which fundamental values may be more contingent than might have been hoped inasmuch as there appears to be an unacceptable degree of freedom for the judge in deciding how conflicts of values will be resolved. The question then becomes one of knowing whether this contingency can be removed.

---

1 Although, as Brian Tamanaha (2007, 5-7) has demonstrated, they disagree about a lot less than they may think.

This paper first of all lays out and expands upon Luhmann's observations on the problems raised for the law (and especially courts) by indispensable norms and more particularly by conflicts between two or more of them. In particular, this part of the discussion proceeds on the basis of an understanding of law's function within Luhmann's approach to society. It then considers a number of the ways in which legal theory has attempted to resolve these problems before considering some recent (and perhaps surprising) thinking on these issues from the common law courts (to which Luhmann makes a number of references in his article). Insofar as neither theory nor practice appears able to overcome the difficulties that Luhmann highlights, conclusions are drawn which suggest that far from being a matter for regret, Luhmann's analysis clarifies the practical limitations on what may be expected in respect of values and identifies the point at which those concerned with the protection of values should focus their attention.

Law's Function, the Question of Validity and Indispensable Norms

Fundamental to any discussion of Luhmann's approach to law is a clear understanding of his view of its *function*. Insofar as his account envisages the functional differentiation of society into autopoietic subsystems, law's function is to stabilise normative expectations over time. »Law consists of the exploitation of conflict perspectives for the formation and reproduction of congruently (temporally/objectively/socially) generalised behavioural expectations« (Luhmann 1987, 27). Law is able to perform this function due to the fact that autopoiesis implies normative (or operational) closure and cognitive openness. In the case of law, normative closure means that »only the legal system can bestow normative quality« on its elements and thereby constitute them as elements«. But the legal system is also simultaneously cognitively open since in the constant reproduction of its elements it needs to be able »to determine whether certain conditions have been met or not« (1987, 20). Thus, normative closure is concerned with the »self-continuation [of the system] in difference to the environment »while cognitive openness« serves the coordination of this process with the system's environment« (1987, 20; 1985, 113f). For the rest of society law's normative closure means simply that it is able to determine in advance whether something will be legal or illegal. This may appear to be a rather minimalist and unambitious view of law's role, but for Luhmann this represents a significant achievement in the evolution of functionally differentiated modern society (Luhmann 1995, 332f). If law were not present to perform this role, then society would be unable to determine in advance whether any planned conduct would be legally relevant, and, if it were, what the attitude of law towards it would be. The apparently minimal role is transformed by this observation into a vital function without which social interaction would be, if not impossible, then practically extremely difficult. In Luhmann's terms such a situation would involve everything being determined at the level of cognition, on the basis of ongoing experience, as opposed to the level of normativity.

Law in Luhmann's understanding, accordingly, plays an important societal role, but accepting his theoretical position is not without significant consequences for *how* it is able to operate. If law is normatively closed and cognitively open, then information is neither transferred from it to other social subsystems nor vice versa in the way that would traditionally be assumed. Insofar as each system makes selections on the basis of its own binary code so it constructs its own reality. In other words, each system produces information *internally*. This does not, however, mean that there is *no* connection with the world outside the system, only that it now becomes necessary to modify substantially the way in which causality is understood:

> a system creates its own past as its own causal basis, which enables it to gain distance from the causal pressure of the environment without already determining through internal causality what will occur in confrontations with external events. (Luhmann 1995, 41; see also 1987a, 335f)

This radically different view of society can give the impression that social subsystems exist in a state of mutual indifference, but this is not the case. Law, for example, cannot get by without society. As Luhmann puts it, the »legal system for its part is probably more dependent than any other subsystem on receiving impulses ... from interaction systems with other functional orientations« (1981, 46). It is important to understand, however, that law is not simply controllable at the whim of other systems. Law itself will make selections on the basis of its own binary code. Equally, despite the fact that society »needs« law to stabilise normative expectations, so this does not mean that other subsystems are in some sense controllable by law. They too will make selections on the basis of their own binary codes: »the operational mode of self-referential systems changes into forms of causality that to a large extent reliably prevent it from being steered from outside« (1995, 41). Society for Luhmann is not, then, composed of mutually indifferent, solipsistic communicative realms, but nor is it composed of open systems susceptible to deterministic analysis and intervention.

The ability of law to perform its societal function of stabilising normative expectations, however, is maintained only insofar as its foundational paradox is not confronted. But what does this mean? What is this paradox? Consider this: the operation of law is about determining what is legal and what is illegal. There are no other alternatives. Thus, the judge in considering a case in effect applies the distinction legal/illegal to a particular set of circumstances. But before that application can be made, there is a logically prior question to be answered: what makes the very application of that legal/illegal distinction itself legal? This, in essence, is a different and more sociologically sophisticated way of asking the perennial jurisprudential question: what is law? Or, to put it in other words, what is it that makes law *law*?

This, of course, is none other than the question of validity about which the naturalists and the positivists have argued for centuries. For the naturalists, leaving aside all the nuances of the various versions of natural law, validity is dependent on some *moral* criterion. For the positivists, again using very broad-brush terms, validity is dependent on pedigree, that is, the fact that a norm has been issued by a source that is *recognised* as a valid legal source. The systems theory approach, however, is not content with either of these answers. It recognises that in each case a line is being drawn in order to respond to the question of validity but that in so doing the question of validity is really only being deferred. Thus, for the natural lawyers, the question that arises is: what makes the *establishment* of a particular moral criterion *legal*? While for the positivists, the question that arises is: what makes the *recognition* of a particular source as a legal source *legal*? Of course, in each case, the theorist will object that this is not really a fair question. In each case, his or her answers were essentially intended as a means of dealing with this tricky situation and of doing so in ways that are broadly acceptable, whether on moral or pragmatic grounds. Raising the validity question again is, as it were, to pick at the scab that theory had helped to form over the wound opened up by the recognition that law needs foundations.

And in fact Luhmann appears normally to have been content to let matters lie in this regard – indeed to have demonstrated theoretically how the legal system avoids any problematical confrontation with the foundational paradox in order that it may maintain operational closure and thus the viability of the system (1989, 145). The answer for Luhmann is that the legal system develops ways of concealing the paradox so that it appears as if its operations are not in fact based on self-reference. In other words, the system develops means of *deparadoxification* (1988). This answer cannot lie at the level of the code. It is the drawing of distinctions between system and environment on the basis of the code that inevitably entails a paradox, namely the question of why its own binary code is not applied to itself. Something else is needed, and in Luhmann's approach this is the *programme*. Whereas a system's code is invariant (and thus to change code is to change system), its programmes *can* change. As King and Thornhill (2003, 60) express it, »programmes are able to give the impression of incorporating universality, finality or perfection by reconstructing them within the legal system.« In short, programmes define what is »correctly« legal and »correctly« illegal (Luhmann 1992, 171f).

So, if this is the case, why does it appear that Luhmann is now, to adopt another metaphor, levering the lid of the can of worms that is the validity question? To be clear, this is not mere mischief making. Luhmann wants to know what the answer to the validity question is because he is interested in what happens when recourse is had to fundamental values in the resolution of some of the most challenging contemporary problems. At the time at which »Are there still indispensable norms in our society« was written, it might have been possible to dismiss the hypothetical terror / torture case that Luhmann refers to as relevant only in the context of an academic seminar. It is not possible to do so now. One does not have to be particularly pessimistic or an adherent of one of the more apocalyptic futurologies (of the »clash of civilisations« (Huntington 2002) variety, for example) to recognise that the sorts of conflicts of fundamental values cases that Luhmann refers to may well be a particular challenge in the years ahead – and all the more so because, at least in Europe and a few other parts of the world, we live in secular societies that have broadly abandoned metaphysical modes of legitimation. It is thus not that Luhmann wants to expose the foundational paradox. Rather he wants to know what the deparadoxification strategy is or will be in contemporary or foreseeable conditions.

As has been hinted at above, the efforts of all legal theorists of whatever persuasion may be read as contributing to the necessary deparadoxification of the legal system. At one level, if a traditional natural law solution could be accepted, then the problem would be dealt with in an incontrovertible fashion. Insofar as the source of validity is divine, then not only is the source readily identifiable but also not open to challenge. The decline of belief and the progressive secularisation of society render these proffered solutions less acceptable. Legal positivistic solutions fare no better, however. Even that purest legal scientist, Hans Kelsen (1961), can do no better in preventing the possibility of an infinite regress in his hierarchy of norms than a basic norm whose validity is *presupposed*. Is legal theory then a dry well in the search for validity? Contemporary positivists may offer some hope insofar as they concentrate some of their efforts on refining Hart's rule of recognition and thus locate the answer to the validity question in the observable actings usually of legal officials (Tamanaha 2007, 10ff). But doesn't that in the last analysis reduce to an analogue of Kelsen's position? Ask the legal officials *why* they accept a particular rule of recognition and the regress continues. Almost against expectation (not least because Luhmann (2008, 24) is so dismissive) it is contemporary natural law that may offer a satisfying answer not only to the immediate validity question but also to Luhmann's concerns about indispensable norms.

Answers from Legal Theory

Confronted with the easy criticisms to which traditional natural law is subjected, John Finnis (1980) has attempted a modern restatement that avoids the usual pitfalls. For him »A theory of natural law claims to be able to identify conditions and principles of practical right-mindedness, of good and proper order among men and in individual conduct« (1980, 18). In order to understand the subtlety of his approach, it is necessary to begin with a discussion of practical reason, that is, with reasons for actions. The basic position on practical reason that Finnis challenges is the classical account provided by David Hume. He, of course, stressed that reason cannot tell us what we *ought to* pursue, only *how to achieve* what we have already decided to pursue. Thus, every reason for action is related to a desire, but reason does not tell us what the desire ought to be. Consequently, for Hume, one desire is as good as another, as reason cannot tell us differently. What is good is thus only ever *subjective*, what any given person happens to desire. Problems arise, of course, if what is desired is not intelligible. Surely reasons only make sense when they are referred to some *objective* concept of good. It accordingly appears that it is not sufficient to begin the analysis with desires, but rather with some conception of the good that is not related to desire; in other words, some notion of *objective* good or goods (1980, 36ff).

This is in essence the starting point for the approach developed by John Finnis. He rejects Hume's conception of practical reason and develops an alternative based on a notion of *objective goods*. By objective goods, he means things that are good irrespective of whether they are desired or not. They are things that are good in themselves, and people desire them because they are good. Subjective goods, by contrast, on this account, are things that are good only because it so happens that a person or people desire them. Recalling that for him natural law is concerned with principles of practical reasonableness in ordering human life and human community, Finnis suggests that there are certain *basic goods*, as far as human beings and human life are concerned. These basic goods are objective insofar as every reasonable person must agree with their value as objects that humans aim for. For Finnis, then, the basic principles of natural law are not moral but *pre-moral*. There is no moral judgement involved. The basic goods are good because everyone must rationally agree that they are objective goals. This resonates with Luhmann's observation that »Values … are valid without justification … In practice, values serve to halt reflection« (2008, 28).

Finnis (1980, ch. 3 & 4) provides us with a list of seven objective or basic goods: life (including ideas of self-preservation and self-determination); knowledge (including for its own sake and not just instrumental knowledge); play (again including for its own sake and without any necessary instrumentality); aesthetic experience; sociability or friendship; practical reasonableness; and religion (defined broadly to include concern with the sorts of questions that would equally interest natural and social scientists). While Finnis (1980, 83) notes that this list of basic goods is stable across a wide range of places and times, this anthropological support is not the justification for the inclusion of the particular basic goods in the list. The basic goods are included because as far as Finnis is concerned they are *self-evident*. In other words, in each case, while it is impossible to *prove* that a basic good is good, it turns out not to be possible to *deny* such a proposition. The argument runs as follows: if we are offering a reason for action, then what we are doing is showing how the action is related to a basic or objective good; it follows that we cannot offer reasons for pursuing the basic or objective goods; they must accordingly be pre-supposed; anyone who genuinely denies that these goods are not important for his or her conduct must, by definition, be unreasonable (1980, 101-103), It should also be noted that Finnis does not see these basic goods as in any sense forming a *hierarchy*. For him, each of them is *equally fundamental* (92-95).

But what does this add to consideration of the sorts of questions Luhmann has posed when he asks about indispensable norms? Well, it is immediately clear that we have here an account of basic values that it is going to be very difficult to contest. Even those who are critical of Finnis concede that he has produced something impressive and important. And while traditionalists may complain that this is an attenuated version of natural law, this is not likely to be a problem for anyone else, but rather a positive advantage. But even if this constitutes a fairly robust account of basic values, one that is not dependent on metaphysics and one that can even be described as pre-moral, it remains to test it in the sort of setting that Luhmann postulates. In order to proceed to that stage, it is necessary first of all to consider what Finnis does with these values as a foundation for a more developed account of natural law.

The next step for Finnis is a series of tests of »practical reasonableness« that are designed to provide answers when applying the basic goods in practice. These tests essentially constitute the next stage in the structure of Finnis's natural law analysis and provide a means of developing the natural or moral law (what ought and what ought not to be done) from the pre-moral first principles or basic goods.

There are nine tests in all (Finnis 1980, ch. 5):

1. One should form a rational plan of life, in the form of a set of coherent intentions and commitments, which should provide a reference for the way in which one lives one's life
2. There should be no arbitrary preferences amongst the basic goods
3. There should be no arbitrary preferences amongst persons
4. One should have a proper sense of detachment
5. One should have a proper sense of commitment (in other words, 4 and 5 taken together mean that a person should be sufficiently flexible to adapt to different circumstances)
6. Efficiency is to be pursued within reasonable limits, but is not itself to be a treated as a central principle
7. There should be respect for every basic good in every action, such that no choice would contravene any basic good
8. There should be consideration for the common good
9. One should follow one's conscience, even where this is (in good faith) in error

At first sight, this last test potentially leads Finnis into difficulty: on the one hand, it is required because to suggest that a person should do otherwise would imply irrational or even immoral conduct; on the other hand, there are people whose conscience apparently tells them that they should, for example, discriminate against others on grounds of race or religion, and so on, which Finnis clearly cannot have in mind.

Closer examination reveals, however, that his set of tests is more watertight. The sorts of behaviour that people might in conscience believe to be right, but which most others would find objectionable appear to be prevented by other tests, such as »no arbitrary preferences among persons«, or »consideration for the common good«. On the other hand, however, people who believe in conscience that discrimination is right would no doubt have a response to those tests as well. The fact that they were discriminating against *all* people of a particular race or religion would indicate that theirs was not an arbitrary preference. Equally, they could, and not infrequently do, defend discrimination on the basis of arguments referring to the common good.

Whatever the problems thrown up by this last test, Finnis claims that, taken together, the basic goods and the tests of practical reasonableness provide society with a means of both avoiding injustice (at least in its more extreme forms) and of grounding fundamental rights. And to a great extent, this next step perhaps deals with the sort of problems just discussed.

Displaying characteristic subtlety, Finnis is able to argue for the existence of absolute rights in a manner that appears to brook no objection. Put simply, his argument is this (1980, 126-127):

1. Through reflection on our engagement in practical reason we all admit that certain basic goods are self-evident
2. Since they are self-evident, it follows that one of the tests of practical reasonableness must be that there should be respect for every basic good in every action, such that no choice would contravene any basic good
3. Where there are duties that admit of no exception, there must logically be correlative rights that admit of no exception

The rights that Finnis generates by this method are as follows (1980, 225):

1. not to be deprived of life as a direct means to an end
2. not to be positively lied to in any situation in which factual communication is reasonably expected
3. not to be condemned upon charges which are known to be false
4. not to be denied the possibility to procreate
5. to be taken into respectful consideration in any assessment of what the common good requires

Few would argue with these rights as rights, albeit that there could be (as is always the case) discussion about whether this is really a full list, whether some of the rights here are actually fundamental or are actually expressions of more basic rights, and so on.

Of greater importance in the context of the current discussion is Finnis's insistence that there should be respect for every basic good in every action, such that no choice would contravene any basic good (the seventh test of practical reasonableness). Critics have pointed out that the foreseeable consequences of many choices harm basic goods. Finnis avoids this problem, however, by allowing choices to be made where the result is that a basic good will be harmed *indirectly*. The basic position then becomes that we may not make choices where a basic good will be harmed *directly* (1980, 225-226).

This seems like a neat escape route until one starts considering more complex examples, including attacks on military targets during war that will predictably produce civilian casualties, and medical decisions relating to saving either the life of the mother or the life of the baby (Simmonds 2002, 117-118). Can one really call the deaths inevitably involved in these cases *indirect* harm? These are tough questions for any theoretical approach, but they are precisely the cases where practice not infrequently looks to theory for guidance. The direct and indirect harm approach advocated by Finnis simply does not seem to provide that sort of guidance. Thus, precisely in the sort of situation postulated by Luhmann, even this most subtle and persuasive of accounts of fundamental values falls short.

In order to be clearer about this, consider what happens when there is a conflict between two or more basic goods. While the seventh test of practical reasonableness requires that there should be respect for every basic good in every action, such that no choice would contravene any basic good and while Finnis is clear that there is no hierarchy among the basic values such that every one is equally fundamental, real life, regrettably, will not play along. The terror/torture example is a case in point. A judge is precisely going to have to rank basic goods. The direct/indirect test might come into play here, but this is surely either going to be a mere fig leaf for a judge's own moral conviction (which fundamental rights are supposed to preclude) or alternatively a worrying chink in the armour of fundamental rights that will allow the state to justify precisely the sort of activity that those rights are supposed to exist to prevent! In short, whatever the decision, even an application of Finnis' approach leaves the question of ultimate validity unanswered in precisely the cases where indispensable norms are expected to come into their own.

Nor is Finnis by any means alone here. Consider, as just one other example, Ronald Dworkin's approach. When confronted by hard cases, judges will find themselves without rules to apply, but they will at least be able to have resort to principles, which, of course, as far as Dworkin is concerned, are integral to the legal system. A principle, for Dworkin, is a standard to be observed because it is a requirement of justice or fairness or some other dimension of morality. Whereas legal rules are applicable in an all-or-nothing manner, principles merely state reasons that argue in one direction or another. Principles, accordingly, argue in favour of a decision, but they do not impose a decision in the way that an applicable rule does. Principles are thus considerations that judges must take into account when deciding cases, but they may be outweighed by other principles.

Equally, they are outweighed by rules that directly contradict them. It is, howe-ver, possible for a principle to prevail over a rule (Dworkin 1978, 22-28).

So far so good, but a problem will obviously arise when more than one prin-ciple might apply as Dworkin himself acknowledges. Clearly a weighing of the different principles will have to take place, but how does Dworkin ensure that the judge in any such case does not decide on the basis of individual prefer-ences or some other extra-legal consideration? His answer is to postulate a hypothetical superhuman judge, Hercules, who has the task of constructing a scheme of principles that provides a coherent justification for common law precedents (1978, 110). Dworkin understands the legal system as a *seamless web* (115) and thus Hercules is guided by a concern with consistency and integ-rity as he performs his task. This approach also leads Dworkin to propose his *one right answer thesis,* in other words, the notion that the answer to any legal question posed to Hercules will be the right one (Dworkin 1986, 235).

There is certainly something intuitively attractive in Dworkin's approach, cert-ainly from the perspective of lawyers. Is it not the case that lawyers routinely operate on the basis that the judicial determination of a case provides the final answer? But once again, when confronted with the very hardest cases, there must be doubts that everything will always turn out as easily as Dworkin implies. Is his direction to the judge to concentrate on consistency and integ-rity any more likely than Finnis' direct/indirect harm test to provide an answer that does not in fact depend on a standard beyond that provided by the legal system? Dworkin might perhaps be felt to have moved things a little further in his acknowledgement that the relative position of principles may change, but the precise ranking in any given situation is no less likely to raise the sort of problems than it did for Finnis. It really does look as if Luhmann was not just being awkward when he noted that »Nothing follows from values to aid in the adjudication of value conflicts. There is, as is often said, no firm hierarchical (transitive) order of such a type that certain values are always preferable to cert-ain other ones«(Luhmann 2008, 29).

Answers from Legal Practice

If legal theory, even in the form of perhaps the most sophisticated and subtle account of basic values, cannot resolve Luhmann's question, then perhaps it may be fruitful to turn to the world of practice. It is a fact that judges do confront cases of the sort that Luhmann postulates where fundamental values are at stake and tough choices have to be made. And, as Luhmann himself has noted, it is a feature of the modern legal system that justice cannot be denied. »Courts have to decide even when they cannot decide, or at least not within reasonable stan-dards of rationality. And if they cannot decide, they must force themselves to be able to decide« (Luhmann 2004, 289) In short, judges cannot duck the tough questions. But how do they do deal with such situations? How do they do what is apparently impossible? In language that would undoubtedly trouble Ronald Dworkin, Luhmann states that »If the law cannot be found, it must simply be invented« (289). In language that might somewhat reassure Dworkin, he continues »The paradox of the undecideable decision has to be unfolded one way or another, and that means the decision must be translated into distinctions which can be managed, for example the distinction between decision and consequence or between legal principle and its application« (289). At various points in his article, Luhmann points to the example of the common law courts and suggests that »Perhaps the development is going more in the direction of precedents, typical of common law, coupled with a correspondingly complex demand for proficiency in decision-making and a less conceptual style of argumentation.« (2008, 30) Is it possible that the common law courts could indeed offer some guidance on the way that the law may deal with the hardest cases?

At one level, it may appear an odd choice to look to, say, the English courts for any such guidance. In a system that glories in an unwritten constitution and the doctrine of parliamentary sovereignty, one may legitimately wonder whether this will really turn out to be a rich source. Might it not be the case that if Luhmann had been a little more specific he would have referred explicitly to, say, the American courts and perhaps indeed have noted a judicial analogue of Weber's English problem? It is certainly true that the English courts are not in a position to carry out the sort of constitutional adjudication that is the norm in, say, the United States (the advent of the Human Rights Act 1998 notwithstanding) and thus may not appear to be an obvious first port of call for an indication of how the common law courts might deal with cases involving fundamental values. It is nevertheless the case that a recent decision does offer a fascinating insight into how the senior judiciary understand the relationship of the courts to the legislature and, more particularly, an indication of how they would resolve conflicts on the basis of an appreciation of fundamental values.

The case in question, *Jackson and Others v Her Majesty's Attorney-General* (2005) at first glance looks rather unpromising with respect to the immediate interests of this paper, concerning as it does a challenge to the validity of the Hunting Act 2004 by which the hunting of foxes using dogs had been outlawed. Even when the grounds on which the challenge was mounted are considered, there appears to be little of relevance here because those grounds were essentially technical. It is a rule of the common law that a Bill requires the consent of both Houses of Parliament, the Commons and the Lords, as well as the Royal Assent before it can become an Act of Parliament. An exception to that rule exists insofar as the Parliament Act 1911 restricts the powers of the upper chamber, the House of Lords, to prevent the passage of a Bill that has the support of the elected chamber, the House of Commons. In short, once any Bill (subject to specified exceptions) had been passed by the Commons a certain number of times within a certain period then it would go forward for the Royal Assent notwithstanding that it had been rejected by the Lords. The Parliament Act 1949 had the effect of reducing the number of times that a Bill had to be passed by the Commons and of shortening the period within which this had to happen for it to go forward for Royal Assent notwithstanding the rejection of the Lords. The Hunting Act 2004 was one of only a handful of Acts to have been passed using the procedures laid down by the Parliament Acts. The complicating factor was that the 1949 Act had itself been made using the procedures of the 1911 Act. It was the contention of the appellants in *Jackson* that insofar as the 1949 Act represented an illegitimate use of the 1911 Act procedures and was therefore not valid law so any Act purporting to have been passed under the procedures as modified by the 1949 Act would similarly be invalid.

The judges of the Appellate Committee of the House of Lords in *Jackson* were able to deal with the case fairly straightforwardly on the basis of the normal rules of statutory interpretation. Thus, the fact that the 1949 Act did not fall into either of the categories of exceptions mentioned by the 1911 Act meant that it did constitute a valid use of that Act's procedures and was accordingly valid law. Consequently, the Hunting Act 2004 was also valid law.

Notwithstanding that fairly straightforward disposal, the judgements produced by the nine judges run to more than forty closely typed pages. While the possibility or otherwise of hunting with foxes is a matter of direct interest to a relatively small minority of the British population, the fact that a procedure exists whereby one chamber of the legislature can force law through against the wishes of the other inevitably gives rise to the postulation of doomsday scenarios where some hypothetical future House of Commons seeks to enact a draconian piece of legislation which threatens fundamental values. Accordingly, the judges in *Jackson* knew that whatever they said in the context of what some might view as a rather singular piece of legislation might well have considerable significance in any future case where the stakes were considerably higher for perhaps the population as a whole. And it is this fact that makes *Jackson* important for the concerns of this paper. Among the various judgements, two in particular stand out: those offered by Lords Hope and Steyn.

Lord Hope's judgement includes analysis of the significance of parliamentary sovereignty in concrete terms and concludes that this does not at all mean that the legislature can simply do as it pleases, but rather must involve some consideration of the public acceptability of what Parliament purports to pass as law. In this regard he notes that »Parliamentary sovereignty is an empty principle if legislation is passed which is so absurd or so unacceptable that the populace at large refuses to recognise it as law« (Jackson 2005, para 120) And he continues later in a similar vein:

> In a democracy the need of the elected members to maintain [the] trust [of the electorate] is a vitally important safeguard. The principle of parliamentary sovereignty which in the absence of higher authority, has been created by the common law is built upon the assumption that Parliament represents the people whom it exists to serve. (Jackson 2005, para 126)

As Michael Plaxton has noted, Lord Hope, in suggesting »that the public will recognise Parliament only if it acts in such a way that it maintains their ›trust‹… appears to toy with the idea of using judicial review to ensure that Parliament does not betray that trust.« The implications of such a suggestion, Plaxton (2006, 256-257) observes, are far-reaching: »If we assume that, among other things, the public trusts the legislature to act in accordance with a particular political morality … it would fall to the courts to test the validity of statutes by determining whether they comply with that morality«.

Lord Steyn, if anything, goes even further when he notes that the supremacy of Parliament, while »still the general principle of our constitution« is nevertheless »a construct of the common law« created by the judges. »If that is so«, he continues, »it is not unthinkable that circumstances could arise where the courts may have to qualify a principle established on a different hypothesis of constitutionalism.« And he continues, even more powerfully: »In exceptional circumstances involving an attempt to abolish judicial review or the ordinary role of the courts, [the judiciary] may have to consider whether this is a constitutional fundamental which even a sovereign Parliament … cannot abolish.« (Jackson 2005, para 102)

This proposed approach by Lords Hope and Steyn may, of course, have less surprise value in an era when the Human Rights Act 1998 is common currency. But it is important to note that these judges seem to be pushing the role of the judiciary to check Parliament beyond circumstances in which rights under the European Convention on Human Rights are asserted. That would be a very singular extension of what many would understand to be the role of the English courts, but is perhaps an indication of precisely what Luhmann had in mind when he made his observations regarding developments in the common law courts. Thus, it would appear that in extreme situations where the legislature has pushed things too far, that would »test the relative merits of strict legalism and constitutional legal principle in the courts at the most fundamental level.« (Jackson 2005, para 101, per Lord Steyn)

Does this mean, then, that if and when questions of fundamental values or indispensable norms arise in the English courts, the judges will have to hand a ready means of resolving conflicts among them insofar as they will utilise some notion of political morality as a measure? The language of Lords Hope and Steyn quoted above would certainly lead one to that conclusion, but in fact that is not the case. As Plaxton has observed, there is a flaw in the argumentation even of Lord Steyn, the judge who seems willing to develop the role of judges furthest: »He, like most of the other members of the panel, rejects the … suggestion that there is a hierarchy of constitutional norms – that some fundamental institutions are more fundamental than others.« (Plaxton 2006, 259-260) This is a major problem since if »validity depends on compliance with some constitutional norms but not others, it must fall to the judiciary to sort out which norms are fundamental and which are not. Yet Lord Steyn rejects this possibility.« (260)

Thus, even in the case that in some respects represents the high water mark of judicial activism in the English courts the problem identified by Luhmann remains. Indeed, not only is there no mechanism for resolving conflicts between fundamental values, there is actually a specific rejection of the possibility of doing this by the judges who otherwise appear most willing to be activist.

It is possible, however, to speculate further than either Lords Hope or Steyn have done. If circumstances are imagined where the sort of judicial activism they envisage would be required, then the necessity of deciding between different values becomes clear. The self-denying ordinance in this regard either has to be abandoned or the judges have to admit that they are not actually prepared to be as activist in practice as they suggested in principle. This observation only moves matters forward so far, however. In effect, it takes one to the position where there is an acceptance that a potential conflict of values will have to be resolved, but it does not indicate how this is to be done. Even if the test of political morality were deployed, the precise nature of this test remains opaque. In essence, one is thrown back on the sorts of problems that beset the theoretical positions, such as those of Finnis or Dworkin.

Conclusion

Having failed, as it were, to obtain any satisfactorily clear answer to the questions raised by Luhmann's article, it is tempting to say that the search for a final answer to the question of validity in the ordering of values is a futile one, that there seems no way to avoid the decisionism or relativism that indispensable norms were supposed to save us from. But what this brief excursion through the realms of legal theory and legal practice has surely shown is that there is no point in regretting the inability to achieve what is impossible. There is no once and for all answer to the question of validity in the ordering of values. Rather it is necessary to be content with the observation that it is the *fact that there are values* that offers the protection that individuals within society seek. The *fact of values* is accordingly as close as it is possible to approach to the inviolate level without risking problems of a confrontation with the paradox. While Luhmann (2008, 29f) himself points to concerns that such an approach must be unsatisfactory, it must equally be acknowledged that his own recognition of the necessity of deparadoxification means that the search for greater detail and greater certainty must be fruitless: one would be thrown back on the problem of the paradox. Thus the level of values becomes inviolate in two distinct senses. It is inviolate in the sense that we cannot know the detail of the ordering of values in advance because it is inviolate in the sense of acting as a bastion for values that by definition are resistant to any ordering in advance. If this seems like an unacceptably fatalistic note on which to end, then one should bear in mind the degree of our responsibility for the protection of values that

Luhmann's analysis highlights. Recall that »Law consists of the exploitation of conflict perspectives for the formation and reproduction of congruently (temporally / objectively / socially) generalised behavioural expectations« (1987, 27). In any given case where a conflict of values is at stake those with an interest in indispensable norms must be alert to the reasoning and argumentation of the judge. It is inevitable that *a* deparadoxification strategy will be in play, but it is not inevitable that *any given* deparadoxification strategy will be in play.

References

Dworkin, Ronald (1978): Taking Rights Seriously. London: Duckworth.
Dworkin, Ronald (1986): Law's Empire. Cambridge, Mass: Belknap Press.
Finnis, John (1980): Natural Law and Natural Rights. Oxford: Clarendon Press.
Huntington, Samuel P. (2002): The Clash of Civilizations and the Remaking of World Order. London: Free Press.
Jackson and Others v Her Majesty's Attorney-General (2005): UKHL 56 (http://www.publications.parliament.uk/pa/ld200506/ldjudgmt/jd051013/jack-1.htm).
Luhmann, Niklas (1981): Communications about Law in Interaction Systems. Pp. 234-256 in: K. Knorr-Cetina/A.V. Cicourel (eds.), Advances in Social Theory and Methodology: Toward and Integration of Micro- and Macro-Sociologies. Boston: Routledge & Kegan Paul.
Luhmann, Niklas (1985): The Self-Production of Law and its Limits. Pp. 111-127 in: G. Teubner (ed.), Dilemmas of Law in the Welfare State. Berlin, de Gruyter.
Luhmann, Niklas (1987): The Unity of the Legal System. Pp.12-35 in: G. Teubner (ed.), Autopoietic Law: A New Approach to Law and Society. Berlin: de Gruyter.
Luhmann, Niklas (1987a): Closure and Openness: On Reality in the World of Law. Pp. 335-348 in: G. Teubner (ed.), Autopoietic Law: A New Approach to Law and Society. Berlin: de Gruyter.
Luhmann, Niklas (1988): The Third Question: The Creative use of Paradoxes in Law and Legal History. Journal of Law and Society 15, 2, 153-165.
Luhmann, Niklas (1989): Law as a Social System. Northwestern University Law Review 83, 1&2, 136-150.
Luhmann, Niklas (1992): The Coding of the Legal System. Pp. 145-186 in: G. Teubner/A. Febbrajo (eds.), State, Law and Economy as Autopoietic Systems. Milan: Guiffré.
Luhmann, Niklas (1995): Social Systems. Stanford: Stanford University Press.
Luhmann, Niklas (2004): Law as a Social System. Oxford: Oxford UP.
Luhmann, Niklas (2008): Are There Still Indispensable Norms in Our Society? Soziale Systeme 14, 18-37 (in this volume).
Kelsen, Hans (1961): General Theory of Law and State. New York: Russell and Russell.
King, Michael/Thornhill, Chris (2003): Niklas Luhmann's Theory of Politics and Law. Basingstoke/New York: Palgrave.
Plaxton, Michael (2006): The Concept of Legislation: Jackson v Her Majesty's Attorney General. Modern Law Review 69, 2, 249-261.
Simmonds, N. E. (2002): Central Issues in Jurisprudence. London: Sweet & Maxwell.
Tamanaha, Brian (2007): The Contemporary Relevance of Legal Positivism. Australian Journal of Legal Philosophy 32, 1-38.

Dr. John Paterson
School of Law, University of Aberdeen
Taylor Building, Old Aberdeen, AB24 3UB, Scotland
j.paterson@abdn.ac.uk

Soziale Systeme 14 (2008), Heft 1, S. 83-101

Niels Werber

A Test of Conscience
Without Indispensable Norms:
Niklas Luhmann's War on Terror[1]

Abstract: In Niklas Luhmann's social theory, the state of exception does not exist. His monographs presuppose the »normal« functioning of communication in world society, and this means that the borders of function systems and the differences between media and codes remain intact. Politics is politics, law is law, etc. But is this still true in the case of large scale terror attacks? In the question he posed to jurists in Heidelberg – whether »indispensable norms« are still valid – Luhmann opens a fissure in the heart of normality. By using the scenario of a »ticking bomb,« Luhmann parades the aporias of function codes before our eyes. The state of exception is normatively undecidable, but requires a decision nevertheless. These are the »hard cases« and the »tragic choices.« The essay plays out various scenarios involving dilemmas of decision in moral, legal, political, and mass-media communication and arrives at a type of »aprincipled maneuvering« that places systems theory astonishingly close to the modes of amoral theories current in the USA since »9/11«.

Ticking Bombs 1: A Test of Conscience at the Draft Board

In 1984, Orwell's year, I received a call to service from the Essen District Military Registration Office. The result of the military medical examination was T2: fit for duty. Thus I was faced with a truly innocuous choice: to enlist for military service, which lasted fifteen months at the time, or to refuse armed service, and do twenty months of civil service.[2] Probably so I could continue to wear my hair long, or due to the herd instinct common to virtually all seniors in the college-prep curriculum, I declined armed service due to »conscientious objection« and was invited to the Reassignment Office, where a committee of officers and citizen observers would review my rationale. There were good and bad reasons for »conscientious objection«; the object was to determine which type of reasons might be attributed to my conscience. To this end the committee posed contrived what-if scenarios to ascertain if, in such and such a case, I might take up arms – for example, to protect my girlfriend from a violent crimi-

---

1 Translated by Todd Cesaratto. Citations of Luhmann's works published in German are translated as well.
2 Compare Luhmann's order (»Gestellungsbefehl«) from 1944 as a much more serious example (Luhmann 1988b, 34).

nal. One of these thought experiments, whose cultural history still remains to be written, offered a variation on what at this time was already an old favorite of novels and war films: the ticking-bomb scenario.[3] Wouldn't you do everything in your power to prevent a weapon of mass destruction from exploding? The clock is ticking and an act of violence is the only conceivable means of salvation. If at that very moment – »just imagine ...« – you had a weapon in your hand, wouldn't you use it to save your life and the lives of hundreds of innocent people?

My answer was affirmative and I passed the test of conscience, because this committee knew how to distinguish between extreme emergencies, emergency aid and self-defense, on the one hand, and the training of a soldier in an army that was in the cold war, on the other. Since a morally interested observer cannot observe a conscience, but only communications attributable to a conscience, hundreds of thousands were confronted with such thought experiments in which they had to handle the communications about moral experience and action being staged in the test as second-order observers. And since the committee consistently presents the problem of moral action as a *conflict of values* to the conscience testee – save lives by becoming a killer yourself or respect terrorists' rights to life and human dignity, even when this might imply the death of hundreds – and still demands explanations (»Reasons of Conscience« in Article 12a/2 of the German Constitution) for the action taken in each paradoxical situation, the conscientious objector has only one choice: Observe how the committee observes him observing a scenario and tailor his morality to »reflect« this appropriately (Luhmann 1989b). Here the etymology of »reflection« certainly springs to mind and the alternate meanings »refract« or »throw back.« The unbending authenticity of a first-order morality – »weapons are bad; I'll never kill; soldiers are murderers; my conscience principally forbids the use of force ...« – did not get one very far here, only straight to a rejection notice since every committee with just a little experience knew how to construct situations that either force one to treat as relative commandments and norms that were just presented as absolute, or place the conscience testee on the evil side of his own morality – for example, for accepting the death of hundreds, hundreds of thousands or maybe just his girlfriend or family in order not to have to scrutinize his own »unconditional« values and norms (»Thou shall not kill!« or »Everyone has the right to life and physical inviolability.«).

---

3   Compare Jean Larteguy, *Les Centurions*, Paris 1960; *Die Zenturionen*, Bonn 1961; *Lost Command*, New York 1966, and its film adaptation with Mark Robson in the starring role, *Lost Command* (1966); in German *Sie fürchten weder Tod noch Teufel*. It is set in the Algerian war. The French officer uses torture in order to prevent an assassination by guerillas. Voilà: the ticking bomb. Although the French army used torture in Algeria, the ticking-bomb scenario is imaginary. See Michael Slackman, »What's Wrong With Torturing a Qaeda Higher-Up?«, *The New York Times*, May 16, 2004. On the absurdity of the scenarios see Jim Henley, »Ticking Bombast. What would you do to save millions of lives?« ReasonOnline, January, 2007 (http://www.reason.com/news/show/117073.html).

All of this suggests a dangerously deconstructive reflection: Can it be immoral to adhere to moral values and norms? These are the questions Niklas Luhmann pursues in »Ethik als Reflexionstheorie der Moral« (1989b; »Ethics as a Reflective Theory of Morality«) and »Are there Still Indispensable Norms in Our Society?« (2008a)

Luhmann states, »Whoever moralizes takes a risk.« Once one takes a moral position in a matter, then one puts one's own »self-respect« on the line. After all, one is a good person, a devout Christian or a humanistic supporter of the constitution, and one expects that the grounds given for one's »personal opinions« will be confirmed by others and honored through »external respect«. In the test of conscience it works the other way around. The example cases should move the testee to relativize his morality; then, in the next step, to demonstrate that self-disclosure regarding his own conscience was false or that his conscience has just the right ability to relativize norms that a soldier needs. Whatever happens, »you went out on a limb with your morality« because it is after all a test of conscience. But it »is difficult to retreat and leave behind the identity one risked« (Luhmann 1989b, 370). Whoever wants to avoid this will be compelled to observe the moral code »good/evil«. The code's various programs now come into view and the unavoidable relativization that attends second-order observation makes possible the question of whether it might not be better to give up the »principles« that one just »slipped on« (436) in order to attain a higher good, namely not to be trained for an occupation of killing of others? One might call these considerations »ethical« because they would venture a moral observation of morality, a weighing of »greater goods« and »lesser evils«. And if this weighing of goods leads to an affirmative result: Would it then not be more clever to observe how the committee manages morality's distinction in order to meet these expectations? Whoever uses such tactics moves along the lines of a reflective theory of morality, a position from which it is quite difficult to say if the theory itself is good or evil. The question posed by Luhmann is precisely the question of whether such reflections must themselves be moral or not. At least one can observe the difference between an »authentic« advocacy of moral convictions (»X is good/bad«) and an observing of observations (»Under what circumstances would the committee think it good if I held X for bad or good?«). If these memoirs are not entirely deceiving, then, tests of conscience represent a sort of training camp for second-order observation. The »lesson« gained there »goes: always reflect the code as a distinction« (Luhmann 1989b, 436).

Even if one really did learn observing the code of morality as opposed to morally observing for the first time at the District Military Registration Office (and not from family or at school), what becomes of the case of the »ticking bomb« under the conditions of second-order observation? Is it a moral case at all? Or is it rather a problem for political decision makers or legal regulation? With morality, Luhmann warns the sciences, we are dealing with »something highly infectious that one should only handle with gloves and sterile instruments,« for »otherwise one will get infected with morality and will expose that which began as a scientific investigation to moral exploitation« (1989b, 359). Morality palpably disconcerts Luhmann because it »contaminates« his theorem of functional differentiation, such that the systems theorist would no longer know if scientific communication might possibly carry a moral parasite in it. Or should the moral code decide scientific questions, as many ethics professionals require? And then what happens to political and juridical questions? Is moral politics good politics? If not, then should politicians and jurists also wear »gloves«? Reflecting on the moral code proves to be a disinfectant, for when one gives or withholds approval, one proceeds cautiously when one knows that the criteria – on the basis of which one finds reasons for showing persons respect or contempt – are groundless, contingent and contradictory (360). Even this caution is still formulated in the context of a morality of morality. But Luhmann's reflective theory of morality departs from this paradigm and sets forth a sociology of morality that is not itself moral (446, 431).

Ticking bombs 2: Indispensable Norms or State of Exception?

In 1992 Niklas Luhmann begins his »Heidelberg University Lecture« with the presentation of a »case« that intensifies the test-of-conscience scenario:

> Imagine: You are a high-level law-enforcement officer. In your country – it could be Germany in the not-too-distant future – there are many left- and right-wing terrorists – every day there are murders, fire-bombings, the killing and injury of countless innocent people. You have captured the leader of such a group. Presumably, if you tortured him, you could save many lives – 10, 100, 1000 – we can vary the situation. Would you do it? (Luhmann 2008a, 18)

This is a lecture and not a test; no one is required here to answer »yes« or »no.« What matters for Luhmann is not so much the decision but which decision-making program is brought into play. Whoever looks around for criteria for making this decision will certainly, as a legal scholar, first consult the German constitution, *Article 1.1:* »Human dignity is inviolable.« Luhmann, who studied law, remarks provocatively: »the layman is at first astounded that the norm is formulated as fact. Is it therefore possible for torture not to violate human dignity?« (2008a, 18). The question is justified however since a dozen years later, after 9/11, the German Federal Government and a majority of the Parliament share a similar mindset as they pass the Air Security Act, which authorizes the air force to shoot down fully occupied civil aircraft in the event of a *renegade* attack. There were protests against the act because the killing of innocent civilians contradicts the constitution, but it was defended by the Federal

Government, among others, before the Federal Constitutional Court with the argument that »the Air Security Act also preserves human dignity. The human dignity of passengers in an airplane struck by a missile was considered.«[4] Killing hundreds of civilians by order of the Federal Government would thus not take away their human dignity! The Federal Constitutional Court had, on the contrary, made clear that even if the »innocent persons« on board were certain that they »were doomed already«, this would in no way change the fact that the »killing of innocent people in an inescapable situation« very much would take away their dignity. For »human life and human dignity deserve equal constitutional protection without regard for how much remains of an individual's physical existence.«[5] This certainly also applies to Luhmann's »case« since, first of all, torture is »totally and absolutely« forbidden by international law, and secondly, torture forcibly violates the human dignity of the person being tortured.[6] Case closed? Perhaps for the German courts, but not for Luhmann, and not for German security politicians either.

Luhmann's consultation of the constitution for the apparent solution to the case serves as a guideline for his actual question: Are there really »indispensable rights that are to be observed regardless of any of the decision's consequences«? (2008a, 18). What the Federal Constitutional Court omits in its reasons for judgment – for example think of all the domestic and foreign policy consequences a German »9/11« would have, which naturally play no role in the cited judgment – Luhmann includes in his considerations. »The terrorists have a nuclear bomb, and it must be found and disarmed. Would you use torture?« Luhmann asks anew (19). What matters is not finding a decision that would hold up in the Federal Constitutional Court, rather, what matters is the »form of the problem.« He goes one step further: Could one maybe be »unjust« when one »distinguish[es] between just and unjust« in an extreme case where one would be right in a »normal case«? (19) Precisely at this point the codification of communication becomes a problem, and it is left open to debate whether or not the distinction between right and wrong is itself lawful or unlawful. This »paradoxicality of the legal system« is generally »invisibilized« and the system continues to follow its codification without its fundamental paradoxicality causing further disturbances (Luhmann 1989a, 64). In a regular court proceeding such considerations are rarely heard. However some take issue with the paradox and problematize a code's »unity of the difference« (Luhmann 1990, 84 fn 17). Whoever observes in

---

4   Federal Constitutional Court, 1 Federal Constitutional Law 357/05 from Feb. 15, 2006, Paragraph 56. The Court is of an expressly different opinion (Paragraph 117) and declares the law unconstitutional and invalid. It does indeed violate human dignity when the state orders to be shot down a plane high jacked by terrorists and used as a weapon.
5   Federal Constitutional Court, 1 Federal Constitutional Law 357/05 from Feb. 15, 2006, Paragraph 131.
6   See Schmahl 2005. See also Federal Constitutional Court, 2 Federal Constitutional Law 1249/04 from Dec. 12, 2004 and on a »Ban of Torture« Federal Constitutional Court, 2 Federal Constitutional Law 1506/03 from Nov. 15, 2003.

this way is bedeviled (85). The semantic traditions of most function codes demonstrate (Luhmann 1988a, 240ff) that the »diabolical« observation of »justifications for the validity of distinctions« is undesirable (Luhmann 1990, 91). This applies to the legal code just as it does to power, truth, money, to codes of art, the education system, religion or morality. The solution that modern society has found for this problem here seems to be very efficient. *El Diablo* is expunged, that is invisibilized, and the paradoxical conditions for symbolic generalization are »protected from latency« (Luhmann 1984, 456ff). This suffices for the »normal case.« Right stays right and what is wrong is legally determined (Luhmann 1993, 143f). But what happens in the case of an exception?

Luhmann normally avoids this concept. Only at a distance does he address Carl Schmitt's »state of exception« concept explicitly (Luhmann 1987a, 11f), and one could certainly discuss his reasons for doing so (compare Wirtz 1999; Werber 1995). The media codes of the function systems are built universalistically and provide for no exception (Luhmann 1988b, 33f; Luhmann 1975). It is impossible to acquire scarce goods on the market without the ability to pay, or for statements to be held as true even though they are not falsifiable. Whoever wants scarce goods needs money and whoever wants scientific knowledge must hold to the code of true / false. Codes play a main role in the emergence of a modern functionally differentiated society (Luhmann 1984, 218f). It is only a »mild exaggeration« to state that not people but codes govern us, and it is not at all an exaggeration to maintain that we were socialized by »codes of difference« and not by persons (Luhmann 1987c 168f). They serve to translate a function into a difference, to cover a specific function realm completely; they select from the environment that which can be internally informative to the system; they are programmable and asymmetrical; thus they outfit communication with a preference – with condensed »probability of acceptance« (Luhmann 1995a, 302).

In particular the »legal system cannot accept exceptional status« (Luhmann 1993, 414). But Luhmann's »case« wants to be just that, an exceptional case that moves the observer – or more exactly, since in his view »neither Kant nor Habermas« count here, the systems theoretical observer – to confront »the problem of the right to break the law« (*das Recht zur Rechtswidrigkeit*; Luhmann 2008a, 31). How do we, he asks the audience, »decide ›hard cases‹ (as Americans would say in their inimitable fashion)« (Luhmann 2008a, 19; see also Luhmann 1993, 314f). He underscores the worldwide »contemporary relevance« of such cases (Luhmann 2008a, 35) and repeatedly recalls the particular difficulty of his scenario – a nuclear bomb in the terrorists' hands, an accomplice in custody, would you use torture? If our society has indispensable norms, then the answer will be »no« under all circumstances. Basic rights are basic rights because they can never be suspended. In contrast to other constitutions, the most important basic rights (Articles 1-20 of the German Constitution) are not open to alteration by lawmakers for all time. If law still reigns then the basic rights are also valid – the constitutionality of all law is assessed according to their measure (Luhmann 1993a, 95f). From the internal view of the law the certainty of »functioning constitutionality« is thus »a functional equivalent for the recognition of human rights and makes it – legally-technically – almost superfluous« (579). *Superfluous* because a constitutional state's legal practices do not normally injure basic rights. But only *almost* superfluous precisely because there are exceptional cases such as the one of shooting down a hijacked civil aircraft.

The German Minister of Defense Dr. Franz Josef Jung gave a speech on Sep. 19, 2007, before the German parliament on the topic of »Ordering Airplanes Highjacked for Reasons of Terror to be Shot Down without a Legal Basis« (www.bmvg.de). The Minister acknowledges the judgment of the Federal Constitutional Court and expressly emphasizes that the planned law for shooting down renegade flights in extreme cases has been declared »unconstitutional.« The »case« has thus been conclusively decided but not resolved as a political problem. Rather the judgment overtaxes politics and puts stress on the structural coupling between the legal system and state-authorized force. Because Jung asks again, what is to be done when terrorists illegitimately use an airplane full of passengers as a weapon; the Federal Constitutional Court's judgment has not done away with the possibility of such a situation. »In this situation, we have to respect the legal order, including human dignity; but we should also remember that we have sworn an oath to prevent harm from coming to the German people.« Incidentally, Jung has also sworn »to preserve and protect the Constitution and the Law of the Federation«, but this makes his point all the more clear. The Minister does not believe that the »situation« can be described and handled in legal terms alone, rather he reserves the right to evaluate the matter politically and decide accordingly: The »defender of the force of order and command« – says Jung using words Luhmann also uses – stands before a »tragic« choice. He makes clear that »after consideration of all perspectives« he would give the order to fire in an »extreme situation,« that is, he would act unconstitutionally, and afterwards accept »political responsibility« for his decision. During a quite fascinating Federal Government press conference on Sep. 17, 2007, a speaker for the Federal Ministry of the Interior indicated (www.bundesregierung.de) that in the case of such a »tragic situation«, the Minister of Defense would be acting on the basis of »an extra-legal state of emergency.« »The prerequisites for this extra-legal regulation,« added Senior Legal Adviser Kaller, »is difficult to describe in detail.« The exception does not permit itself to be legally regulated, which rests on the logic of an »extra-legal state of emergency.« Politics reserves for itself the right to make decisions that do not correspond to the High Constitutional Court's interpretation, that is, that the legal code cannot comprehend. This fact seems so sinister to politicians that the »extra-legal state of emergency« is maintained to be in no way the absence of all »legal regulation« but rather »a legal option« – and indeed an option for the Federal Minister of Defense. Said a bit more pointedly, the disposition over life and death turns the Minister into a »sovereign in the sense that the decision about the critical situation, even if it is the exception« – is his (Schmitt 1976, 38). That the Minister will accept responsibility after the fact will not at all diminish the carnage typically expected during states of exception: The air force »is deployed and wreaks all sorts of destruction« perhaps people are even killed, etc. All of this can no longer be made undone« (Schmitt 1985, 126). From the irrevocable wrongs that could conceivably accrue with the implementation of such »measures« in an »extra-legal state of emergency« it does not however follow – neither for Carl Schmitt and maybe not for the Federal Government too – that they were »unconstitutional from the beginning« since this would lead to the »absurd conclusion« that the Constitution established for the protection of the German people only »permits measures without effects or consequences« (127). For Schmitt the decisive factor is the efficiency with which a situation can be resolved and a state of normalcy can be restored. The Ministers of Defense and of the Interior have also avowed that they will not content themselves with »measures without effects or consequences« and are determined to suspend »indispensable norms« in extreme cases.

This would certainly be an opportunity to address »hard cases.« Is this what Luhmann meant when he confronted his audience with the possibility that in the most extreme case of a ticking bomb that it is perhaps wrong to insist upon the distinction between right and wrong, and that one must consider other options that are not to be »morally discrediting one« prematurely (2008a, 19-20)? Obviously Luhmann holds it for conceivable that essential basic rights must be canceled in certain cases because they cannot hinder »innocent-bystanders« from falling victim to »the fanaticism of terrorists« (33). Does Luhmann become a theorist of the state of exception here, and is thinking in terms beyond values and norms all the easier for him when nothing of them remains in his sociological reflection of morality which could be used to orient decisions?

The problem of the exception is briefly mentioned by Luhmann in the monograph *Law as a Social System* and then broadly *excluded*. »Human rights injuries of unambiguous blatancy« – these would be: »the state-supported disappearing of persons, forced deportations and expulsions, illegal killing, incarceration, torture with the knowledge or under the protection of state organs« – would take place *elsewhere*, namely where constitutionality is not guaranteed and states are unable or unwilling to settle human rights violations with *normal* constitutional means« (Luhmann 1993, 579, italics NW). Luhmann is not speaking here of the zones of exclusion that he describes in »Beyond Barbarism« for he adds that »such violations are widespread, that is to say, common in the majority of states« (579). From here it follows that the zones in which people cannot count on the sovereign power respecting, preserving and protecting their basic rights is relatively large. In an »extreme situation«, to quote the Minister once more, this could happen to any airline passenger in the skies over Berlin.

Luhmann does not pursue this thought any further – which would put him in proximity to Giorgio Agamben's considerations of »naked life« – because he actually has high hopes that these zones will disintegrate. The globalization of constitutionality into a »world legal system« has indeed not yet been realized but does lie in the developing global society's logic of evolution. One has only to wait – and in the meanwhile lead black sheep onto the right path with »sanctions« and »assistance.« Wherever communication takes place, that is, in modern society's entire »realm of inclusion ..., the normal conditions for stability reign« (Luhmann 2008b, 45). Since systems theory knows no spatial dimension of communication (Werber 1998), it is understandable that Luhmann does not follow his own observations to realms that elude the logic of functional differentiation or that call this logic into question (see Luhmann 1995b).

Thus Luhmann pursues the exceptions' spatial dimension only half-heartedly; certainly he considers it plausible that »injuries to human rights« can occur in spite of »functioning constitutionality«, or, formulated more precisely, that »injuries to human rights« are covered rather than condemned by »positive law« (Luhmann 1993, 579). These exceptional cases do not allow mitigation via spatial or temporal distinctions because they pertain to constitutional law itself and they must be treated with non-normal constitutional means. Luhmann suggests what might be understood by this: A quasi-juridical »solution« to the problem of legal injury to the constitution that disregards »all legalistic considerations based on Article 1 of the Constitution,« namely:

> Allowance of torture through internationally supervised courts, closed-circuit surveillance of the scene in Geneva or Luxemburg, long-distance supervision via telecommunications, transferring the just / unjust distinction onto the victim's option of being either hero or traitor. Taken all together, not very satisfying solutions. But it is equally unsatisfying to do nothing at all and thereby sacrifice innocent-bystanders to the fanaticism of terrorists (Luhmann 2008a, 33).

More humanitarian torture with judicial permission conducted by certified experts whenever possible and of course with medical oversight. Luhmann's suggestions seem as if taken directly from today's headlines. A critical review of the U.S.-American »ticking-bomb« controversy ends with the admission that the question is not at all whether torture is permissible under extreme circumstances, but rather only if torture is to be regulated or not:

> In some circumstances, though, our only real choice, in terms of both national security and moral consequences, will be between controlled and uncontrolled torture. We gain nothing by pretending differently. In the struggle against deadly terrorism, some of world's most civilized democracies are themselves unwilling to shrink from doing what they think is necessary. Such are the times in which we live. (Slater 2006, 215)

This is no extremist position. Since 9/11 prominent jurists and political scientists have advocated it in the form of various strategies. The spectrum runs from an endorsement of the legal regulation of torture in the most extreme emergencies (Alan M. Dershowitz, Richard A. Posner) to notions that reject legal regulation, but at the same time concede that it could be necessary to do what must be done (»bad acts«, »dirty hands«) in exceptional cases (Michael Walzer, Michael Ignatieff, Jean Bethke Elshtain).[7] Must? Since one can obviously refrain from doing what others believe they must do, we are clearly dealing with the need to make a decision. But on the basis of what norm? When disregarding constitutional, basic and human rights is supposed to be the »lesser evil«, must there not also be »greater goods«? Here the discussion gets ensnarled in an endless spiral that, on the quest for a highest norm, winds toward the infinitude of a heaven of values. Luhmann has no doubt that this quest for a »norm that evades all conflicts of interest« will produce no results (Luhmann 2008a, 34). There will be no ethically or legal-philosophically satisfying resolution of the case. The matter is normatively »undecidable« (19). But it must be decided because the bomb is ticking.

But how? Let us suppose that the decision is made against torture for normative reasons (morality, law, international contracts, good manners) (Bellamy 2007 523) or, in the German case, against the shooting down of the renegade plane. This would not solve the problem. One would have to reckon with test cases that perhaps basic values could not handle (Luhmann 2008a, 19f). Would society lose hope in its basic values in the case of a catastrophe – the nuclear bomb explodes, the plane full of passengers crashes into a stadium, etc. – that could have been prevented, hence the presentation of the case, via the suspension of these basic values (compare Derrida 2003)? Luhmann does not direct his question at the Federal Constitutional Court, whose answer is already known and which is not responsible here, but rather at society. The law recognizes no »exception« to the »rule« (Luhmann 2008a, 29), but law is not everything for society. From a »sociologist's distance«, Luhmann wants to determine whether the communication off »›indispensable norms‹ finds success in a society« or not (21). In the case of Police Vice President Daschner, who threatened a stubbornly tight-lipped kidnapper with physical pain in order to discover the victim's hiding place, a Forsa survey from 2003 showed that 63 percent of Germans were against punishing Daschner for using torture. He had done the right thing. It was a matter of saving an 11-year-old boy. But if it were a matter of a major city full of innocents – women and children? Might there not even be – in conjunction with the media's coverage of the case – a political majority supporting illegal, unconstitutional decisions? And would not the prospect of an election victory be a motive for assuming »political responsibility« for such decisions?

7   See exemplary texts like Ignatieff 2004; Dershowitz 2002; Bellamy 2007; Hannah 2006.

Luhmann directed his question regarding the indispensability of norms at society. This brings the mass media into play, whose construction of reality and scripts are decisive in underwriting society's self-understanding. What society knows about society, indeed about the world it constructs, it knows through the mass media (compare Luhmann 1996, 9; Luhmann 1997, 1106). Society observes itself in the mass media and thus creates its own reality, the reality of society (1096ff). This also applies to the evaluation of »hard cases« because the mass media enable a »very original type of norm production« that does not rely on legal texts, but rather responds to »scandalous events« (deportations, disappearing of persons, political murder …). Since under the pressing demands of a concrete situation, one cannot embark upon a worldwide quest for a »norm that evades all conflicts of interest« (2008a, 34), Luhmann seems to prefer relinquishing the production of norms to the mass media. Are the media the functional equivalent of a sovereign, namely an instance that decides »ad hoc« in view of the concrete »situation« without drawing conclusions for the next case? It sounds cynical but may suit society's reality better than the hope that a »uncoerced discourses [will lead] to a reasonable result that will produce consensus« among all involved (35). »Would you do it?« Luhmann suggests that this decision would be made not only out of consideration for basic rights, but with a view toward the mass media. They have already tested serious cases.

Ticking Bomb 3: Tests of Conscience in the Mass Media

Before captivated media audiences, politicians, scientists, talkshow hosts and celebrities discuss »what-if« questions. Imagine: a plane is full of passengers. On board there is a »dirty bomb« and a handful of terrorists who want to detonate it at a sold-out football game or in a shopping district. Would you order the plane shot down, Mr. Schäuble? Mr. Baum? Ms. Künast? Mr. Primor? On Sep. 23, 2007, Anne Will of the *Anne Will* TV show asks this question. Various opinion-research institutes pose the same question to the public: Would you shoot the plane down, yes or no? In September the majority is evidently against it. Can »indispensable norms« be deduced from this or merely an insufficient depiction of the scenario? Even Anne Will's guests are supposed to answer with a clear »yes« or »no«, presumably so that the hostess has the opportunity to ask follow-up questions: You would really have a passenger plane shot down – with all of those innocents people on board? You would really fold your hands in your lap and just sit there as determined terrorists murdered hundreds of passengers, countless football fans and themselves? Is that not … evil?

None of the guests walk into this fairly obvious morality trap. In their statements each guest takes pains to »demoralize« the question and to separate his own person from possible interpretations of the situation. »The bomb is

ticking! Shoot it down?« Personal involvement with indisputably moral questions – it's a matter of people's lives, any one of us could be on that plane
or in the stadium with which it collides – is cautiously avoided by resorting
to the seemingly neutral ground of legal questions and expertise, reciting the
position of the courts and other institutions. The guests sidestep »risking their
own identity.« Without morally jeopardizing »one's own person«, one can cite
Federal Constitutional Court decisions or discuss more technical questions like
how a plane can actually be shot down without incurring collateral damage in
the crash zone, who is liable for damages according to civil law, or what is the
appropriate warning time between the alert and missile launch, and whether
this even allows the on-site authorities sufficient time to inform a minister
and act according to his orders. Audience members reject these de-moraliza-
tions as evasions. They wants to see »individual moral judgments prefabricated
and assigned to each participant« (Luhmann 2000, 308f). They are not disappointed.

The discussants are guests on a talk show and each of them knows that the
mass media call for another form of complexity reduction than the First Senate
under the leadership of the Federal Constitutional Court President. Whoever
desires the audience's applause, and already senses electoral success behind
such acclaim, must speak pointedly, aggressively and polemically. »Sacrificing
people's lives is contrary to our Constitution.« Or: »We want freedom *and* security.« Who would deny this? »Like stars in the heavens there are countless values. Therefore basic values are needed for emphasis. Here traditional concepts
like freedom, equality, justice, peace, security, dignity, welfare, and solidarity
are used to designate special status« (Luhmann 2008a, 28). Each guest reaches
into the well-stocked value chest and what inevitably follows is the demon-
stration of a conflict of values, for the rhetorical eminence of values contains no
information whatsoever regarding the primacy of one over the others. »Nothing follows from values to aid in the adjudication of value conflicts.« There is
no hierarchy that provides for »freedom [being] more important than security
in every case, peace always more important than freedom, justice always more
important than peace, etc.« The »adjudication« of these value conflicts remains
»unregulated« (29), Luhmann writes – and indeed they are lawfully, morally,
legally-philosophically and ethically unregulated. In contrast the mass media
make possible their own type of norm production, as seen on the *Anne Will*
show.

Bringing basic values into play does not suffice; rather the mass-media scripts
suggest that the political adversary holds a different view and is more or less
for the sacrifice of lives or against securing freedom. Both variations garner
applause: conspicuous demands of respect for one's own moral position and
unmistakable contempt for the opposing moral position. Television in particular
loves conflicts and scandals that lend themselves to a moral inflection because
these situations depict those involved as moral agents to whom norm viola-

tions and controversial decisions can be attributed (Luhmann 2000, 308f). The mass media – out of time considerations alone – cannot »fully illuminate the complex back stories that might have motivated if not forced the moral agent to do what he did.« Nonetheless they must situate the case, scandal, norm violation or decision in a story with a beginning, middle and end; thus motivation gets assigned to the good or bad character of the *dramatis personae*. Mass media »coverage« uses morality as a mechanism for the reduction of complexity, and when persons can provide »an occasion for respect or contempt«, their stories will be reported (Luhmann 1996, 64f). One can easily gather from the 207 viewer comments on the *Anne Will*-Blog, posted by the ARD, that this works not just as a script – most bloggers characterize the acting Minister of the Interior as evil, the Minister of the Interior, ret., as good – but also that moralization is adopted as a procedure. Just like on television: One disputes credibility, discredits positions as wicked or dishonest, and denies opponents' ability to speak to the topic.[8]

That this procedure relies on a specific mass-media format is also probable because other formats lead to other reactions. The »round table« format staged by the mass media predictably leads involved parties to a respectable consensus. The »round table« allows participants to be depicted as equal, which makes an unequal distribution of respect and contempt difficult, and it suggests »full inclusion« as if all parties always participate in achieving consensus. Every time the result is a praiseworthy compromise among reasonable persons – and if negotiations fail, they are certainly not portrayed as »round-table« discussions. That parties who reject »round-table« negotiations deserve contempt is de facto unquestionable according to mass-media logic. Jürgen Habermas's expectation – that in »the public light citizens [would] interact with each other as equals« (1990, 57) and in such an assembly decide questions of power, showing each other mutual respect and thus arrive at an uncoerced agreement – corresponds to the format of a »round-table« interaction. Consensus in a matter results from »the force of a better argument« in a public discussion (Habermas 1990, 119). Observing the mass media, however, shows the opposite to be the case.

»Especially conspicuous,« Luhmann (1989b, 444) writes on Dec. 31, 1987, after a look at the newspaper, »is the way politicians fire morally charged broadsides at each other, the way pleas and invective make reference to moral judgments, and the way opponents reciprocally refute each other's ability to make judgments.« Here one could add that the opposite also occurs: Politicians, tariff partners, enemies in civil war, or protectors and pollutors of the environment offer each other mutual assurances of respect, serious intent and honest effort, but that this format also moralizes. In this case the belief is roused that the good will of all participants will find a solution acceptable to all – that thus the

---

8 http://annewill.blog.ndr.de/2007/09/23/mit-minister-oder-ohne/#comments (accessed Oct. 9, 2007).

matter must not be *decided* in the sense that the decision would exclude other previously possible options, which others might have preferred. The »round-table« format conjures away the basic problem of the political and the medium of power (see Schmitt 1991; Luhmann 1988b). It is swept off »the table« of the mass media, but not, however, out of the world. The reality of all the Afghani ethnicities and groups' miraculous consensus that the St Petersburg summit so suggestively represented is indebted to this format; and now as the mass media are reporting that the St Petersburg agreement is not being upheld, they remind us that important actors were not even at the table and that the »moderate Taliban« must now participate in new multiparty compromise negotiations. After the round table is before the round table. Rebuffing an invitation to the national dialogue can only be interpreted as proof of evil within this media format. That the »round table« in fact stages accord that is not yet implemented lies in the format's blindspot.

According to its own self-description the *Anne Will* talk assists in the formation of political opinions. This opinion formation resorts to moral scripts. »Supported by the mass media, morally charged conflicts are in any event staged before audiences presumed competent in making judgments.« The reciprocal discrediting went so far that none of the participants can seriously qualify as »electable.« Luhmann suspects that maybe moralization occurs in the General Assembly of the Bundestag because »people are obsessed with the idea of being able to bring the audience as *moral* authority over to their side.« Potentially public media exchanges could thus aim primarily at having audiences condemn the position of the political opponent and respect one's own. Luhmann shows disgust for the possibility of a moral infiltration of the political:

> But a political election *may not be permitted* to form a government on the basis of a moral qualification or disqualification; for that would simply imply that the morally disqualified candidate is unelectable, that is: He may be part neither of government nor of opposition in hopes for change of government. That ruins one if not the deciding, structural achievements of democracy: the facilitation of an orderly change of power at the system's highest level and the (relative) independence of this change in power from the power of those governing at the time (Luhmann 1989b, 444f; italics NW).

Once again Luhmann is driven to expressing anxiety over the fact that the de-differentiation or the contamination of the code will threaten the function system, as though this could not be entrusted to the autopoesis of society, which could find other ways of connecting communications with communications, for example in the form of networks (compare Baecker 2005, 198, 234) or, as Cologne Sociologist Erwin Kurt Scheuch would say, »factions«.

It is in any case established that politics fails to keep morality at a distance, at least in the mass media. It appears difficult to resist the temptation to proffer one's opponent for the public's contempt. One maintains that the opponent's proposed technical, juridical or political handling of the matter does not deserve respect, but rather is cynical, cowardly, opportunistic or otherwise dishonest. Rejecting morality seems impossible, since »everyone who does this will be judged negatively by morality, which can only judge according to two values and has no third value at its disposal for the requested distance to morality« (Luhmann 1989b, 445). As soon as someone demands respect for his opinions or actions – simultaneously risking contempt for his person – moralization also occurs; thus his attitude in the matter is moralized as well. Once morality is in play, every attempt to assume an amoral or immoral perspective – to deal with the matter »beyond good and evil«, so to speak – is inevitably branded evil or bad. Maybe our society does not need indispensable norms. But as soon as the mass media take on the »hard cases« – which will always happen since these hard cases make great news – they are inevitably moralized and connected to persons. The public's respect or contempt for these persons is translated daily into tangible electability statistics. It is what it is, but should one hold this to be good? Should the ratings and votes of viewers decide the »hard cases« because they represent a majority that could support a certain decision in a certain case in a certain situation? This too is the theme of novels (Spinrad 1994; Stephenson 1994). And it makes the scenario suspenseful at least. Luhmann concluded his Heidelberg talk with the statement that in »hard cases« a sociological description of problematic decisions is more helpful than a juridical exegesis of the constitution or a discussion of values. »Ultimately, the question this situation confronts us with is: What can we do? But before we can ask this, there is a vital preliminary question: How can one observe and describe adequately?« (Luhmann 2008a, 35).

A Society without Indispensible Norms

This is certainly correct, but Luhmann's descriptions avoid the paradoxes of law only at a price, a price that Luhmann does not name explicitly, and he does not indicate whether he intends to pay it. Both his reflections on morality and his deconstruction of the law end with the state of exception. This is the consequence of his »diabolical« look at the codification of the law and the amoral possibilities in deciding »hard cases.« The price consists in an endangerment to Luhmann's desired theoretical architecture: globalization of the mode of functional differentiation (Luhmann 1997, 162ff). Luhmann does not close his eyes to exceptions to the rule, but does everything he can to make his descriptions of these cases finally prove the rule that »world society« is functionally differentiated: »A general diagnosis would therefore have to state that world society has adapted itself to the functional differentiation of systems, but in many functional domains (including economics, politics and law) such an evolutionarily improbable form of differentiation cannot assert itself – but neither can any other!« (Luhmann 2008a, 31). Finally even the mafia must conduct its affairs according to the fact of functional differentiation (Luhmann 1995b).

Luhmann shows outright bitter ridicule for positions that contradict these suppositions, for example »economic politics.« »As the rain dance ritual serves the Hopi Indians, talk of economic stimulus, securing Germany's position, job creation, etc., fulfills an important function – the function of giving people the impression that something is being done and politicians are not just waiting for the problems to solve themselves,« though precisely this »is still the *best* solution that we have at the time« (Luhmann 2000, 113; italics NW). The »best« still means: do not even try that which is impossible anyway, that is, intervention in one system (the economy) with other system-specific (political) operations. Autopoetic systems are just that: »perfectly autonomous« (126). As the basis for this Luhmann cites the »self-referential closure of the economy«, which for its own – not for political – reasons shifts its bases of operations or creates jobs and does so without any causal dependency on political decisions. The »differences that the economy creates and leaves behind cannot be decided by political vote« (113). One can vote for parties from the government or opposition but not for economic success, technical advances, freedom or security. It is noteworthy: Although systems theory normally comes across as purely descriptive sociology, which in contrast to its »critical« counterparts does not wish to offer advice, one can extrapolate from Luhmann's writing something like a pathos of autonomy and a corresponding ban on intervention. Luhmann warns outright of a disintegration of difference between the various function codes. »When a communication procedure cannot observe and respect this difference, it can only lead to confusion« (Luhmann 2000, 392). Behold the difference, is his commandment. This yields a contradictory result. After his deconstruction of the legal code and warning about morality, Luhmann elevates functional differentiation itself to a norm and demands it be respected.

What does this have to do with our topic? My thesis is: Only amidst complete differentiation of function systems, in a state of their »perfect autonomy«, can our society dispense with »indispensable norms.« The law judges, politics decides, morality evaluates. The function codes tailor whatever happens so that it can be settled juridically or politically with »*normal* constitutional means« (Luhmann 1993, 579; italics NW). This however is not the case, and Luhmann's theory faces the imposition of formulating exceptions that cannot be placed back into the parameters of functional differentiation via a self-explanatory linkage. This applies to systems theory's tentative considerations along the lines of spatial exclusion, as well as its observation of the ominous »endangerment« of a system's »self-referential reproduction« through the excessive demands of its environment (Luhmann 1987, 150). The »hard cases« are introduced by Luhmann expressly as an example of such excessive demands. It does not matter how the »tragic choice« plays out, the law cannot solve legal cases and the political system cannot solve extreme cases without respectively revoking the conditions of functional differentiation and established structural couplings. That, in every situation, governmental politics attempts to externalize (extralegal state of emergency) or exclude (Guantanamo) these cases is an index for this »endangerment's« reality. Communicating openly about cases that compel the law and politics to observe their own paradoxical and contingent existences is no alternative to governmental or judicial statements.

The bomb is ticking, the terrorists are in your grasp. Torture could save lives. »Would you do it?« Luhmann's reading of the ticking-bomb scenario extends beyond the parameters of basic values and basic rights, and into a theory of the exception. Leaving the choice of exceptions to the mass media does not solve the problem, for their original type of norm production cannot serve as a substitute program for making political or legal decisions without cancelling the »perfect autonomy« of function systems. Therefore the »ticking bomb« is a »hard case« not just because law and politics are overtaxed by the imposed decision, but the decision confronts systems theory itself with a »tragic-choice.« Either one lets the judges look over the constitution and pass judgment, thereby obligating future, collectively binding governmental decisions. Then one stipulates functional differentiation as »the normal condition of stability« of social systems (Luhmann 2008b, 45), the Federal Constitutional Court does its duty – but the nuclear bomb explodes and society is overburdened by the consequences of adhering to indispensible norms. Or one »reflects on the conditional parameters« of making a decision and discovers a »capacity for maneuvering without principles«, a sort of opportunistic »use of tactics« to »prevent the momentary worst-case scenario.« In this »maneuvering without principles« Luhmann sees an alternative to normative decision-making programs (»constitution«) and to surrendering political decisions to the mass media (»public opinion«). A »use of tactics« without relying on indispensable norms or moralizing public opinion is the recommendation of an »ambitious sociological theory« (Luhmann 2000, 168). Since 9/11 more governments have followed this recommendation of governing pragmatically and decisively – freed from norm- and value-based considerations – than Luhmann could have guessed. In a different theoretical language one would call such an opportunistic, flexible, reactive mode of operations normalistic (Link 1997) or governmental (Foucault 2004a; Foucault 2004b; Hardt 2003; 2004). Matthew Hannah's analysis of the »ticking-bomb« dispositive relies entirely on theory inspired by Foucault and Agamben. Important for my reading of Luhmann is the parallel between a governmental normalism and a politics of »maneuvering without principles.« According to Jürgen Link this means developing an ability to handle traditions and norms cognitively rather than normatively. The opportunistic handling of values could become the motto for a »flexible normalism«, which, following Link, is »made in the USA« and currently »on the path toward dominance« (Link 1997, 312).

The agents of such a »flexible normalism« are forever functionally, pragmatically, boldly, soberly, adaptively and efficiently adjusting their conduct to each new situation in order to achieve their objectives. Jack Bauer from the TV series 24 epitomizes this figure. Everyone knows what he would do if the bomb were ticking: »Whatever it takes!«[9] In such a dire situation society finds itself in a state of exception without indispensible norms. The normalistic handling of an extreme situation is far removed from the »normal conditions for stability« of a functionally differentiated society. One would have to reckon with the suspension or the confusion of the function codes. A »maneuvering« politics could make itself thoroughly at home there.

References

Baecker, Dirk. (2005): Form und Formen der Kommunikation. Frankfurt a.M.: Suhrkamp.
Bellamy, Alex J. (2007): Dirty Hands and Lesser Evils in the War on Terror. British Journal of Politics and International Relations 9, 509-526.
Derrida, Jacques (2003): Schurken. Frankfurt a.M.: Suhrkamp.
Dershowitz, Alan M. (2002): Why Terrorism Works: Understanding the Threat, Responding to the Challenge. New Haven, CT: Yale University.
Foucault, Michel (2004a): Geschichte der Gouvernementalität I. Sicherheit, Territorium, Bevölkerung. Vorlesungen am Collège de France 1977-1978. Frankfurt a.M.: Suhrkamp.
Foucault, Michel (2004b): Geschichte der Gouvernementalität II. Die Geburt der Biopolitik. Vorlesungen am Collège de France 1977-1978. Frankfurt a.M.: Suhrkamp.
Habermas, Jürgen (1990): Strukturwandel der Öffentlichkeit. Untersuchungen zu einer Kategorie der bürgerlichen Gesellschaft. Frankfurt a.M.: Suhrkamp.
Habermas, Jürgen (1992): Faktizität und Geltung. Frankfurt a.M.: Suhrkamp.
Hannah, Matthew (2006): Torture and the Ticking Bomb: The War on Terrorism as a Geographical Imagination of Power Knowledge. Annals of the Association of American Geographers 96, 622-640.
Hardt, Michael/Antonio Negri (2003): Empire. Die neue Weltordnung. Frankfurt a.M.: Campus.
Hardt, Michael/Antonio Negri (2004): Multitude. Krieg und Demokratie im Empire. Frankfurt a.M./New York: Campus.
Ignatieff, Michael (2004): The Lesser Evil: Political Ethics in an Age of Terror. Princeton, NJ: Princeton University Press.
Link, Jürgen (1997): Versuch über den Normalismus. Wie Normalität produziert wird. Opladen: Westdt. Verlag.
Luhmann, Niklas (1975): Einführende Bemerkungen zu einer Theorie symbolisch generalisierter Kommunikationsmedien. Pp. 170-192 in: N. Luhmann, Soziologische Aufklärung 2. Opladen: Westdt. Verlag.
Luhmann, Niklas (1984): Soziale Systeme. Grundriß einer allgemeinen Theorie. Frankfurt a.M.: Suhrkamp (Social Systems. Trans. John Bednarz J. & Dirk Baecker. Stanford: Stanford University Press, 1995).
Luhmann, Niklas (1987a): Archimedes und wir. Interviews. Berlin: Merve.
Luhmann, Niklas (1987b): Machtkreislauf und Recht in Demokratien. Pp. 142-151 in: N. Luhmann, Soziologische Aufklärung 4. Opladen: Westdt. Verlag.

---

9 Jane Meyer, Whatever It Takes. The politics of the man behind 24, in: The New Yorker, February 19, 2007.

Luhmann, Niklas (1987c): Widerstandsrecht und politische Gewalt. Pp. 152-170 in: N. Luhmann, Soziologische Aufklärung 4. Opladen: Westdt. Verlag.
Luhmann, Niklas (1988a): Die Wirtschaft der Gesellschaft. Frankfurt a. M.: Suhrkamp.
Luhmann, Niklas (1988b): Macht. Stuttgart: Enke.
Luhmann, Niklas (1989a): Am Anfang war kein Unrecht. Pp. 11-64 in: N. Luhmann, Gesellschaftsstruktur und Semantik, Vol. 3. Frankfurt a. M.: Suhrkamp.
Luhmann, Niklas (1989b): Ethik als Reflexionstheorie der Moral. Pp. 358-447 in: N. Luhmann, Gesellschaftsstruktur und Semantik, Vol. 3. Frankfurt a. M.: Suhrkamp.
Luhmann, Niklas (1990): Die Weisung Gottes als Form der Freiheit. Pp. 77-94 in: N. Luhmann, Soziologische Aufklärung 5. Opladen: Westdt. Verlag.
Luhmann, Niklas (1993a): Das Recht der Gesellschaft. Frankfurt a. M.: Suhrkamp (Law as a Social System. Trans. Klaus A. Ziegert. Oxford: Oxford UP, 2005).
Luhmann, Niklas (1995a): Die Kunst der Gesellschaft. Frankfurt a. M.: Suhrkamp (Art as a Social System. Trans. Eva Knodt. Stanford: Stanford UP, 2000).
Luhmann, Niklas (1995b): »Kausalität im Süden.« Soziale Systeme 1, 7-28.
Luhmann, Niklas (1996): Die Realität der Massenmedien. Opladen: Westdt. Verlag (The Reality of Mass Media. Trans. Kathleen Cross. Stanford: Stanford UP, 2000).
Luhmann, Niklas (1997): Die Gesellschaft der Gesellschaft. Frankfurt a. M.: Suhrkamp.
Luhmann, Niklas (2000): Die Politik der Gesellschaft. Frankfurt a. M.: Suhrkamp.
Luhmann, Niklas (2008a): Are There Still Indispensable Norms in Our Society? Soziale Systeme 14, 18-37 (in this volume).
Luhmann, Niklas (2008b): Beyond Barbarism. Soziale Systeme 14, 38-46 (in this volume).
Schmahl, Stefanie / Steiger, Dominik (2005): Völkerrechtliche Implikationen des Falls Daschner. Archiv des Völkerrechts 43, 358-374.
Schmitt, Carl (1985): Der Hüter der Verfassung. Berlin: Dunckler & Humblot.
Schmitt, Carl (1991): Der Begriff des Politischen. Berlin: Dunckler & Humblot.
Slater, Jerome (2006): »Tragic Choices in the War on Terrorism: Should We Try to Regulate and Control Torture?« Political Science Quarterly 121, 191-215.
Spinrad, Norman (1994): Pictures at 11. New York: Bantam.
Stephenson, Neal / George, J. Frederick (1994): Interface. New York: Bantam.
Werber, Niels (1995): Von Feinden und Barbaren. Carl Schmitt und Niklas Luhmann. Merkur. Deutsche Zeitschrift für europäisches Denken 9 / 19, 949-957.
Werber, Niels (1998): Raum und Technik. Zur medientheoretischen Problematik in Luhmanns Theorie der Gesellschaft. Soziale Systeme 4, 219-232.
Wirtz, Thomas (1999): Entscheidung. Niklas Luhmann und Carl Schmitt. Pp. 175-197 in: Albrecht Koschorke / Cornelia Vismann (eds.), Widerstände der Systemtheorie. Kulturtheoretische Analysen zum Werk von Niklas Luhmann. Berlin: Akademie Verlag.

Prof. Dr. Niels Werber
Droysenstr. 2, App. 31
D-10629 Berlin
niels.werber@rub.de

Soziale Systeme 14 (2008), Heft 1, S. 102-109

William E. Scheuerman

»Against Normative Tone-Deafness«

Abstract: Luhmann's essay eerily anticipates the post 9/11 argument – now widely endorsed in the United States – that even the fundamental moral prohibition on torture is by no means necessarily sacrosanct. Despite what appears to be an assault on traditional modes of moral reflection, Luhmann's critique itself implicitly rests on traditional forms of weak (and probably utilitarian) moral argumentation. Luhmann argues that we need to acknowledge the existence of irrepressible »tragic choices«, yet his own apparent (but by no means consistent) hostility to »old European« moral rationalism precludes him from fully understanding the nature of such tragic moral situations.

Reading the late Niklas Luhmann's essay »Are There Still Indispensable Norms in Our Society?« (2008; first published 1993), one is immediately struck by its eerily prescient character. Despite the deeply abstract contours of his remarkable theoretical edifice, Luhmann clearly had his hand on the public pulse, as even his most difficult writings always grappled, however indirectly, with contemporary political and social trends. This article is no different. Since the terrorist attacks of September 11, 2001, a global debate has quickly unfolded concerning precisely that troubling prospect with which Luhmann begins his reflections: if thousands of lives could be saved, might it be appropriate for state officials to torture captured terrorists? The German *Basic Law* would condemn your actions, and strict statutory bans even in common law-oriented legal systems unambiguously prohibit torture, notwithstanding some of Luhmann's potentially misleading comments about such systems. But might not a state official quite reasonably consider the employment of what U.S. Vice-President Dick Cheney now euphemistically describes as »alternative« forms of interrogation? If so, does it make sense to assert that modern society rests on any sacrosanct or at least indispensable norms, since the prohibition on torture would seem to fall into the category of absolute and thus inviolable norms? What could be more essential to a decent political and social order than a strict prohibition on torture?

Since the 9/11 attacks, U.S. jurists have grappled with the disturbing possibility that torture might be justifiable in the face of dire existential threats to public order (see Levinson 2004). This legal debate has hardly occurred in a political vacuum. Indeed, substantial evidence suggests that it has contributed to major shifts in U.S. policy, according to which forms of interrogation long widely condemned by international lawyers have been embraced by the Bush Administration as part of the »war on terror« (Danner 2004). I mention this not because I intend to smear Luhmann's name by cheaply linking his serious theoretical reflections to the pathologies of present-day U.S. policy, however. His general point hardly relies on the speculative and empirically dubious assumption that torture can provide useful rather than misleading information, a presupposition brilliantly decimated two centuries ago by the great Italian Enlightenment legal thinker Beccaria, and whose suspect character has been corroborated by substantial historical and social scientific research. (Not surprisingly, the Bush Administration has yet to provide reliable evidence that its »alternative« interrogation methods have generated positive results, even in the narrow terms defined by the Administration.) If I understand Luhmann correctly, the torture example is only one (though perhaps not the best) illustration of his broader claim that any notion of the indispensability of norms to modern society can no longer rely on »conclusive formulas for an edifice of norms, nor of principles, nor of a basic norms, nor even of a highest value that encompasses and trumps all others.« (Luhmann 2008, 35) Luhmann's social theory has always taken a deeply anti-normative form. In this spirit, the essay expresses serious doubts about the indispensability of any »redemptive, conclusive formula, a [normative] system in the case of Kant's or a general law, valid a priori« (2008, 20) to contemporary society.

Yet it still makes sense to dwell for a moment on the parallels between Luhmann's starting-point and the post 9/11 U.S. legal debate. Like Luhmann, participants in that debate are busily deconstructing the modern humanitarian idea that even a norm as seemingly foundational as the torture prohibition is somehow indispensable. In a spirit of hard-headed »realism« by no means alien to Luhmann, they delight in shredding familiar dogmatic moralisms: the anti-normative character of their reflections hardly directly mirrors his, yet thematic overlap remains. Not surprisingly perhaps, his argument may be vulnerable to a point easily made about the U.S. jurists. Their assault on the strict torture ban is hardly an attack on »norms« *per se*, but instead an argument which itself obviously takes a normative character. They unleash familiar (and, frankly, oftentimes weak) utilitarian (and consequentialist) arguments against a demanding (and probably quasi-Kantian) interpretation of the torture ban, typically arguing that torture might, in extreme cases, prove justified because it would best serve the »public good« or »national security,« e. g., some »greater good« which supposedly trumps the manifest evils of torture. A deep commitment to a utilitarian ethics represents the best way to minimize the unnecessary loss of life in the face of existential threats to the political community, and such an ethic rightly possesses a certain primacy in relation to rigid general legal norms which, as we know since Aristotle, sometimes fail to do justice to the idiosyncrasies of the particular case. From this perspective, the point is not that modern society can do without indispensable norms, but instead that we need a more nuanced understanding of the normative structure of moral and legal reasoning in order to grapple with the unavoidable limits of any rigid system of general statutory legal or constitutional norms.

Critics of this position then typically shift the terms of debate to more familiar ground: how *sound* are the utilitarian arguments that are being posited? Even if it remains indisputable that *every* legal system inevitably faces hard cases in which general legal norms provide only limited guidance, for example, might not a *loosening* of the strict ban on torture in fact generate »worse« normative consequences, that is, *increase* the unnecessary loss of human life? In other words, one line of argumentative attack takes the form of asserting that those who challenge the inviolability of the torture ban are advancing an inconsistent and ultimately misbegotten utilitarianism. Others attack their utilitarianism head-on. But *all sides* in the debate recognize that competing *normative* models of practical reasoning are at stake.

Now Luhmann very well might find himself alarmed by the general texture of this exchange, having famously argued that »the moral code can act like a bacterial infection« that dangerously pollutes the autonomy of competing codes in the context of social complexity and functional differentiation (Luhmann 2000, 211f). Yet his reflections here repeatedly reproduce traditional normative categories. Torture arguably only represents a paradox or »tragic choice« in the first place because, as Luhmann and some U.S. jurists now note, it is at least conceivable that it *might* »save many lives,« in other words, because of an implicit moral commitment to the sanctity of human life. Torture may be justified, in other words, because our fidelity to the »norm« or »value« of preserving human life potentially trumps normative bans on physical or psychological abuse. In cultures which lack a basic moral commitment to the value of preserving human life, torture would simply not generate the same quagmires that it necessarily poses for us: one would simply practice it, as was too often the case in pre-Enlightenment Europe, as a matter of course. To retort that the moral commitment to saving »many lives« lacks any basis in our (e.g., western modern) moral heritage, and instead is built into the codes that govern our legal or political systems, if indeed this is how Luhmann might respond, reproduces precisely that »other-worldliness and ignorance of law« he polemically attributes to proudly normative theorists like Kant and Habermas.

This observation points to a more fundamental weakness in Luhmann's otherwise prescient observations. As mentioned, the famously anti-normative orientation of his social theory is again on full display here. Unfortunately, his arguments provide more than sufficient ammunition to those who have always worried about this facet of his thinking.

Quite correctly, Luhmann (2008, 22) notes that when one »attempts at identifying and establishing indispensable norms, one's attention will likely be drawn, even today, to natural law.« The discourse of natural law long dominated western political, moral, and legal thought; its language and categories provided the framework by means of which indispensable norms were postulated. But for Luhmann (2008, 24) »natural law remains only an empty shell«, having failed to secure a suitable home in either the basic consciousness or the institutional structures of modern society. Natural law influenced the emergence of modern law, and increasingly out-of-date jurists still praise its virtues while doing battle with their positivist foes, but natural law remains a dead horse, fundamentally incongruent with functional system differentiation and the temporal structure of modernity. If I understand him correctly, his point is not only that natural law has been subject to what Weber famously described as the process of »disenchantment,« but that its normative kernel was effectively obliterated by this process as well. Consequently, it never gained real footing in modern society. In Luhmann's (2008, 25) own language: the semantics of natural law correlated well »with the imperative of stratified differentiation« characteristic of »noble« or aristocratic societies, but not with modern forms of functional differentiation. Natural law, consequently, can provide no basis for deriving or establishing indispensable norms.

On this point, as on so many others, Luhmann's analysis seems reminiscent of Weber's. Unfortunately, it no less problematically precludes an alternative interpretation of the complex and multi-faceted tradition of modern natural law.

In Weber's famous account in *Economy and Society* (1979) of the development of modern natural law, he argued that a perfectly formal or value-free model of the social contract freed from any substantive natural law elements was necessarily incoherent. Such a view of the social contract would have to depend on a notion of natural law made up »entirely of general legal concepts devoid of any content« (1979, 868) Its presuppositions would have to be so abstract that they would only generate the most trivial conclusions. The only coherent version of modern natural law necessarily rests on substantive (but ever less sturdy) ideas of natural law. But since, for Weber, the process of disenchantment inevitably denies substantive natural law any normative bite, the most one can say is that »natural law dogmas influenced more or less considerably both [modern] lawmaking and lawfinding.« Yet since »all metajuristic axioms in general have been subject to ever continuing disintegration and relativization ... [they] have lost all capacity to provide the fundamental basis of a legal system.« (1979, 874) In other words, natural law shaped modern institutions, as Luhmann similarly notes, but it can no longer provide a reliable normative basis for legal or practical decision making. For Weber (1979, 868-879), the »substantive« moral ideas about »reason« and »nature« which grounded natural law in its most developed Enlightenment-era manifestations simply failed to withstand the battering ram of *Entzauberung*.

To be sure, Weber's argument raises legitimate concerns about formalistic conceptions of the social contract; those conceptualizations remain controversial today (Benhabib 1989/90). Nonetheless, this reading of modern natural law

and – in particular – its mature formulation as Enlightenment-era social contract theory prematurely forecloses another plausible competing interpretation.
One instead could argue, building on Rousseau, Kant, and countless writers
inspired by them, that the normative kernel of the social contract ideal was
the simple but decisive intuition that legitimacy derives from a formal decision
making process in which participation is genuinely free and equal: only those
norms can be considered normatively acceptable if they emerged in a process
of decision making which we can fairly describe as meeting demanding yet
universally acceptable standards of freedom and equality. In short, we *might*
be able to free modern natural law of problematic premodern assumptions no
longer tenable in the context of our disenchanted universe, while salvaging
the basic idea of the social contract as an inspiration for a model of normative
legitimacy resting on a set of formal procedures securing the free and equal
participation of everyone.

Of course, this suggestion raises at least as many tough questions as it answers.
With Weber (and, prior to him, Hegel), one might ask whether such strict formalism and proceduralism could ever be theoretically coherent. In addition,
one would have to show how this version of modern natural law managed
successfully to gain a foothold in modern consciousness and practice. It would
be silly to downplay the difficult intellectual challenges at hand. Nonetheless,
it is precisely this path which has been pursued – in my view, with at least
some success – by a broad range of thinkers and intellectual traditions. Among
contemporary social philosophers, Habermas and Rawls come immediately to
mind. But many others might be mentioned in this context as well.

Unfortunately, Luhmann's essay never really considers this developmental possibility. Its only references to Kant and Habermas are highly polemi-
cal. Luhmann misleadingly accuses Habermas, for example, of neglecting the
dilemmas posed by »the right to violate the law.« (2008, 31) Especially in light
of Habermas's detailed 1980s discussions of civil disobedience, as well as his
more recent interventions on the problematic legality of NATO intervention in
former Yugoslavia, this is a peculiar criticism (Habermas 1983; more recently,
see Habermas 1999). Luhmann's quick comments do not do justice to Habermas's impressive *Between Facts and Norms* (1996). Kant's idiosyncratic critical
reflections on a »right to revolution,« I might similarly point out, have recently
been placed in a sympathetic light by a leading left-wing German political theorist (Maus 1992). More fundamentally, Luhmann's curt discussion of natural
law seems unfairly uninterested in a variety of impressive attempts to rework
the fundamental ideas of natural law while simultaneously respecting the unavoidable complexity and contingency of contemporary social life. In this tradition, one might also place the leading postwar U.S. natural lawyer, Lon Fuller,
whose work has been experiencing something of a revival in the last decade or
so (Witteveen / Burg 1999).

At times, Luhmann's critical survey of natural law echoes the normative reduc-
tionism of orthodox Marxism: for Luhmann, the semantics of natural law
provided something like a »normative« superstructure to aristocratic society,
but this »superstructure« apparently lost its fundamental »basis« with the
shift from stratification to functional differentiation. »Freedom and equality
are made abstract norms,« not mainly, as Luhmann (2008, 26) suggests here,
because of the functional needs of a changing society, but also by means of an
immanent cultural and intellectual development from which we continue to
benefit. Even if Luhmann is undoubtedly right to claim that many elements
of traditional natural law were integrally linked to premodern social experience (this is hardly a novel observation, by the way), should we be so willing to
abandon its normative legacy altogether? Is there nothing substantial we can
salvage from it?

Of course, attempts to rework the heritage of natural law have become suspect
to some today because they appear linked to a »human rights fundamentalism,« destined to culminate in an irresponsible »military humanism« according to which (western ideas of) human rights can and should be foisted on
»outlaw« states by military means, typically employed to the disproportionate
advantage of the great powers. Military intervention under the auspices of protecting human rights, of course, raises difficult moral and political questions,
many of which seem to possess precisely that tragic character which Luhmann
hopes to recall. But one should probably note that the most subtle discussions
of the »tragic choices« entailed by humanitarian intervention have been under-
taken by those who refuse to abandon the normative heritage of western moral
law thinking altogether (Wheeler 2003).[1] For example, the violent practices of
the great powers in Yugoslavia, Iraq, and elsewhere are best criticized from
within the horizons of normative ideals of popular sovereignty, the rule of law,
and human rights. On one critical reading, »military humanism« depends on a
deeply *problematic* and intellectually tendentious interpretation of the best way
to preserve traditional western normative ideals. It privileges »human rights«
(and their self-named guardians) over democratic legitimacy and the rule of
law,[2] in reality making a mockery of many noble normative intuitions. Blame
for the systematic bombing of civilians, to put the point bluntly, cannot be easily placed at the doorsteps of Rousseau or Kant.

So like Weber, Luhmann is vexed by the possibility that his intellectual opponents obscure the »tragic choices« that we face. He wants a theory that rests on
a deep appreciation of the inherently tragic contours of modern life. To be sure,
this is a legitimate concern. However, I wonder whether his own deeply anti-

1 Wheeler, I think, provides a superior understanding of the paradoxes of humanitarian intervention to realists like Danilo Zolo (2002).
2 On this tendency, see Brunkhorst 2005. Even more pointedly, see the work of Ingeborg Maus,
   a Kantian who opposed the NATO intervention in Yugoslavia. See the interview with her in
   Oliver Tolmein (Maus 2000).

normative instincts can possibly do justice to the deep tragedies with which we inevitably find ourselves struggling. To put the point rather bluntly and crudely: in western thought, an appreciation of tragedy in human existence has often-times presupposed a demanding moral code. For example, early modern Euro-peans (and ultimately many others as well) came to worry about *Raison d'Etat* and »the illegal breaching of the law by the holders of the highest political power« not simply because it violated the just-unjust system code's structure, but instead because such acts violated our deepest moral commitments: when rulers appealed to reason of state to massacre political opponents in the name of »necessity,« they did so in conflict with the deepest tenets of Christianity. We now similarly worry about torture not because of its incompatibility with mod-ern functional differentiation, but instead because it goes against what remains of the great moral teachings of our tradition.

In a powerful but unfairly neglected little book, *Scientific Man Vs. Power Politics*, Hans J. Morgenthau (1946) argued that precisely the *decline* in the contempo-rary world of a demanding moral ethos, according to which others must be treated non-instrumentally as *ends-in-themselves*, was the source of our lapsed appreciation for the many tragic choices we face. Only if we maintain fidelity to strict moral ideas, can the depth of the tragedies with which we are constantly confronted become plain to us in the first place. We should worry, as Weber argued, about the unintended *consequences* of our political choices, not sim-ply because we strive for consistency, but because they risk undermining our deepest moral commitments: »We want peace among nations and harmony among individuals, yet our actions end in conflict and war. We want to set all men free, but our actions put others in chains as others do to us.« (Morgenthau 1946, 188) Morgenthau went so far as to assert that significant strands of tra-ditional Christian and Jewish religious thought were more alert to the intrin-sic quagmires of human action than what he decried as modern »scientism«: they forthrightly recognized »the existence of two forces – God and the devil, life and death, light and darkness, good and evil, reason and passion – which struggle for dominance of the world.« (1946, 205) Like Weber, he believed that disenchantment necessarily undermined the religious foundations of much western moral thinking. Yet he still worried that too much of modern thought had thereby thrown the baby out with the bath water, glibly discarding core moral insights before proceeding disastrously to downplay the unavoidable tensions between the quest for power and morality. Far too often, political actors consequently reduce politics to morality (and embrace a simple-minded moralism) or, no less troubling, morality to politics (and thus opt for *Realpoli-tik*). *Both* tendencies ignore the tragic choices we face; both are politically and morally irresponsible.

To be sure, much more needs to be said about the complex nexus beween »tragic choices« and morality. Luhmann would rightly warn us of the potential dangers of any endeavor to salvage traditional moral and normative ideas at the cost of sacrificing the contingency and complexity of modern social life. By the same token, it remains unclear whether »tragic choices« can really be quite as tragic as Luhmann seems to believe in the context of a theory that downplays the far-reaching moral and normative impulses that continue to shape so many different arenas of modern social existence.

References

Benhabib, Seyla (1989-90): In the Shadow of Aristotle and Hegel: Communicative Ethics and Current Controversies in Practical Philosophy. The Philosophical Forum 21, 1-2, 1-31.

Brunkhorst, Hauke (2005): Solidarity: From Civic Friendship to Global Legal Community. Cambridge, USA: MIT Press

Danner, Mark (ed.) (2004): Torture and Truth. New York: New York Review of Books.

Habermas, Jürgen (1983): Ziviler Ungehorsam. Testfall für den demokratischen Rechtsstaat. Wider den autoritären Legalismus in der Bundesrepublik Pp. 29-53 in: Peter Glotz (ed.), Ziviler Ungehorsam im Rechtsstaat. Frankfurt a.M.: Suhrkamp

Habermas, Jürgen (1996): Between Facts and Norms. Contributions to a Discourse Theory of Law and Democracy. Cambridge: Polity Press.

Habermas, Jürgen (1999): Bestiality and Humanity: A War on the Border Between Legality and Morality. Constellations 6, 3, 263-272.

Levinson, Sanford (ed.) (2004): Torture: A Collection. New York: Oxford University Press.

Luhmann, Niklas (2000): Answering the Question: What is Modernity? An Interview with Niklas Luhmann. Pp. 195-223 in: William Rasch, Niklas Luhmann's Modernity: The Paradoxes of Differentiation. Standord: Stanford University Press.

Luhmann, Niklas (2008): Are There Still Indispensable Norms in Our Society? Soziale Systeme 14, 18-37 (in this volume).

Maus, Ingeborg (1992): Zur Aufklärung der Demokratietheorie. Rechts- und demokratietheoretische Studien im Anschluss an Kant. Frankfurt a.M.: Suhrkamp.

Maus, Ingeborg (2000): „Wer den Weltstaat etablieren will, riskiert Krieg." Pp. 71-84 in: Oliver Tolmein (ed.), Welt Macht Recht. Konflikte im internationalen System nach dem Kosovo Krieg. Hamburg: Konkret Verlag.

Morgenthau, Hans J. (1946): Scientific Man Vs. Power Politics. Chicago: University of Chicago Press.

Sanford, Levinson (ed.) (2004): Torture: A Collection. New York: Oxford University Press.

Scheuerman, William E. (2007): Was Morgenthau a Realist? Revisiting Scientific Man Vs. Power Politics. Constellations 14, 506-530.

Weber, Max (1989): Economy and Society, ed. and trans. Claus Wittich and Guenther Roth. Berkeley: University of California Press.

Wheeler, Nicholas (2003): Saving Strangers: Humanitarian Intervention in International Society. Oxford: Oxford University Press.

Witteveen, Willem J. J./Burg, Wilbrun V. (eds.) (1999): Rediscovering Fuller. Amsterdam: Amsterdam University Press.

Zolo, Danilo (2002): Invoking Humanity: War, Law, and Global Order. London: Continuum.

Prof. William E. Scheuerman
Faculty of Political Science, Indiana University
1100 7th Ave., Bloomington, IN 47405
wscheuer@indiana.edu

Soziale Systeme 14 (2008), Heft 1, S. 110-125

Costas Douzinas

Torture and Systems Theory

Abstract: Niklas Luhmann's attack on the rhetoric of the ›indispensable values‹ brigade is important and timely. Self-evidently good norms have political usefulness but no philosophical value. However replacing values with rights and entrusting decisions to lawyers displaces rather than solves the problems of indeterminacy and conflict of law and rights. The (falsely) ascetic commitment to description coupled with the acceptance of the social order makes systems theory useless as a tool for improving society. Philosophy tends the distance between the naturally and socially given and the eternal aspiration to resist and transcend it, by exploring both the justice internal to law and the justice which holds the whole of law to account.

1. A ticking bomb?

One can only admire Niklas Luhmann's prescience. Many years before 9/11, an eon before Abu Ghraib, Guatanamo Bay and ›extraordinary renditions‹ became household names, to open an essay on ›indispensable values‹ with a discussion of the ›ticking bomb‹ hypothesis is quite prophetic. Would one torture a terrorist suspect who may have knowledge about the whereabouts of a bomb about to go off and kill »10, 100, 1000« innocents? Would the answer change if the immediate family of the hesitating torturer was involved or »if the terrorists have a nuclear bomb?« (Luhmann 2008, 18, 19) Luhmann bravely and prophetically anticipates some of the proposals we have been hearing recently. Torture can be allowed if regulated and supervised by »internationally supervised courts, closed-circuit surveillance of the scene in Geneva or Luxemburg, long-distance supervision via telecommunications, transferring the just/unjust distinction on to the victim's option of being either hero or traitor.« (33) Luhmann adds without much explanation that these solutions are not satisfactory (morally, one assumes) but they become inevitable if one realises that »doing nothing« would sacrifice »innocent-bystanders to the fanaticism of terrorists« (33).

This is as strong an opening in an essay on norms and values are you are likely to come across. The choice of example to illustrate the malleability of ›indispensable norms‹ is brave but troubling. Indeed, torture in one of the few acts that the post-WWII western consensus found totally abhorrent. Torture was seen as part of a past that the West had left behind for good. A number of international treaties explicitly banned torture and a whole convention was dedicated to the abolition of the practice. In Europe at least torture seemed a relic fit for the history seminar. Article 3 of the European Convention on Human Rights not only bans »torture, inhuman and degrading treatment« but also makes the prohibition absolute, disallowing its suspension even in times of war or emergency »threatening the life of the nation« (Art. 15).

It was understood, of course, that in extreme cases, certain exceptions might be necessary. The Israeli Supreme Court for example had allowed, in *Hamdan*, the internal security forces to apply »moderate physical pressure« during the interrogation of suspects.[1] This blanket authorisation, which was condemned by the UN Committee on Torture was repealed in 1999 when widespread abuses against Palestinians were uncovered by human rights organizations.[2] Indeed, this juridical reversal demonstrates the slipperiness of the legal slope. Mild torture in extreme cases of a ›ticking time bomb‹ (Hamdan, the torture victim, according to the court »possesse[d] extremely vital information, the immediate procurement of which would prevent an awful disaster, would save human lives, and would prevent very serious terrorist attacks«) can easily mutate into extreme torture techniques widely applied. No information leading to the avoidance of disaster was discovered by the torture of Hamdan.

Delivered first as a lecture in December, 1992, Luhmann's (2008) piece was published in 1993. Yet it comes straight out of current debates. In the last few years, the hypothesis has been a mainstay of newspaper commentators, moral philosophy seminars and conferences on applied ethics, one of the main ways through which professional moralists have come to discuss the morality and legality of torture in the ›war on terror‹ and not only. Lawyers, such as Alan Dershowitz (2002) and liberal commentators, including Michael Ignatieff (2004) and Bruce Ackerman (2006), are prepared to enter into debate about the morality and legitimacy of torture and to develop detailed ways of legalising it through ›torture warrants‹, ›sunset clauses‹ and judicial supervisory regimes. These procedures introduce an element of judicial or other external supervision and therefore make the exercise of torture ›limited‹ and ›lawful‹.

We can understand the ›ticking bomb‹ scenario as a game played in University seminar rooms. As every law professor knows, a good ›problem question‹ on an exam paper should be able to compel the ›right‹ answer. We have no evidence that information about ticking bombs was ever acquired by torture, including in Israel. The trick is that we have to say yes or no to an unreal situation that never happens. The answer appears to be the outcome of moral deliberation, reasoned argumentation and choice as befits the seminar room; but it would take a moral absolutist of heroic proportions to argue anything other than ›yes‹. The appearance of freedom is as false as that which accompanies, according to Luhmann (2008a, 45), the »supply-society« leaving the individual »with mean-

---

1 The Hamdan case, HCJ 8049/96.
2 Public Committee against Torture in Israel et al, HCJ 5100/94 et al.

ingless decisions«. The choice is forced; the scenario is constructed in such a way as to make torture pre-emptively justified. But this undergraduate game has dire consequences. It lowers the threshold of acceptability of torture and makes it a topic apt for civilised conversation and moralistic disputation. One of the few moral certainties of our civilisation is on the retreat.

Why should Luhmann choose such a problematic example to illustrate his argument about ›indispensable norms‹ also known as human rights? One obvious answer is that the ban on torture is precisely the most ›indispensable‹ of norms and therefore the best test case for his critique of the idea. But it also serves the wider purpose of bringing together a number of strands in the history of ideas, legal history and jurisprudence which help illustrate his own systems theory. Let us briefly follow some of these steps.

2. Indispensable norms or fundamental rights?

Luhmann's concern, typical of a German educated in law, is with ›indispensable norms‹ (constitutional rules for example), the values lying behind them (human dignity, freedom or equality) and the permissible and necessary balancing (›tragic choices‹) when these norms/values clash amongst themselves or with other public policies. Luhmann's warnings against the triumphalist excesses of the values, ›indispensable norms‹ and rights brigade is extremely timely. His indictment is long and compelling.

Values are essential for political manifestoes and constitutional court decisions because they are presented as self-evident and self-evidently good. One is for peace, freedom and humanity and not for war, slavery and the inhuman. While values have no need for justification, they can justify any number of policies. Their political usefulness is therefore great but their philosophical value limited. Their incontrovertible ›goodness‹ serves to stop reflection about their nature or import. The great and proliferating number of values, their abstraction and vagueness mean that while they are endemically in conflict, they offer no intrinsic advice about its resolution. Values allegedly help make decisions indisputable; in reality, they are of no use in deciding specific issues. As a result, value conflicts are treated at the level of the individual case which, under-determined by grand principle, operates in a situational and casuistic context in conditions of »self-generated uncertainty«. Values, supposedly necessary for decisions, »bring this necessity into the form of contingency« (2008, 29).

One possible response to the problem of undecidabilty would be, according to Luhmann, to take the legal route: concentrate on the individual case, follow the elaborate procedures and protocols the law has developed for resolving conflicts and remember that a decision must be made. Luhmann mentions certain legal techniques for resolving normative clashes which resemble our own ›presumptions in interpretation‹.[3] Instead of constructing ever more complete and hierarchical lists of values, with their foundational, basic or ground norms (an exercise that will inevitably fail), a more appropriate strategy would move »in the direction of precedents, typical of the common law, coupled with a correspondingly complex demand for proficiency in decision-making and a less conceptual style of argumentation« (2008, 30). The civil law of fundamental values and basic norms should try to approximate the common law model.

The relationship between civil and common law, this ›peculiarity of the English‹ according to Max Weber, is too complex and evolving to be discussed here in any detail. To test the advice in our area of immediate interest let us turn briefly to the case-law that comes closest to the ›conflict of values‹: human rights. By combining high value and legal technique, rights-based adjudication may be the answer to the problems that under-determined values and indispensable norms create but cannot resolve.

If we turn to the Anglo-American discourse of rights, the German rhetorical excess of values is repeated and even exceeded. For the rights fanatics, rights trump policies, give right and certain answers to hard cases, they unbelievably enjoy ›objectivity‹ and promote the values of dignity, autonomy and equality. We live in the age of rights, we are told. The North and the South, left and right, state and church, globalising imperialists and anti-globalisation protesters, first world liberals and third world revolutionaries, they all use the language of rights. In our age of ›posts‹, where the ›end of history‹ alongside modernity, class, ideology and something called ›the human‹ has been proclaimed (rather hastily; Fukuyama, its celebrated proposer, has recently admitted that reports of the death of history have been premature), rights are the last universal vocation, the only institution that allegedly enjoys catholic approval. Rights are the ideology after the death of ideologies, the only ideology or ›idolatry‹ in town, according to Michael Ignatieff, its apologist in chief.[4] But can rights give ›right answers‹ to the hard choices of our day and replace the difficulties of values and norms?

The jurisprudence of human rights shares the problems Luhmann identifies in the field of fundamental norms and values. Human rights provisions more than all other law are profoundly ambiguous and must be interpreted in complex political and legal situations. Human rights are the one area in which the realist and critical legal claims have been almost universally confirmed (Kennedy

---

3 Such presumptions assisting judicial interpretation when more than one meanings can be attributed to a statutory provision include the following: when two statutes are in conflict Parliament must be presumed to have repealed the earlier Act (the so-called ›repeal by implication‹); Parliament must be presumed not to wish to violate international legal obligations; or, the use in an Act of Parliament of the masculine pronoun ›he‹ must be presumed to include the feminine ›she‹, unless clearly indicated to the contrary. There are many such presumptions, some of which contradict each other. As is obvious by the examples given, their assistance in deciding cases involving conflict of values is strictly limited.

4 I use the term ideology here in its strict Althusserian definition, as the ›imaginary way in which people relate to their real conditions of existence‹.

1977, 304-9; Koskenniemi 1999; Kennedy 2001). In brief summary, the critics argue that human rights provisions are indeterminate; that they are always subjected to wide and similarly indeterminate restrictions;[5] that rights are inescapably involved in conflicts with other rights (freedom against security, free speech and press against privacy) or with the same rights of others; that their open-ended language means that they acquire meaning and effects in acts of interpretation and application, in which all kinds of non-principled considerations are involved; finally, that the context of application is much more important than the text of the provisions.

The claim, for example, in Article 2 of the European Convention on Human Rights that ›everyone has a right to life‹ gives no answer whatsoever to questions about the legitimacy of abortion, euthanasia or the use of lethal force by the military against civilians and the security services against presumed terrorist threats.[6] Human rights provisions do not wear their meaning on the sleeve of the relevant treaty clause. Whether, for example, events in Rwanda amounted to genocide (according to the Security Council they did not) or whether the persecution of Albanians in Kosovo amounts to a ›humanitarian catastrophe‹ (no according to the Security Council, yes according to NATO) is not answered by treaties and conventions but by the politicians, diplomats or judges interpreting them in the context of state interests. As an international lawyer put it »any substantive issue could be labelled as a human rights violation« (Tomasevski 2000, 405). If one combines this recognition with law's intrinsic indeterminacy, which means that »the legal argument inexorably and quite predictably allows the defence of whatever position« (Koskenniemi 1999a, 351, 354), it becomes clear that the trust put on lawyers' ability to resolve conflict through the tool of human rights is seriously misplaced.

Replacing values with rights and entrusting decision-making in hard cases to lawyers does not solve the problems Luhmann rightly identifies. Indeed, if that were the case, if technical solutions at the individual level could respond to the ills of domination and exploitation, violence, war and the ›end of history‹ would be nigh. Does the ubiquity and inflation of rights discourse mean that

---

5 The right to freedom of expression in Article 10 ECHR is subjected to such ›formalities, conditions, restrictions or penalties as are prescribed by law and are necessary in a democratic society in the interests of national security, territorial integrity or public safety, for the prevention of disorder or crime, for the protection of health or morals, for the protection of the reputation of the rights of others, for preventing the disclosure of information received in confidence, or for maintaining the impartiality of the judiciary.‹ A cynical soul might observe that every possible restriction on speech can be justified under this litany of exceptions.

6 In a number of cases the European Court has stated that states retain a ›margin of appreciation‹ (in other words discretion) in deciding their obligations under the Convention (Handyside v. UK, Series A, ECHR, No 24, Judgment of 7 December 1976); that ›even if one assumes that Article 2 protects the unborn life, the rights and interests involved have been weighed against each other in a reasonable way‹, (Open Door Counselling Ltd v. Ireland, ECHR, Series A, No 246, Judgment of 29 October 1992); that ›the value of life to be protected can and must be weighed against other rights of the person in question‹, (McCann and others v. UK, ECHR, Series A, No 324, Judgment of 27 September 1995).

we have transcended conflicts of interests and the clash of ideas? A cursory perusal of the daily news indicates not. Luhmann agrees; his diagnosis of the world order is even more accurate today than at the time of the writing. Economic development takes place through the exclusion of masses of people; democracy is imposed through despotism and invasion; rights are guaranteed through dissent and resistance (2008, 32). He is right to dismiss the cosmopolitan solutions of Kant (universal rights guaranteed by world federation) and Habermas (rights legislated through deliberative democratic procedures) for being naive and ignorant of the law (Douzinas 2007, ch. 7). Reason, uncoerced communication, basic values or fundamental rights cannot pacify conflict or remedy massive injustice. Legal technique cannot cure deep and widening domestic and international rifts. Freedom is far too general a concept with many antagonistic conceptions (consider the irreconcilable interpretations held by the American government and the insurgents in Iraq) and equality (before the law) far too formal to guarantee anything more than the most generic recognition of personhood. Luhmann is absolutely right in his critique of values although he should not expect much better from the jurisprudence of rights. As he emphasises, the right not to be tortured does not mean just that – people are tortured all the time. The boasting, rationalisation and bad conscience of the values enthusiasts have been often repeated by the human rights brigade.

3. Rights and systems theory

What is the import and function of rights according to systems theory? For Luhmann, rights offer a programme for the »unfolding of paradoxes«. In this they resemble values: the persistent contingency of what is presented as necessary ironically makes »the indispensability of norms – that is the autopoiesis of the system« (2008, 30). Rights give objective validity to subjective entitlements, they recognise individuality socially and make »the individual's unsociability the basis for regulating the legal system of society« (35). This is a rather modest account with one major advantage: it does not confuse what the Europeans call ›subjective rights‹ with ›fundamental‹ or human rights. Subjective rights were created by the early modern legal system. The rise of the legal form of rights is a clear indication of the emergence of capitalism and its close companion, individualism. Marx famously said that commodities cannot go to the market and sell themselves, the indispensable action of capitalism. They must be taken there by people (legal subjects) exercising rights. Rights and legal persons claiming them are the logical prerequisites and outcomes of a market economy and a positive legal system which, to meet capitalist needs, regulates social life by means of general precepts. Rights follow rules, but there is nothing glorious or exalted about them. They are the indispensable building blocks of a socioeconomic system based on the market and of a legal system that facilitates it.

In Luhmann's felicitous phrase, rights turn ›the individual's unsociability‹ into the basis of the social bond.

Human rights are different. As a positive legal institution, they are a sub-category of rights, protecting certain important claims, commonly against state powers. Luhmann emphasises the paradoxical nature of rights and distinguishes them from human rights (2008, 33f). His followers (Verschraegen 2006; Teubner n.d.) who have written more extensively about rights tend to be more lyrical (and less realistic. I am not qualified to judge whether they remain faithful to the canon). According to Gert Verschraegen (2006, 105, 106, 110, 113-5), human rights enable and legitimise free choice, strengthen the dominant characteristics of free inclusion and social mobility and constitute the unnoticed and elementary condition for participation in modern society. While the pre-modern individual was subjected to total social inclusion, the functionally differentiated modernity makes social inclusion heterogeneous. Rights are a compensation for the loss of total inclusion and fixed social position. People have now access to various systems such as education, the economy, law, politics, etc. which allow them to follow their personal preferences and free them from moral precepts. In this sense, human rights protect both individual spheres of influence and the differentiation between different systems by imposing a self-limitation on the political system.

The slide from rights to human rights is evident. The theory of the disciples becomes an example of the ills the master identifies in the rhetoric of indispensable norms. How can we resist this over-inflation of rights discourse? If human rights are given to people on account of their humanity and not of membership in narrower groups such as citizenship, ethnicity or class, we may conclude that human rights do not exist: those who have only humanity to protect them, the ›unlawful combatants‹ of Guatanamo Bay, the migrants who drown in the Mediterranean or get blown up in the minefields of the Greco-Turkish border trying to get to the ›promised land‹ of Europe, the ›one use humans‹ of the refugee camps, all these *homines sacri* of the new world order have no ›human‹ rights and therefore no humanity. Or, it may make us realise that rights do not belong to humans or may not »protect the freedom and interest of individuals« as Verschraegen (2006, 207) claims; rather rights construct our ›humanity‹ as a receding horizon, as a humanity that is always still to come.

Either way, the claim that the purpose of rights is to protect the differentiation of functional systems is not convincing. Natural and human rights have been won through struggles and campaigns for their recognition or expansion. I have not come across yet any protest banners demanding that ›system differentiation‹ be protected. This is not a facetious point. The attempt to turn rights into institutions policing the borders of systems necessarily falls into the most ahistorical type of naturalism. »Constitutional and human rights are not a creation of the law« argues Verschraegen (2006, 103) »but are pre-legal as a social institution, as a self-protecting device of society«. This is 18th century naturalism of the most naïve kind craving for pre-legal and pre-social institutions but without the attendant social contracts. One should be reminded however that without the struggles of dissidents, rebels and revolutionaries, none of these institutions would have arisen.

Luhmann takes a different tack in this article. He believes that the use of human rights should be restricted to the worst cases of injury to dignity and atrocity and that the tendency to turn them into a rule-book for global social work should be resisted. The juxtaposition of human dignity with social work is troubling. It harks back to the old debate about negative and positive freedom and the Cold War argument that social and economic rights are not proper rights because, unlike civil and political rights, they are not justiciable (legally enforceable) and potentially violate individual freedom. Warming to this theme, Luhmann disparagingly and distastefully adds that human rights are the »foundation for poorer countries' demands on richer countries« (2008, 34). To avoid this expansionist use of human rights by the poor to seek redress for past injustices, Luhmann proposes that the language of rights should be replaced by that of human duties. This is clearly a Sisyphean task for a legal system based on the principle of the rights of the ›unsociable individual‹. Indeed a right-based legal system cannot support independent duties and responsibilities; the only duties it understands are those imposed on third parties as a result of the operation of rights. And this is why Luhmann bizarrely argues that the most important ›human‹ duty is that of states to provide order, if need be by torturing its enemies.

At this point, the critical legal position has to abandon the fellow-travelling with systems theory. We have covered quite a lot of common ground at the level of description or observation. But when Luhmann moves to the normative position (as all trained lawyers are likely to do even when they protest their prescriptive agnosticism), the conservative nature of systems theory emerges clearly.[7] If antagonistic values, conflicting norms and contradictory concepts clash and cannot be synthesised or made to cohere at the level of the individual decision, Luhmann's advice is to return to legal technique. This is because the law has historically exhibited the ability to co-opt and integrate counter-principles and antinomian practices and has promoted its autonomy and closure in this manner. The example offered is the recognition that, since Rome, the law can be violated for ›reasons of state‹, a state of exception or emergency can be declared and an ›eminent domain‹ created in order to serve supreme public ends (*salus populi*). Luhmann proposes the extensive adoption of this technique as an antidote to the exaggerated rhetoric of values and human rights. The unlawful can be legalised, the outside domesticated, if it is imported into

---

7 Chris Thornhill (2006, 99) after a careful reading of Luhmann's political theory finds its implications problematic. These include an »attachment to nineteenth century models of administrative positivism and limited state-legalism« and the »obvious appeal of some of his ideas to quite standard versions of reactionary theory (especially neo-liberalism)«.

the law and regulated. Torture, by definition illegal and abhorrent, can become lawful, if it is supervised or certain procedures are followed. This approach brings the exception or negation of law into the legal system and allows its bipolar coding of lawful/unlawful to reveal fully its paradoxical nature.

According to Giorgio Agamben and much contemporary critical theory, the legalisation of the unlawful and the wholesale normalisation of the exception have happened already (Agamben 1998; 2005; Hardt/Negri 2000). As Walter Benjamin (1999, 38) put it starkly, a propos of the Third Reich, the state of exception has become permanent. Luhmann does not refer to Carl Schmitt and his famous definition of the Sovereign as he who can suspend the law in order to save it (Schmitt 1985, 46).[8] Giorgio Agamben's extensive programme of research around the figure of the Sovereign and the state of exception has shown that this suspension of the law is a permanent characteristic of western polities: it grounds politics on the programmatic exclusion of certain people (the *homines sacri*) from the domain of legal protection. Order is based on exclusion; meaningful life on meaningless existence. It is not so much that the law adopts the exception in order to achieve functional differentiation; rather the law is based on this originary exception.

We can now understand the importance of the ›ticking bomb‹ scenario. Its narrative construction leads inexorably to the justification of torture. Its inevitable conclusion meets the realism of the observational technique and deconstructs the idealistic rhetoric of the ›indispensable norms‹ brigade. But it does much more. It introduces the paradoxical nature of decision-making (system theory's mainstay) and places the theoretical premium not on the bodily integrity of people (who, in systems theory, are the ›environment‹ of the functional systems) but on the integrity of the systems themselves for which the maintainance of order is supreme necessity (»the state organization ... first and foremost [is] ... the international address for questions about the provision of order« (Luhmann 2008, 35)). Human rights are turned into the state's duty to protect the *ordre publique* in a dance macabre of paradoxicality. But there is a different kind of paradox that permeates the operation of human rights to which we now turn.

4. The ›shell‹ of natural law

Luhmann's attack on the rhetoric of indispensable norms is important and timely. It is prefaced by a brief and rather clichéd review of the history of natural law from Plato to Nato. Natural law, in its various transfigurations, is presented as the main source of fundamental values. The brief history concludes with the ringing declaration that natural law is »an empty shell of a word, applicable in

---

8 For an excellent discussion of Schmitt's theory of sovereignty see Rasch 2005.

flowery phrases … nothing results from the historically deducible meaning of natural law that could answer our question as to the validity of indispensable norms« (2008, 24).

Indeed, natural law may be an empty shell or a ›floating signifier‹. It is true that the author of natural law and the content of its rules have changed considerably throughout history. Successive versions have been discredited, fallen into disrepute or disuse. Luhmann is right that none of the earlier versions could survive the change in social conditions which gave it substance and legitimacy. The purposeful cosmos of the Greeks, ordered by *dike* and implanted in the *physis* of all things animate and inanimate; the philosophical cosmopolitanism of the Cynics and the spiritual *logos spermatikos* of the Stoics could not survive the Roman positivisation of *dike* into *jus* and the turning of cosmopolitanism into imperialism. Christian natural law could not survive the disenchantment of the world and the cold critical eye which invented theodicy and completed God's trial with the ›death of God‹. Similarly, the ideal natural rights proclaimed in the great revolutions of the 18th century could not survive the final triumph of capitalism in the 19th and the rise of mass democracy in the 20th century. Natural rights mutated from grand statements of revolutionary fervour into the legal canons, protocols and procedures of human rights inscribed in laws, constitutions and international treaties. The positivisation of natural rights repeated earlier examples: the age of rapid industrialisation and colonial expansion which followed the revolutions needed strong governments, social engineered and productive populations, control and pliable bodies in the place of rebellious and romantic dissidents.

It is true that in all these mutations, established powers displayed a great ability to assimilate natural law to their cause. We no longer believe in a purposeful cosmos, an overarching reason, divine legislation, natural entitlements, or asocial needs and desires. It could not be otherwise. Most striking however is that despite the successive deaths of its authors, despite the repeated and inevitable rejections of every specific content, the ›empty shell‹ keeps coming back. The eternal return of natural law is more interesting than the passing away of every single one of its versions. In the latest mutation, international law has replaced God as the author of superior law (human rights); this source will also fade away in time. But the wide acceptance of human rights, the latest great bonanza of naturalism, tells a different story from Luhmann's dismissal of the tradition. What survives the various historical incarnations of natural law and their rejection or transcendence by later generations is precisely the ›shell‹ of natural law, a form, an attitude that unites its differing versions despite their widely differing content. To understand this we need to take a different approach to the history of the idea.

For Greek philosophy, nature (*physis*) and its law are born together in an act of resistance against traditional authority. In pre-classical Greece, law and convention, right and custom were identical; the root of all authority was the ancestral. The philosophical ›discovery‹ of the idea of nature brings this claim to an end. Nature is a critical concept; it must be discovered because it is occluded by a combination of convention, law and ancestral authority. By discovering nature, Plato and Aristotle departed radically from that tradition. For the classical philosophers, nature is not just the physical world, but a term of distinction, a norm or standard used to separate the work of philosophical and political thought from what obstructs or hides it, namely the combination of customary law and conventional opinion. Philosophy now appeals from the ancestral to the good, to that which is good intrinsically, to that which is good by nature (Bloch 1988, 91).

Nature is philosophy's tool, its ›discovery‹ and elevation into an evaluative standard and weapon against convention emancipates reason from the tutelage of power and gives rise to natural right. Nature presents itself as what was hidden by culture because philosophy cannot come into existence or survive, if it submits to ancestral or conventional authority. Philosophy and nature are born against the law. To this day when knowledge and reason are subjected to authority they are called ›theology‹ or ›legal learning‹ but they cannot be the philosophy practised by the Greeks (Bloch 1988, 92). In this sense, turning nature into norm, into the standard of right was the greatest early step of rational civilisation but also a cunning trick against priests and rulers. The Sophists used nature against custom and law. In setting *physis* against *nomos* and individual opinion against tradition, they gave *physis* a normative meaning, in which ›to reason‹ meant to ›criticise‹ (1988, 7-9). Socrates and Plato, in turn, deployed nature to combat the moral relativism of the Sophists and to restore the authority of reason. Their response to the Sophist challenge was to re-establish the normative character of nature by showing that, far from contradicting law, it sets the fundamental norm of each being. This is how nature, this most cultured of concepts entered the world: as a critical idea that expresses resistance to the sclerosis of established powers and the intolerance of received opinion.

We can observe a similar process in modernity. Natural rights in the 18th century and human rights after Word War II were invented to protect people and arm them in their struggle against unjust power. They may have been co-opted by imperial and disciplinary projects; their positivisation may have turned them into legitimation tools for socio-political‹ arrangements and ideological weapons against those who disagree with the West. It is true, as Luhmann insists, that natural rights have been repeatedly ›politically assimilated‹. They began as a means of expressing moral and political dissent and rebellion against existing authorities only to be appropriated by these very authorities as instruments for consolidating and justifying their power to promote their own partial interests. But as the current expressions of the naturalist legacy they retain a distance – even if minimal – from the reality of social relations, legal rights and imperial aspirations. Natural right and its descendents enters the historical agenda directly and indirectly, disguised as religious duty, legal right or political ideology, every time people struggle »to overthrow all relations in which man is a degraded, enslaved, abandoned or despised being.« (Bloch 1988, xxvii-xxix) This was the case in the great revolutions of the 18th century, in the post-WWII ›never again‹ declarations, in popular uprisings against fascist and communist rule in the late 20th century, and every time the oppressed, exploited and dispossessed invoke them in their struggles. Human rights, whether positivised or not, belong to a long and honourable tradition of dissent, resistance and rebellion against the domination of power, the oppression of wealth, and the injustice of law. They are parts of the legacy of the left.

This is what I mean by the ›shell‹ of natural law. In its various permutations, it has marked a distance between the naturally and socially given and the eternal aspiration for its transcendence. Natural law is one main expression of the often reasoned and always felt ›sense of injustice‹. What is important about natural law is not so much its changing authors or content (today the different types of human rights) but its persisting form: the desire to resist, criticise and change the existing world for a better place. This is what Luhmann rejects by turning natural law not into a ›shell‹ but into a meaningless, amorphous skin.

5.   Justice and law between systems and deconstruction

Human rights are full of paradoxes. Rights give objective existence to subjective entitlements. The duty-bearer who must deliver individual entitlements is the state; but it is law, the language of the state, that enforces these rights. The greatest paradox is that after their positivisation, a statement of right refers both to a legal entitlement and to what a higher source (nature, morality, international law etc) demands. When a Chinese political dissident claims that he has the right to free speech, he is both wrong (he evidently does not under extant law) and right. His assertion is against the current state of law but this is not just a moral claim; it is a call to arms for the reform or transformation of the political and legal system. In this usage, the naturalist or moral element of human rights is an integral part of the whole and is in permanent tension and occasional conflict with their putative legal status.

This confounding of the real and the ideal is characteristic of human rights discourse. The very nature of rights is paradoxically both of the law and of something beyond it, call it justice if you will. Against the moral poverty of legal positivism (law and morality are totally separate) and the moral imperialism of rights fanatics (all law is moral and rational), the critical legal position makes the relationship between law, justice, and force, the key of political philosophy and jurisprudence (Douzinas/Gearey 2005, ch. 1 & 4). For the positivists, justice is identified fully with the law. Legality, the rule of law, the impartiality of the judiciary, the following of formal procedures, this is the essence of justice. Any contamination of law by value will compromise its ability to turn

social and political conflict into manageable technical disputes about the meaning and applicability of pre-existing public rules. Morality as much as politics
must be kept at a distance; indeed the main requirement of the rule of law is
that all ›subjective‹ and relative value should be excluded from the operation
of the legal system. This insulation of law from ethico-political considerations
allegedly makes the exercise of power impersonal and guarantees the equal
subjection of citizens and state officials to the dispassionate requirements of
the rule of rules as opposed to the rule of men.

In the positivist worldview, law is technical reason, a poor remnant of the *orthos
logos* and *recta ratio* of the classics. Justice on the other hand is associated with
emotions and passions. To assert that a legal system is unjust, says Alf Ross
(1958, 274), is an »emotional expression ... To invoke justice is the same thing
as banging on the table: an emotional expression that turns one's demand into
an absolute postulate.« Non-formal conceptions of justice are »illusions which
excite the emotions by stimulating the suprarenal glands.« (275) When »someone says ›that thing is unjust‹ what he means is that the thing is offensive to
his sentiments.« (Hayek 1972, 168 fn 30)

The similarities between this crude positivism and systems theory are remarkable. The bipolar code guaranteeing the closure of the legal system is that
of lawful/unlawful. Justice, on the other hand, is one of the values Luhmann
strongly dislikes and suspects. The emphasis on legal technique, judicial competence, rules of interpretation and legal procedures repeats the main preoc-
cupations of positivist jurisprudence. The function of rights as promoters of the
differentiation and closure of functional systems moves in the same direction.
For Luhmann, the just/unjust bipolarity was highly problematic (2008, 2) and
has been abandoned in favour of the legal (lawful/unlawful) coding. While
systems theory attacks the excesses of the neo-Kantians, it fully adopts a strict
and simplistic law/morality divide evident in early legal positivism.

This approach to law is both cognitively wrong (deciding what is lawful is
impossible without an evaluation about the moral, just or desirable outcome)
and morally impoverished (it reduces morality either to private ›subjective‹
choices and/or to a predication of legality). It became the legitimation and rationalization of the great atrocities of the 20th century. The eternal return of (new
versions of) naturalism despite its repeatedly proclaimed ›fallacy‹ indicates that
law and morality are not opposed. They are linked in inner paradoxical ways.
For the Greeks and Romans, justice was the prime, albeit missing, virtue of
the polity and the spirit and reason of law. A just constitution was a legitimate
constitution and a just legal system has a valid claim to the obedience of its
citizens. We find similar ideas in the writings of the common lawyers. Justice is
cumulatively the foundation, the spirit and the end of the law. As law's imme-
morial and unwritten foundation, justice links the common law with divine
will and its expressions in nature and reason. After the Reformation, justice as
equity is explicitly associated with the divine order and becomes law's spirit.

When law and justice, in the form of equity, are in conflict, the law must give way to higher reason. In all these formulations, justice is seen as the »primitive reason« (Finch 1627, 57) of law, its virtue and ethical substance, an ideal or principle that gives rules their aim and limit and remedies their defects. But justice is also something outside or before the law, a transcendent principle that gives it overall direction, a higher tribunal or reason to which the law and its judgments are called to account. In this sense, a law without justice is a law without spirit, a dead letter, it can neither rule nor inspire.

Modernity repressed the inner link between law and justice to its detriment. We could describe postmodern jurisprudence as the latest return of the repressed. In our disenchanted world, the transcendent must be found in the immanent, the principle of justice in history. When law violates its established procedures and harms someone; when it does not recognize or uphold rights which have been given already or are reasonably expected; when it breaches basic principles of equality and dignity – in all these cases the law acts unjustly according to its own internal criteria of justice. We can call this first type of justice, legal justice, because it is internal to the law and operates when the law matches its own standards and principles.

But legal justice is only one facet of justice. A different conception has inspired the jurisprudence of deconstruction from Jacques Derrida to Jean-Luc Nancy and critical legal theory. It starts from the statement of Emmanuel Levinas that justice operates in the relationship to the other person. The other is a singular, unique finite being with certain personality traits, character attributes and physical characteristics. But to me, this finite person puts me in touch with infinite otherness. According to phenomenology, I cannot know the other as other, I can never comprehend fully her intentions or actions, I can never have an appropriate adequation or presentation, because no immediate access or perception of otherness exists. We need criteria in order to be just to the other but they are not readily available. Indeed any attempt to turn justice into a theory (as some Marxists did) or a series of normative statement and commands (as Kantians do) is necessarily a violation of justice. Theories and laws need to be applied; but every application would turn the uniqueness of the other into an instance of the concept or a case of the norm and would immediately violate their singularity. The principle of justice is respect the singularity of the other – a very different axiom from Luhmann's access to many functional systems.

The infinite dwells in the finite, justice dwells in the law but also challenges the law since the law forgets the infinity of the other. The law has to deal with many others and it must compare and contrast them. To do that it puts them on the same scale and compares them by using rights, duties and other common denominators that allow the different to become similar and the other same. Justice is immanent to the law, but this immanence means that law is unequal to itself; it contains within itself what opens to a new law, a new politics, a new place or non-place (utopia). Justice lies within the law as a gap, a chasm that judges both specific instances of injustice and violence but also the overall direction of the law. Both inside and outside, justice is the horizon against which the law is judged both for its daily routine failings and for its forgetting of justice. Whether we see the law as a historical institution or as a system of rules and decisions, the deconstruction of its operations discovers either the violence of origins in its daily operations or unravels the ordered bi-polarities (fact-value, public-private, objective-subjective, lawful-unlawful) and shows that they cannot stabilize the legal system.

According to Michael King (2006, 47), law has »only two ways of responding to perturbations from its environment – one is not to recognise the issue as relevant to law; the other is transform it into an issue which can ultimately be resolved through law's coding of lawful/unlawful.« If this is the case, systems theory is unable to ›observe‹ the internal split of human rights, their double reality partly positive law and partly a distancing from and judging of positivity as part of its nature. No bipolar code can account for their integral ›moral‹ component which doubles the legal condition: it can neither be accepted as relevant to law nor can it be resolved through the lawful/unlawful coding the very operation of which it is meant to challenge perpetually.

The ›ticking bomb‹ hypothetical and the domestication of torture indicate the limits of liberal theory. The value/rights idealists (the neo-Kantians Habermas, Dworkin etc) identify rights with right and improbably believe that reason and principle have all the answers. They are proven daily wrong but this only makes their claims louder and shriller. The systems realist, on the other hand, anxious to prove the probity of his theory, leaves us cynically exposed to the dictats of power, if its exercise seems to confirm the autopoietic prescriptions. As Luhmann keeps insisting, the question »[w]hat can we do?« must be preceded by »how can one observe and describe adequately« (2008, 35) as if, at the beginning of the 21st century our lack of knowledge is the main impediment to action. As King (2006, 52) honestly admits, »Luhmann's *usefulness* might well lie in the *uselessness* of his theory as a blueprint for improvement of social systems.«

For the neo-Kantians, norms and rights have all the answers. For the systemics, reason is no panacea for our ills and every line of resistance becomes a further twist in the paradoxical operation of systems. In both cases, we are left with not much hope; Luhmann is at least honest about it. We need more, however, if we are to resist the brutality of our times. Hegel famously said that the owl of Minerva flies at dusk. It may be that at this late stage the modernist priority of knowledge over action or of *techné* over praxis is in the process of being reversed against the advice of systems theory – and this is the unacknowledged wisdom of our age.

References

Ackerman, Bruce (2006): Before the Next Attack. New Haven: Yale University Press.

Agamben, Giorgio (1998): Homo Sacer. Sovereing Power and Bare Life. Stanford: Stanford University Press.

Agamben, Giorgio (2005): State of Exception. Chicago: Chicago University Press.

Benjamin, Walter (1999): Theses on the Philosophy of History. Pp. 253-264 in: W. Benjamin, Illuminations (Harry Zohn, trans). London: Pimlico.

Bloch, Ernst (1988): Natural Law and Human Dignity (D.J. Schmidt, trans.). Cambridge, MA.: MIT Press, 1988

Dershowitz, Alan (2002): Why Terrorism Works. New Haven: Yale University Press.

Douzinas, Costas (2007): Human Rights and Empire: The Political Philosophy of Cosmopolitanism. London: Routledge-Cavendish.

Douzinas, Costas / Gearey, Adam (2005): Critical Jurisprudence. Oxford: Hart.

Finch, Sir H. (1627): Law, or, A Discourse Thereof in Four Books. London: Society of Stationers.

Hardt, Michael / Negri, Antonio (2000): Empire. Cambridge, MA.: Harvard University Press.

Hayek, Friedrich von (1972): Law, Legislation and Liberty. London: Routledge & Kegan Paul.

Ignatieff, Michael (2004): The Lesser Evil. Edinburgh: Edinburgh University Press.

Kennedy, David (2001): The International Human Rights Movement. Part of the Problem? European Human Rights Law Review 3, 245-267.

Kennedy, Duncan (1977): A Critique of Adjudication. Cambridge, MA: Harvard University Press.

King, Michael (2006): What's the Use of Luhmann's Theory? Pp. 37-52 in: Michael King / Chris Thornhill (eds.) Luhmann on Law and Politics. Oxford: Hart.

Koskenniemi, Martti (1999): The Effects of Rights on Political Culture. Pp. 99-116 in: Philip Alston et al (eds.), The European Union and Human Rights. Oxford: Oxford University Press.

Koskenniemi,, Martti (1999a): Letter to the Editors of the Symposium. American Journal of International Law 93 / 2, 351-361.

Luhmann, Niklas (2008): Are There Still Indispensable Norms in Our Society? Soziale Systeme 14, 18-37 (in this volume).

Luhmann, Niklas (2008a): Beyond Barbarism. Soziale Systeme 14, 38-46 (in this volume).

Rasch, William (2005): Sovereignty and its Discontents. London: Birkbeck Law Press.

Ross, Alf (1958): On Law and Justice. London: Stevens & Sons.

Schmitt, Carl (1985): Political Theology: Four Chapters on the Concept of Sovereignty. Cambridge, MA.: MIT Press.

Thornhill, Chris (2006): Luhmann's Political Theory: Politics after Metaphysics? Pp. 75-99 in: Michael King / Chris Thornhill (eds.), Luhmann on Law and Politics. Oxford: Hart.

Tomasevski, Katarina (2000): Responding to Human Rights Violations: 1946-1999. The Hague: Martinus Nijhoff.

Verschraegen, Gert (2006): Systems Theory and the Paradox of Human Rights. Pp. 101-127 in: Michael King / Chris Thornhill (eds.), Luhmann on Law and Politics. Oxford: Hart.

Teubner, Gunther (n.d.): Human Rights Violations and Private Actors. Frankfurt a.M.: Ms.

Prof. Costas Douzinas
Professor of Law and Director Birkbeck Institute for the Humanities
Birkbeck College, University of London
Malet Street, London WC1E 7HX
c.douzinas@bbk.ac.uk

Soziale Systeme 14 (2008), Heft 1, S. 126-141

Hans-Georg Moeller

»Human Rights Fundamentalism«
The Late Luhmann on Human Rights

Abstracts: The essay starts by discussing the question if the debate between Luhmann and leftist social theory was primarily ideological in nature or not. It is stated that Luhmann's own interest in the debate was not so much to pursue a political dialogue, but rather to expose the theoretical flaws of his opponents in order to provoke a paradigm shift in social theory. By referring to Luhmann's treatment of the issue of human rights in his later works, I try to illustrate how he attempted to »deconstruct« the arguments of his intellectual adversaries. Luhmann makes use of semantic-historical and functional analyses of this politically successful concept so that its paradoxical aspects become obvious. This, in turn, »desubstantializes« the concept and shows how it is used as a rhetorical device that expresses a certain value-fundamentalism and is supposed to support the utopia of all-inclusion.

I.

Niklas Luhmann became famous as a theorist through his debates with the political left, personified by Jürgen Habermas, in the early 1970ies. I think it is quite important to be aware of this historical background when analyzing Luhmann's writings not only of this period but also later, up to his death close to the end of the millennium. This background explains, firstly, the extremely technical and conceptual nature of his texts. The leftist movement of the sixties and seventies (in Germany and France) was primarily an intellectual affair, lead and fuelled by academics. These academics continued the tradition of European Marxism that had largely been a highly »scientific« enterprise – or at least largely conceived of itself as such. I remember the huge posters displayed on the *Autobahn* in Eastern Germany at that time which said: »The teachings of Karl Marx are omnipotent because they are true.« Despite the perhaps unintended religious undertones of this slogan, it was meant in a scientific way, for Marxism was supposed to be strictly based on social science. Its truth was, exactly in the Luhmannian sense, a scientific truth, not one of revelation. Luhmann always understood himself as a social scientist too, and he was competing with the social scientists of the left. In joining the debate – and in trying to win it – he had to adopt its scientific codes and manners of communication, he had to work from within the already established system and, so to speak, infiltrate it by »marching through the institutions.« The largely unappealing style of his early writings, which he never fully managed to abandon, was affected by the system of communication within which these texts were produced. Luhmann was expressing a different theory of society, of course, but he did so within the already established scientific structures.

Seen from this perspective it is evident why he was labeled »conservative«. He was, obviously, not on the left and did not share most of the Marxist premises. According to the codes of the time, if one was not »progressive« in the Marxist sense, one had to be »conservative«. There was no other category available. One could therefore leave it at this and simply stick to a general categorization of Luhmann's project as a rightist alternative to leftist models. I think, however, that this is by no means the whole story and that it misses the radicalism of Luhmann's project. Luhmann was not simply trying to offer a counterpart to the dominant leftist social theories of his time; rather, he was trying to subvert the whole discourse and effect a »paradigm change« in the Kuhnian sense. He wanted to establish a social theory that would make the previous theoretical frameworks obsolete and a phenomenon of the past that could no longer be taken seriously. Or, as he put it in the first chapter of *Die Gesellschaft der Gesellschaft* (»The society of society«). He wanted to make it obvious that the hitherto generally accepted social categories were no longer »*theoretisch satisfaktionsfähig*«, which literally means that they lacked the dignity necessary to be accepted as an opponent in a duel (1997, 31). Luhmann wanted to demolish fundamentally the respect for the dominant social theories of his era and demonstrate that they were neither in accord with the times nor at Luhmann's own level of theoretical sophistication. As he stated frankly in a late interview (1996, 71): »I do not, as one should in a good controversy, profit much from reading Habermas.«

I think that this »revolutionary« intention, historically grounded in his debates with the left in the seventies, is an important key for understanding the writings of the late Luhmann, i.e. everything after *Social Systems* (first published in 1984).[1] In these later works he focuses more and more on the inadequacy of the dominant sociological theories and concepts and their inability to conceive of current social problems in an intelligent way. Monographs on topics that were at that time fashionable – namely »risk society« (1993) and the environment (1989) – serve the function of exposing the theoretical weakness and backwardness of the left. Luhmann obviously does not intend to offer merely a competing »rightist« view, but to go beyond the left-right framework altogether. In his later writings he explicitly and implicitly focuses on the theoretical poverty, the pompous moralizing, the utopian character, and, above all, the outdated humanism of the prevalent leftist and liberal discourse.

---

1 Interestingly enough, the introductory chapter of this book (1984, 15-29) is entitled: »Paradigm Change in Systems Theory.«

An issue that deserves special attention in this context is the notion of »human rights«. It is certainly one of the most successful »progressive« political concepts. Human rights are all the craze. Demanded by all sorts of activisms, protests, and revolutions they became one of the most precious and undisputed political values of our times, enshrined in constitutions, embraced by the United Nations, frequently in the headlines of the mass media, and deeply settled in the hearts of many. Luhmann sets out to »deconstruct« this prominent notion, and this deconstruction has to be understood, I believe, in connection with the just mentioned fourfold displeasure with mainstream leftist-liberal thought.[2] I will briefly outline this fourfold displeasure with respect to the issue of human rights here before discussing Luhmann's general analysis of the history and function of the concept of human rights in more detail in the main body of this paper.[3]

In a short remark, made in passing on the final pages of *Die Gesellschaft der Gesellschaft*, Luhmann lumps together three of the most basic intellectual cornerstones of modern Western social thought. He states that the Cartesian subject, the idea of human rights, and the Habermasian declaration that modernity is a project that still awaits completion are all representative of a much too static understanding of society (1997, 1143-1144). These commonly accepted claims, namely that the human subject is of core importance in society, that there is some ultimate dignity or value attached to it, and that human subjects can establish a rational and intersubjective discourse that will lead to a more liberated society are, in Luhmann's view unable to do justice to the dynamics and complexity of our social world. He therefore sides with the postmodernists' attempts to overcome traditional »modernist« social theory, even though he disagrees with their implicit assertion that the modern age has come to an end. Luhmann believes that we still live in modernity, but that modern theorists have not yet adequately understood the reality of our modernity. We therefore need a theory that, paradoxically, parts with its modern predecessors in order to come to a better grasp of the functioning of modern communication sys-

---

2 Luhmann explicitly relates to Derrida's program of deconstruction with respect to his own analysis of human rights. While Luhmann approves of the method of deconstruction, he does not approve of the term. (Perhaps because he did not invent it himself, see Luhmann 1995, 235). In any case, I will use the term here, but in inverted commas.

3 I would like to note that my understanding of Luhmann's views on human rights is quite different from that of Gert Verschraegen (2002; 2006). Verschraegen argues in favor of human rights as a useful legal tool to preserve and enhance functional differentiation and seems to imply that his views are in line with Luhmann's. In my view Luhmann has a much more critical and ambiguous position on human rights and, in particular, is unable to appreciate their humanist undertones. The difference between Verschraegen's and my view might, however, not only be related to different preferences with respect to humanism, but also to the different textual material we work with. Verschraegen relies mostly on the early Luhmann, namely the book *Grundrechte als Institution. Ein Beitrag zur politischen Soziologie* (1965) whereas I concentrate on the late Luhmann and texts published in the 1990ies. So there are about three decades between the materials we focus on. Perhaps Luhmann has developed his »radical« stance on humanism and related subjects only in his later years.

tems such as the economy, the mass media, and the legal system. The internal dynamics and evolution of these systems as well as their mutual relations are too intricate to be questioned with such »simplistic« concepts as that of human rights.

In a passage in *Law as a Social System* (2004), Luhmann speaks quite sarcastically about the moralizing attitude that is often attached to the communication about human rights – and which therefore goes beyond the domain of law and becomes more of a rhetorical gesture than an actually functional contribution within the legal system. When Luhmann (2004, 468) states that »human rights have … a market as never before« he seems to have the often grandiloquent and appealing – but not necessary very precise – speeches and communiqués of politicians and activists in mind, and he characterizes this discourse as such:

> It is not merely that one has values; rather, that one must have them and impress them on others. The normative institutionalization of value committees extends to morally motivated programmes of demand. Hence one not only has to extend one's own values to include the values of others (in the interests of the poor, the disadvantaged, the hungry, the >third world‹), but one must also join in these demands in order that others commit themselves to these values as well. However, this form of normative expectation of normative expectation lies largely beyond the established juridical world of forms and is also directed against the law. Legal or illegal – what counts is humanity. (Luhmann 2004, 468)

Another problem of human rights that Luhmann observes is their counterfactual or utopian character. Human rights, although typically claimed in a present tense format (»all men are created equal«), tend to be quite apart from the actual social (and legal) realities. They seem not to define a present state of affairs but a goal for the future. They are, therefore, utopian in nature. Luhmann states in *Die Gesellschaft der Gesellschaft* (writing about the 19th century):

> To the same degree as the theory of natural, innate, and inalienable human rights becomes a success it becomes evident that it is useless for interpreting actual law (that, for instance, in the USA still acknowledges slavery). Instead it only allows for outlooks towards a future that is constitutionally and politically projected. *Therefore* human rights can be proclaimed as being *unlimited*. (1997, 992-993; emphasis in the original; my translation)

Human rights can be declared to be unlimited since they are actually not meant as a formulation of the state of affairs, but as »work in progress«. In actual law, there are always restrictions and modifications of human rights – in the present-day United States as well as in the times after the revolution. Human rights can be labeled »unlimited« not because they are, but because they ideally will be.

The main problem Luhmann has with human rights, resulting from the foregoing analysis, is that they are conceived of as *human* rights. It is the implicit humanism in human rights that the self-proclaimed »radical anti-humanist« (1997, 35) Luhmann cannot accept. Human rights conceive of our social reality in human terms. They necessarily imply that our society is constituted by human subjects with their »natural« characteristics and they propose to be immediately derived from these supposed natural characteristics. Luhmann does not share a humanist concept of society and suggests that society does not consist of human beings, but in communication. This fundamental disagreement with respect to what society is makes it practically impossible for Luhmann to accept the doctrine or »philosophy« of human rights. Luhmann, as I will argue, does not disagree with the contents of human rights – and who would do that – but with their principles. Since human rights are so much intertwined with humanism, it is no surprise that they are often used in moral contexts and not necessarily in »purely« legal ones (even though they are labeled »rights«). They are probably less a legal matter than a semantic device of appealing to humanist values. Their semantic or rhetorical aspects make them ill suited, from Luhmann's perspective, for a theory of law. While humanists might claim that human rights are the foundation of »liberal« legal systems, Luhmann seems to be saying that while they serve as an utopian project within the legal system they do not reflect the functioning and the reality of this system. As Luhmann stated in the passage quoted above, when it comes to human rights it does not matter so much what is »legal or illegal – what counts is humanity.«

II.

Luhmann's »deconstruction« of human rights consists of two steps, as is often the case with his deconstructions of other still widely popular Enlightenment concepts. He firstly traces the historical semantics of the concept back to early modernity and dissects its usage and development so that its contingencies, ambiguities, and correspondences with social structures become visible. Secondly, he describes how the concept actually functions in contemporary society. This is to say that after tracing its historical evolution, he shows that the concept has no universal or fundamental essence whatsoever, but is entirely contingent upon social circumstances that are subject to change. In this section I will outline Luhmann's version of the history of the semantics of human rights and in the following one I will examine Luhmann's view on the function of human rights in our times.

Luhmann understands the historical semantics of human rights in the context of the semantics of values and »indispensable norms«. Evidently, human rights have been conceived of as »indispensable norms« and inferred from fundamental values. If proclaimed as »indispensable«, however, a norm or a right becomes non-contingent or necessary. If it is indispensable, it has an absolute and principal foundation. Luhmann, the theoretician of contingency, is obviously skeptical with respect to claims of necessity and he is interested in finding out how such claims were justified. His interest in human rights therefore focuses on the problem »whether and with which semantic means the legal system can establish the *indispensability* of norms« (Luhmann 2008, 22), or, in other words, on the »problem of the justification of human rights« (1995, 229; my translation). It is no surprise how Luhmann will answer this self-imposed question: The legal system can do so only by way of the »unfolding of a paradox« (*Paradoxieentfaltung*). Accordingly, Luhmann depicts the semantic history of human rights as a history of paradoxes. The seemingly fundamental and non-contingent nature of human rights is thereby thoroughly »deconstructed«.

»Justification« in the above quotation translates the German word *Begründung*. Luhmann explicitly stresses that he uses this word in a twofold sense, both meaning the establishment of *validity* and the provision of *reasons* (German: *Gründe*) for this validity. According to Luhmann this semantic process of »justification« involves what he calls *Paradoxiemanagment*, i. e. the managing of paradoxes. Human rights are, according to Luhmann, based on a paradox (which, for Luhmann, is *not* scandalous, but rather the rule for social constructions). The semantic history of this concept is, accordingly, a history of various and changing forms in which the paradox occurs and different strategies of dealing with it. In times of a semantic crisis the paradox becomes obvious and new ways of coping with it are developed so that it no longer appears paradoxical. In this manner the semantic history of human rights is a history of several appearances and disappearances of paradoxes. The various paradoxes of human rights are, according to Luhmann, based on the following problem: subjective rights become valid only as objective rights: »When the individual claims *his* right as his *own* right, it will fail just as Michael Kohlhaas did.« (Luhmann 1995, 231; my translation) Human rights are explicitly individual rights – but they can only be claimed non-individually. One is doomed to fail, as Michael Kohlhaas did in Kleist's famous story, if one idiosyncratically demands and actually fights for what one – however »justly« – believes to be one's individual right. Human rights are always generalized; I cannot claim them simply »as myself,« but only, for instance, as a woman, as a worker, or as a member of a racial minority. In that way, one has actually to disavow one's unique individuality in order to be able to rely on human rights. A subject can only claim them »objectively« in the form »as X«.

Luhmann identifies exactly three concrete historical situations of the appearance / disappearance of the paradox of human rights.[4] I will briefly summarize these three forms of the »unfolding of the paradox« identified by Luhmann.

---

4 There are two texts by Luhmann tracing this three-step process: *Das Paradox der Menschenrechte und drei Formen seiner Entfaltung* (1995) and section 5 in chapter 12 of *Law as a Social System* (2004).

The first crisis that made the paradox of human rights appear was the break-down of concepts of »natural law« in 16th century Europe and the simultaneous emergence of theories of a »social contract«. Normally it is assumed that the modern focus on the individual led to the concept of the social contract. The social contract was conceived of as a contract between individuals to secure their common well-being. Luhmann, however, likes to see it the other way around. He believes that the theory of the social contract led to a concern for the individual. For him the main question arising from theories of social con-tract is: What about the individuals once they have made the social contract? Luhmann states:

> This before/after problem is answered by the doctrine of human rights through a distinction between human rights and rights that are contractually constituted. And this happens not according to the pattern natural state/civilized state, but with the paradoxical form of the unity of this difference. Human rights are rights that can be salvaged from the natural state into the civilized state ... (1995, 232; my translation).

Luhmann seems to be pointing out that the social contract theory radically departs from earlier theories of natural law. The social contract is, obviously, a product of civilization. Social contract rights are *not* natural rights, but rights that cancel out natural rights. Paradoxically the social contract seeks to pre-serve what it nullifies, namely the natural interests of humans that supposedly precede and lead to the social contract in the first place. In this way the social contract establishes natural rights by abolishing natural rights.

The second semantic crisis occurred, according to Luhmann, in the second half of the 18th century. Luhmann refers to such groundbreaking documents as the American *Bill of Rights* and the French *Declaration of the Rights of Man*. The par-adox associated with these documents is that human rights are understood as »pre-positive« rights that, however, only become rights when they are trans-formed into positive rights. One can, once again, refer to such formulations as »all men are created equal« in the *Declaration of Independence*. The law refers to some supposedly universal and eternal truth that nevertheless can only be actualized if specified and applied in concrete and particular terms. Luhmann explains the problems involved in this paradoxical situation as such:

> This solution is no longer a convincing one. Its problem is that it enacts supposed meta-positive law as positive law, which cannot be adequately explained by the advantages it offers of having texts available for interpretation. Its great disadvantage is that the whole apparatus of text-based validity can be translated onto the level of a global system only with great difficulty and with many inadequacies. (2004, 483)

Luhmann again stresses the fact that the declared »meta-positive« validity of human rights has to be »positivized«. This leads to great problems on a global scale. Today there is, to a certain degree, a global consensus on »meta-positive« human rights, but different nations and different states have very different opinions on exactly which positive rights should be inferred from that »meta-positive« right.

This situation leads to the present state of affairs in which human rights tend to be brought to attention only when they are violated. Through the mass media there is a widespread awareness of human rights, but only in a negative form, an awareness of a lack. No one really knows exactly what human rights are, but everyone can see the violations: genocide, torture, imprisonment without trial, extralegal killings, etc. These violations are obvious and we are confronted with them every time we watch the news. They are even labeled as such, but which exact law is violated often remains in the dark. Luhmann states:

> In this situation, human rights law hardly appears to benefit from the clarity of its basic principles and the precision of the relevant texts, but from the evidence of human rights violations. In view of all sorts of horrific scenes, no further discussion is necessary. (2004, 484)

And he summarizes: »of course, it is also a paradox to say that rights are implemented only by their violation and the corresponding outrage« (2004, 487).

The »unfolding of the paradox« of human rights has to be, as mentioned above, understood in the context of the problem of »values« and »indispensable norms.« The search for human rights and the paradoxes arising from this search mirror, according to Luhmann, a general quest for guiding principles, for universal values, or for »categorical imperatives.« This quest, Luhmann suggests, was misguided from the beginning:

> For it could well be that a long tradition burdens us with an error in controlling the way problems are posed. Perhaps we are still expecting, but probably without much hope for success, a correspondence between decision and principle, a redemptive, conclusive formula, a system in the sense of *Kant's* or a general law, valid a priori. However, the final ground of all deciding lies not in a principle but in a paradox. (2008, 20)

The paradoxes that occurred in the semantic history of human rights are rooted in a pseudo- or post-religious – or perhaps better: secularized – search for redemption. They are rooted in the hope of finding and defining some sort of ultimate (moral) ground from which all legal matters can be derived. This ultimate ground appears nowadays in the form of supposed »foundational values« (*Grundwerte*). The problem with these values, as with human rights, is that there is a consensus on their validity (everybody wants peace, not war; democracy, not dictatorship; freedom, not restriction; life, not death, etc.), but no actual justification of their validity. They are so obvious that no one dares to question them, and if one would do so, one would probably appear immoral

and a heretic. Indeed, questioning the justification of these secular values may
be as dangerous today as the earlier questioning of the existence of God. Luhmann states:

> Values ... are valid without justification – as the observation of commu-
> nication, as it actually occurs, shows. But then it is not possible to request
> justification for values. In practice, values serve to halt reflection. (2008, 28)

The problem with values, however, is that there are as many of them as »stars
in the heavens« (2008, 28). Quite regularly we are confronted with »collisions of
values« (Wertekollisionen) and in the absence of any identifiable »super-value«
it is, in case of such a collision, always impossible to make a decision based on
ultimate values. Ultimately, there is no foundational value that could possibly,
like Plato's idea of the Good, provide the source for a definite answer for us.
How to choose between life and liberty or between democracy and peace? Of
course, such choices are always made and have to be made, but they are not
made according to a universal standard that would guide the decision. Luhmann states:

> Value collisions can only be decided ad hoc, because one requires evidence
> derived from the situation in order to justify the consideration of values,
> which applies a fortiori if more than two values are in play (2008, 29).

This is the same paradoxical state of affairs that we face with respect to human
rights:

> Values are *necessary* in order to give decisions recourse to indisputability.
> Decisions however bring this *necessity* into the form of *contingency*. The
> necessity of adhering to values becomes for its part a contingent evaluation
> – when it comes to deciding – which can turn out differently depending on
> value constellations, the site of decision, and influences on the course of
> decision (2008, 29).

»Foundational values«, »indispensable norms«, and human rights face the
same dilemma, namely the transformation of necessity into contingency
whenever they are applied. This paradox is, for Luhmann, not tragic. We can
still make »informed« decisions just as we have always made them. We can live
quite comfortably with the paradox and its various »unfoldings«. Perhaps we
should simply call off the search for the most foundational value of all and for
the ultimate origin of human rights to save us some trouble.

> Realistically viewed, it is not a matter of conclusive formulas for an edifice
> of norms, nor of principles, nor of a basic norm, nor even of a highest
> value that encompasses and trumps all others. But it is also not a matter
> of postponing decision until uncoerced discourses have led to a reasonable
> result that will produce consensus among all sagacious individuals who
> only require certain procedural guarantees for this. Viewed cognitively, it

concerns paradoxes – the self-blockage of knowledge that is not resolvable logically, but only creatively. (2008, 35)

With this final jab at Jürgen Habermas, the neo-Kantian rationalist, universalist, and moralist, Luhmann encourages us to embrace and live with the paradoxes that society has created.

III.

After analyzing Luhmann's survey of the historical semantics of human rights I will now take a look at his understanding of their actual function. Why was it socially necessary to invent them? What were the structural conditions that made them possible? While the context of »values« provided the framework for Luhmann's approach to the semantics of human rights, the framework that one has to look at when it comes to their function is the issue of social inclusion (and exclusion).

Once more, Luhmann takes on a historical perspective, and, once more, he focuses on the period between the 16th and 18th century in Europe that, for him, is the period in which stratified differentiation was replaced by functional differentiation. Stratified differentiation is identified as the structure underlying the feudal and aristocratic society of medieval and early modern Europe. Social inclusion under conditions of stratified differentiation is, as the term says, achieved by positioning a person at a specific place within a specific stratum. This happens normally simply by birth. By being born, one is born into a specific family and this family occupies a specific position within a specific social stratum. One's social placement is more or less entirely dependent on the family one is born into and on what status one's birth supplies one with within that family (for instance it makes a big difference if one is born as the oldest son or as a daughter). This mechanism of social inclusion by birth was, obviously, rather rigid. Once included, it was quite difficult to change one's status and there were not many options available for exchanging one inclusion with another. One cannot change one's birth. The most practicable alternative was to wave one's inclusion completely and choose exclusion instead, for instance by becoming an outlaw.[5]

With the breakdown of stratified differentiation and the emergence of functional differentiation the conditions of inclusion change dramatically. Luhmann states:

---

5   Luhmann develops his theory of inclusion and exclusion in various texts, most importantly probably the section on *Inklusion und Exklusion* (section 3 in chapter 4) in *Die Gesellschaft der Gesellschaft* (1997) and the essay (1995a) with the same title in *Soziologische Aufklärung 6*. The article *Beyond Barbarism*, included in this volume (2008a), also discusses this subject. For a comparative study see Rasch 2000, 108-123.

> With the functional differentiation of the social system the regulation of the relation inclusion/exclusion has been transferred to the function systems and there is no longer any central agency (as much as politics like to see itself in this function) that supervises the partial systems in this respect. If and how much is available to anyone is decided within the system of economy; which legal claims one can make with which prospect of success is a matter of the legal system; what counts as a work of art is decided within the system of art; and the system of religion provides the conditions under which the individuals can conceive of themselves as religious. (...) Since participation is possible under all these conditions, one can submit to the illusion of a state of inclusion that had never been reached before. (1997, 630; my translation)

In contemporary society, inclusion is up to the function systems. One becomes a student by being admitted to school – and everyone can be admitted. One becomes a patient by being admitted to hospital, and again, everyone can be admitted. Similarly, everyone can file a lawsuit or run for office. The function systems shape one's social identity. They provide one with a job, with property, legal and political status, etc. Social inclusion is no longer regulated primarily by the family, but by the social systems. And what counts is no longer one's birth, but one's *career*, the path – or rather: the various paths – one takes within the function systems.

While the function systems, as Luhmann states, are, on principle, open to everyone (and therefore »Barbarians« no longer exist),[6] this is in fact by no means the case. Not everyone goes to school, can vote, owns property, etc. Therefore, paradoxically, even though the function systems are ready to include everyone, they in fact exclude many:

> Function systems, when operating rationally, exclude persons or marginalize them so drastically that this has consequences in regard to getting access to other function systems. No education, no work, no income, no regular marriages, children with no birth certificate, no passport, no participation in politics, no access to legal advice, to the police or to the courts – the list can be extended and it concerns, dependent on the circumstances, all marginalizations up to total exclusion. (1997, 630; my translation)

It is quite obvious that not only inclusion, but also exclusion currently takes place on a massive scale. And exclusion from one system (no education, for instance) can easily lead to exclusion from others (as Luhmann says: no work, no passport, etc.).

The revolution of social inclusion and exclusion that took part with the change from stratified to functional differentiation is, according to Luhmann, the background that explains the function of human rights. Human rights are the »ide-

---

6 See the text *Beyond Barbarism* (2008a) in this volume.

ology« that goes along with the new (counterfactual) openness for all-inclusion. Luhmann states:

> The function of a semantics of inclusion is taken on in the 18th century by the postulate of human rights. (1997, 628; my translation)

Or, a little more precisely:

> Human rights correspond exactly to the structurally induced open-ended character of modern society. If individuals are to attain access to all function systems in their respectively different ways, and if, at the same time, their inclusion is internally controlled in these functional systems by deciding what is seen as equal and what is not, with the help of function criteria – if all this is part and parcel of the structural imperatives of modern society, it is impossible to say in advance who has to say what or who has to contribute what. Under these circumstances, assumptions about what constitutes human ›nature,‹ and about which rights logically accrue according to that nature, are at best picturesque details in judicial reasoning. Functionally, human rights are designed to keep the future open for the diverse autopoietic reproductions of respective systems. (2004, 135)

Human rights make everyone available for any sort of inclusion into any system. Race, gender, pedigree, etc. are no longer criteria that play any decisive role in the function systems. The color of your skin ultimately does not matter and has no specific value in any of the codes of the contemporary function systems. It is therefore not because of »human nature« or any ultimate moral foundation that we are all equal before the law and all other systems, it is because these systems are entirely indifferent towards such criteria. They can only apply the criteria that they produce themselves (guilty / not guilty; good grades / bad grades; more votes / less votes, etc.), but not those inherited from the past. Freedom and equality are therefore, for Luhmann, not some lofty values that we finally managed to cherish and translate into law, they are rather the semantic adornment of the structural indifference, and, as I think I can say with Luhmann, inhumanity of the function systems. No function system really cares who you actually are – so that you can be anything. There is nothing in which the function systems are less interested than »human nature«. As Luhmann states:

> Freedom means: that the ordering of persons (no longer: families) in society is no longer determined through social structures, but proceeds by a combination of self-selection and external selection. Equality means: that no other principles of inclusion are accepted than those that the function systems themselves determine. (1997, 1075; my translation)

Freedom and equality, the great values associated with human rights, are, according to Luhmann, devoid of any »humanist« contents. They fulfill the function to keep the systems going. Freedom means that it is not determined by anything »natural« or »innate« which career I am going to take, but by my decision, for instance, to go to this or that school, and by the decision of this school to accept me or not. Equality means that the old »human« characteristics (gender, race, etc.) are not those that the function systems have developed and that therefore can now be considered as entirely irrelevant.

Luhmann discusses the function that human rights fulfill only with respect to the all-inclusion that the function systems suggest. He does not, however, comment on the function they might fulfill with respect to the actual exclusion that takes place. The all-inclusion that they, on principle, are supposed to guarantee is therefore likely to result also, and paradoxically, in exclusion.

Two well-known contemporary examples may illustrate this paradox with human rights. One of the most celebrated rights in Western societies is that of free expression. But since this right too has to be specified, it has to be specified exactly what counts as free expression and what not. In practice, these specifications differ from country to country. In Germany not only printing but also possession of Hitler's *Mein Kampf* is illegal, whereas in many other nations, such as the USA, this is allowed with reference to the human right of free speech. In the USA, however, the death penalty is widely legally practiced, whereas in Germany and most of Europe it is considered as a violation of human rights. Nazis in Germany are not legally permitted to plead their case by invoking human rights. In the USA, conversely, a large number of convicts have to do without (at least some very basic) human rights. Human rights are, as mentioned above, in fact never unlimited. Not everybody can in every situation claim »all« human rights. The specific limits of human rights, however, are not necessary, but highly contingent. In any case, they seem not only to be able to embellish the indifference of the function-systems semantically and celebrate their supposed all-inclusion as a great humanist achievement, but also to justify exclusions that are socially or politically desirable. In Germany, there is a certain social consensus that Nazis cannot be accepted as »normal« citizens. Therefore they are excluded from the benefit of what is otherwise claimed as a universal human right. Once you lose the right to free speech, however, it is, in line with the domino effect mentioned by Luhmann, quite easy to lose your job as well, your political position, and perhaps even your wife. In the USA the same is the case with people who commit major crimes – with the important difference, however, that after losing their life, there is nothing left for them in society to be excluded from.

IV.

At the beginning of this article I pointed out that, in my view, Luhmann's theory, particularly in his later years, has to be understood in the context of his earlier criticism of the political left. I argued that instead of offering a »rightist«

or »conservative« alternative, he intended to thoroughly deconstruct the leftist (Habermasian) approach and to demonstrate that it represents an outdated, utopian, and moralist way of thought that can no longer be taken seriously. He intended not only to defeat, but, basically, to take apart the dominant intellectual attitude of his day and to replace it with a much more adequate theory that would go far beyond the traditional humanist concepts of society (and reality). Human rights are one of the most successful concepts brought forth by the »progressive« forces. A thorough deconstruction of popular leftist ideas could therefore not spare human rights. In a quite remarkable passage towards the end of *Die Gesellschaft der Gesellschaft*, Luhmann once more takes apart the »progressive« notions of freedom and equality and stresses that they led to the postulate of human rights. In this context he states that the human rights discourse in our days often appears as »human rights fundamentalism« (*Menschenrechtsfundamentalismus*; 1997, 1022). I think that this provocative term summarizes rather nicely the result of his deconstruction of that idea. The problem with human rights is that they are supposed to be »natural«, »indispensable«, based on »principles«, and are supposed to have »unlimited« validity. They are claimed to be much more than a contingent social construct, namely an ultimate norm that everybody should strive to realize. Luhmann identifies such claims, quite rightly, as, ironically, another type of »fundamentalism«. Even though human rights are often used in arguments against various types of (religious) fundamentalisms, they represent merely a secular version of a belief in universal and necessary principles. Luhmann, of course, is a theoretician of contingency and cannot accept this (or any other) »fundamentalism«. Therefore his analysis of human rights aims at disclosing their paradoxical character. Instead of being »regulatory ideas« or »components of the concept of communication« human rights are a »self-made product of society« (*Eigenleistung der Gesellschaft*; 1997, 35) – which of course means that they are subject to a continuous remaking.

It is important to stress that while Luhmann is quite appalled by »human rights fundamentalism«, he nevertheless has nothing at all against what is practically done with their help, i.e. such things as opposing torture, genocide, etc. Luhmann is obviously not in favor of doing away with their contents, he is just dismayed with their theoretical justification. Perhaps one can infer from Luhmann's deconstruction that human rights as such are not really necessary. We do not need to suppose some inalienable natural rights in order to make, for instance, torture illegal. We do not need to refer to lofty universal principles in order to prevent genocide. Such terrible things can be dealt with, and perhaps even more effectively, by means of »simple« positive law. As Luhmann said in one of the quotations cited above, the problem with human rights is that they pretend to go »beyond the established juridical world of forms« and thus to be *more than* law. They pretend to be more fundamental and less variable. Human rights fundamentalism is therefore not really helpful in legally prohibiting torture or genocide; and it may actually obstruct the acceptance of laws because of the universalist claims involved, which are unlikely to be shared by everybody. It is probably much more pragmatic simply to say that torture is against the law than saying that it is a violation of a universal right. Why not admit the unfounded, contingent, and paradoxical character of laws (and all other social constructs)? It is neither legal nor illegal to distinguish between what is legal and illegal, but this does not prevent us from making this distinction, it rather enables us to do so. Similarly the contingency of human rights does not prevent us from making laws against torture and genocide but makes it an easier task. Human rights fundamentalism is a semantic burden that, for moral purposes, many like to carry, but that is certainly not necessary for making actual laws.

Instead of the leftist-progressive reliance on »universal principles«, on rational necessity, and on moral obligations, Luhmann argues for a »cool« and modest, and even ironical (paradoxical) approach to human rights. Theory cannot find an ultimate justification for human rights; it can only describe their history and function. This leaves legal practice free to do what it deems right rather than having always to reassure itself of the foundations claimed by philosophers. Autopoietic law does not need moral or political philosophers to establish universal guidelines and principles, it can – and does – construct these itself.

Human rights fundamentalism that tries to impose itself on the law – or even ignore the law and do what it deems right anyway and outside the law – is not a solution, but a source of social problems. One could witness in recent years how the invasion of a foreign country was explicitly justified by human rights and in defiance of international law. The most extensive war so far in this century – the war in Iraq – was, in Britain even more so than in the USA (where justifications based on self-defense and national interests were much more prevalent), a war fought by self-proclaimed defenders of human rights. It is ironical that the »left« (represented by Tony Blair) in this conflict showed itself to be even more »human rights fundamentalist« than the »conservatives« (represented by George Bush). I think it is quite likely that Luhmann would not have been surprised by this development. In fact, one may even read his deconstruction of »progressive« human rights fundamentalism as a quite prophetic criticism of the dangerous and aggressive form that it took on in Britain.

References

Luhmann, Niklas (1965): Grundrechte als Institution. Ein Beitrag zur politischen Soziologie. Berlin: Duncker & Humblot.

Luhmann, Niklas (1984): Soziale Systeme. Frankfurt a. M.: Suhrkamp (Social Systems. Trans. by John Bednarz Jr. & Dirk Baecker. Stanford: Stanford University Press, 1995).

Luhmann, Niklas (1989): Ecological Communication. Trans. by John Bednarz Jr. Chicago: University of Chicago Press.

Luhmann, Niklas (1993): Risk: A Sociological Theory. Trans. by Rhodes Barrett. New York: De Gruyter.

Luhmann, Niklas (1995): Das Paradox der Menschenrechte und drei Formen seiner Entfaltung. Pp. 229-36 in: N. Luhmann, Soziologische Aufklärung. 6. Opladen: Westdt. Verlag.

Luhmann, Niklas (1995a): Inklusion und Exklusion. Pp. 237-264 in: N. Luhmann, Soziologische Aufklärung 6. Opladen: Westdt. Verlag.

Luhmann, Niklas (1996): Protest. Frankfurt a.M.: Suhrkamp.

Luhmann, Niklas (1997): Die Gesellschaft der Gesellschaft. Frankfurt a.M.: Suhrkamp.

Luhmann, Niklas (2004): Law as a Social System. Trans. by Klaus A. Ziegert. Oxford: Oxford University Press.

Luhmann, Niklas (2008): Are There Still Indispensable Norms in Our Society? Soziale Systeme 14, 18-37 (in this volume).

Luhmann, Niklas (2008a): Beyond Barbarism. Soziale Systeme 14, 38-46 (in this volume).

Rasch, William (2000): Niklas Luhmann's Modernity: The Paradoxes of Differentiation. Stanford: Stanford UP.

Verschraegen, Gert (2002): Human Rights and Modern Society: A Sociological Analysis from the Perspective of Systems Theory.« Journal of Law and Society 29, 258-281.

Verschraegen, Gert (2006): Systems Theory and the Paradox of Human Rights. Pp. 101-125 in: Michael King/Chris Thornhill (eds.), Luhmann on Law and Politics. Critical Appraisals and Applications. Oxford/Portland: Hart.

Professor Hans-Georg Moeller
Department of Philosophy, University College Cork
1 & 2 Lucan Place, Western Road
Cork, Ireland

Soziale Systeme 14 (2008), Heft 1, S. 142-156

Andreas Philippopoulos-Mihalopoulos

On Absence: Society's Return to Barbarians

> »... Because the barbarians are to arrive today;
> and they get bored with eloquence and orations.
>
> Because night is here but the barbarians have not come.
> And some people arrived from the borders,
> and said that there are no longer any barbarians.
>
> And now what shall become of us without any barbarians?
> Those people were some kind of solution.«
>
> Constantinos Kavafis (1908): Waiting for the Barbarians

Abstract: The inclusion of exclusion in autopoiesis is a far-reaching step that demands a revisiting of the concept of autopoietic society. This article proposes a radicalisation of the concept on the basis of an acknowledgment of the impossibility of communication with the excluded. This acknowledgement conditions society from within. It is built upon the Luhmannian description of Barbarism as the included exclusion, and is further conceptualised as its excess, as a ›space of absence‹. Within autopoiesis, absence is described as an *aporetic* rather than a paradoxical structure, a *memento vanitas* that irritates the system from within, constantly reminding it of its limitations.

I. Barbarians either side

For the poet Constantinos Kavafis, waiting for the Barbarians is not unlike Becket's waiting: messianic, never to arrive, yet already here. The anticipation brings the city to a standstill while at the same time promising to deliver it from such a standstill. The city anticipates the Barbarians, not in horror, it has to be said, but out of fascination and hope for a solution. They would be the solution to the paradox, the *anti*-civilising coup, the moment in which the paradox will be finally addressed and forever banished – or so the desire for the Barbarians dictates.

Luhmann does not wait for the Barbarians. His city operates only in the present, quietly going about its dissimulation, constantly checking itself for consistency, and therefore, never waiting. The future is here, juxtaposing itself between realisation and failure of future projects (Luhmann 1998), and everything that can be predicted, has been predicted. The Barbarians represent no risk or desire for the system, because their advent has already been anticipated. But in this way, any solution the Barbarians might have given (we will never know) lies together with the problem. The Barbarians bring both. A double negative bind that cannot be resolved from the inside – but then again, there is no outside. Luhmann's city has no room for its outside, yet it does understand exclusion. In fact it practices exclusion, it nominates the Barbarians, although it does not wait for them. Exclusion is internalised to the point that it can be internalised, namely, a stroll to the edge of the city, barely past the gate – this is where exclusion stops.

Where, then, is the other side of the boundary in Luhmannian society? A definition of society no longer has any need for the barbarians, since all its exclusions have been internalised. But would a confrontation with the Barbarians be a riskier than anticipated event? Could it be the case that the barbarians have neither left nor arrived, but have always been lurking like a *memento violentiae* within the system? This article will be dealing with such a conceptualisation, questioning some of the boundaries of Luhmannian society, and tracing an understanding of inclusion / exclusion that is reminiscent of a trauma, both in terms of the theory, and the reality that the theory describes.

II. The Direction of the Return

In conceptualising the Barbarians as the definitional opposite of Hellenes, the Hellenic identity was aspiring to an all-encompassing universality. The fundamental distinction between Hellenes and Barbarians was based on the phonetic impression that the Hellenes had of the Barbarians' languages: a recurrent ›bar-bar‹ that could only be included in the Hellenic linguistic sophistication as its antipodes. But, as Koselleck points out (Koselleck 2004; see also Åkestrøm Andersen 2003), the aspiring universalilty quickly transcended the territorial to include the temporal. The asymmetrical counter-concept of Barbarism served to privilege, not just the space of the city but also the present (as opposed to past) Hellenic time.[1] Thus, the concentration of historical and geographical preference found its expression in the leap outside the preferred space and time and into a construction of an outside (the Barbarians / the barbaric time) that remained off bounds. Just as Barbarism, the claim to universality could also only be observed from outside, indeed from a different time altogether. Such a leap, however, has the effect of drawing the outside inside, within the *form* of aspired universality. If a form is an inoperational unity of two counter-values,[2] its operationality is conditioned upon one of its sides being marked. Although

---

1 Cornell 1992, has criticised Luhmann's presentocracy from a feminist/deconstructive point of view; although valid, the critique is not always framed. See Philippopoulos-Mihalopoulos 2009, for further discussion.

2 Luhmann, following Spencer Brown, describes form as a total gesture that includes both selected and non-selected spaces (both marked and unmarked, but before their marking) in one inoperable unity – ›inoperable‹ because the system cannot operate with unities, only with distinctions (see Luhmann 1990; 1993).

universality can only with great conceptual difficulty and self-delusion claim operationality, the case remains that unless the unmarked space is included in the marked, the marked can never rest on its laurels, however contingent these may be.

The above can also be put in a more radical way: the unmarked space is included in the marked as *telos*. Luhmann calls this external reference, but here I would like to take it a little further and posit the illusion of teleology in an attempt to capture the instrumentality of the counter-concept within the systemic construction. In systemic terms, teleology does not determine an absolute direction (Maturana/Varela 1972, 85) but a circularity between two values: marked and unmarked circularly swap positions. As soon as telos is ›achieved‹ (and one value becomes marked), marking changes side and lands on the other side (unmarked) *in order to* mark it. This, however, means that telos can never be fully achieved, since its unmarking (or to recall Kierkegård (1985), the »suspension« of its marking (see also Philippopoulos-Mihalopoulos 2003)) is the precondition for the other telos (the previously unmarked space) to be achieved, and for contingency to be structurally and not only symbolically valid. Thus, telos is defined in opposition to the suspendability of the conditions of the unmarked which have to be in place in order for telos to be achieved. The effect of the circularity is an each time differently nuanced concept of telos:[3] in the Barbarians' case, and at least before Cavafis, Buzzati (1940) or Coetzee (1982), telos is the *end* of it all, and therefore something to be avoided; in other cases, telos is understood as the desired destination towards which every necessary suspension is encouraged. Of course, the two are mutually inclusive. The ideality of the included telos can be understood by the system variably as the unity of the system, memory, or destabilising threat. Whatever its function, telos is included as an unmarked space within the marked side of the form precisely because of its ideality, and regardless of the positive or negative (in other words, redundant or variant) effect it may have on the system. Ideality, therefore, not as ›ideal‹ but rather as a utopia, a non-topos, which teleologically determines reality as its other side: ideality as the unmarked space of reality's temporal and spatial presence. In that sense, the Barbarians' role for Hellenic identity was not only a destabilising threat but also an (equally destabilising) desire for unity. Such a unity is not to be imagined with the Barbarians, but through and against them. ›Through‹ because of the necessary leap outside, and ›against‹ because of the Barbaric counter-concept function.

Thus, teleology is constructed internally, as the instrumental leap towards the future (cognitively appearing in the form of environmental irritation), and an illusionary understanding of unity (e.g., for and within the legal system, justice is presented as the unity of the system (Luhmann 2004)). In any case, teleology

---

3   And according to the programme that links it to its environment and determines the values of the systemic code.

requires the construction of another state, be that of a future state of the same, or a different state to be achieved. It also requires a direction. For these reasons, a system constructs its other side within in order to be able to suspend itself for the sake of the unity of its self-description. If the environment of a system is constructed by the system itself as an internal other-reference,[4] then it would seem that any exclusion of the system is to be sought within the system itself. This is an inclusive exclusion, and has been described by Luhmann as the outcome of the transition from stratification to functional differentiation.

To this, however, one must note an embedded direction, a kind of structural predetermination that decides (follows, reiterates, performs) the facility of being marked. It is, after all, the Hellenes in whose distilled space and time the marking always returns. To put it differently, the problem remains even after the inclusion of telos within the system: there is a consistent and semantically conclusive return to the marked space that points to the particular space's ›facility‹ to be marked, with an ensuing compromise of the contingency of crossing. This ›homecoming‹ is faithful to Spencer Brown's *modus operandi* of a form: that the totality of space (marked and unmarked) is contingent on the starting point, on the direction of the first distinction.[5] As Luhmann says in *Beyond Barbarism* (2008), Barbarians do not characterise themselves as barbarians. But they have to be included, in their exclusion, on the marked side of the form: they are the contrary that has been ingested.[6] This external reference forms part of the system's self-description and guarantees the projection of unity within – it is the necessary boundary, which determines what has already been domesticated. But what is missing from this domestication is precisely the non-domesticated.

I shall return to the non-domesticated shortly. Before that, however, a brief word on the variety of perspectives, which is habitually presented as plausible antilogos, but can no longer be considered relevant when it comes to exclusion on a societal level precisely because of the apparent inclusion of all perspectives. Luhmann admits that exclusion from one social system escalates to intensification of exclusion via repetition in other systems.[7] Society integrates more efficiently when it comes to integrating exclusion – what Luhmann (2008, 45) calls »negative integration« in *Beyond Barbarism*. Negative integration is the outcome of a society that cannot let go of its exclusions. At the same time, the realisation that »functional differentiation cannot … realize the postulated full-inclusion« (2008, 45) pushes Luhmann into positing a different level on which

---

4 For a staunch declaration of this, see Nobles / Schiff 2006.

5 Spencer Brown 1969; see also Rasch 2002, 22. However, see Wagner 1997, for a critique of the Luhmannian directionality that is not to be found in Spencer Brown.

6 The marked determines what the unmarked stands for, and while one is implied in the other, their relation is one of *englobement du contraire* (›ingestion of the contrary‹), an enlightened colonisation and a safe strategy of description. See Dumont 1966, 107, cited in Luhmann 2002.

7 »Exclusion integrates with greater force than inclusion« (Luhmann 1997, 631).

the distinction inclusion / exclusion is to be operating (»the guiding difference of the next century«; Luhmann 2008, 45). From that meta-level, inclusion / exclusion is supposed to be filtering what is to be valid for each functionally differentiated system (Luhmann 1997, 632). In this way, though, at least two of the grand concepts of systems theory are being thrown into a ›new‹ meta-context: society and functional differentiation are now required to swim in the larger ocean of inclusion / exclusion. It would not be out of place to conceptualise the emergence of inclusion / exclusion, not as a new thing, but simply a new thing in the theory: inclusion / exclusion appears to be a spectre of promises past that is here to haunt Luhmann's work and allow a flow of previously unencountered apparitions of bodies and spaces to enter his texts. If I am not mistaken, *Beyond Barbarism* is the first English appearance of a text by Luhmann that refers explicitly to exclusion.[8] Filling a small gap until the eventual translation of *Die Gesellschaft der Gesellschaft* (1997), this text addresses criticisms on Luhmann's allegedly inadequate engagement with human marginalisation, while at the same time creating new space for sustained doubts on the ability of the theory to remain as convincingly all-inclusive as when exclusion did not feature so insistently.[9]

The distinction is encountered in earlier works by Luhmann. The concept of ›total inclusion‹ for example is one such instance. ›Total inclusion‹ is described as the fixity of social position in a stratified society, which disables one from social mobility (Luhmann 1999). A historically defined and contained inclusion has been employed by Luhmann as a means of showing how exclusion of the human agent from modern society was the only way in which the human was allowed mobility and at the same time inclusion in the function systems – notably through the mechanism of human rights. It is unclear, however, whether the present (1992) mere positing of a meta-level in a tight and functionally differentiated autopoietic universe can make room for yet another ›filter‹ for systemic autopoiesis. In other words, it may indeed be the case that systems theory is put under considerable stress if it is required to accommodate the return of a total inclusion and maintain its structures intact. For is it not the case that the present frozen state of inclusive exclusion constitutes precisely such a ›total inclusion‹, especially since inclusion / exclusion has become a potential candidate for the meta-difference of functional differentiation (Luhmann 1997, 632), and exclusion has become a totalised operation reduced to an external reference within society? It is in this context of a certain theoretical anxiety that two questions are hesitantly but vociferously murmured within systems theory. First, is society still a relevant term to describe the total sum of social systems together with their other-references? And, second, if Barbarians have indeed been included in their exclusion, why is it that systems theory cannot

---

8   As first translated and published in Moeller 2006, 261-272.
9   This line of criticism has been best expressed by Neves 2001.

see them? In other words, if Barbarians are no longer outside the city gates, if all exclusion has been ›hospitalised‹ by a society who sees it as a problem to be dealt with (and the operative word here is ›sees‹), why is it that this theory that attempts to describe society in its elusive totality still does not see the Barbarians? Could it be that the Barbarians are still lurking out there, but no ›other‹ society can be found to protect them from autopoietic society's avid inclusion?

III. Beyond Society

I will deal with the question of society first by revisiting Luhmann's description of the term and its instrumental (in the sense of teleological) value for the theory. Indeed, it seems that society is an epistemological necessity of sociology (and as regularly stressed, Luhmann does not do anything except sociology). According to Luhmann (1995, 408), sociology *needs* a concept to express »the unity of the totality ... of social relations, processes, actions, or communications.« Luhmann himself acknowledges that his chosen definition of society has been guided by the attempt to avoid the practical difficulties of social constructivism (see Luhmann 1985; 1988). But what is the price for such an epistemological concession? Autopoietic society filters out what is to be considered as relevant (or not) by social systems. It is »the social system whose structure regulates the ultimate and basic reductions to which other social systems can be attached. [It] guarantees for the remaining systems an almost domesticated environment of reduced complexity« (1985, 104). It is precisely this filtering that constitutes the problem: society is a mode of resistance against systemic self-questioning. Luhmannian society is the womb of selections, in which systems and their environment cohabit. In this womb, the cognitive openness of the system manifests itself on a contingent basis, which, properly thought, should not exhaust itself in the contingency of the marking between two values, but in its consistent movement between two sides: one that contains what retrospectively can be observed as marked; and the other that retrospectively can be observed as markable. The markable side contains the fan of probabilities in a horizontal, non-hierarchical, non-prioritised telos (in the sense of non-topos). Thus, contingency cannot be limited by anything but the system itself, and always in the system's absence. The system cannot control its environment, only believe that it can. Any attempt to contain contingency feeds the illusion of a containable horizon, which, nevertheless, appears to the system as the only horizon available. The partiality of societal horizon (potentially attributed to the sum of communications and only them (Luhmann 1997, 90), or to the absolute closure of the societal system,[10] or simply to an epistemological misconstruction of necessity on behalf of autopoietic theory itself) maternally

---

10 »Society is completely and without exception a closed system.« (Luhmann 1995, 409)

feeds its wombed beings with what is best for them. Autopoietic society risks being a partial description of the way society operates because of the impression of efficacy of domestication for the various social systems.

No doubt, any potential impression of societal essence is explicitly denied by Luhmann (1997, 90). Society is an aggregation of its systems and their communications, and receives its limits from the boundaries of these systems. But even if it is the ›total sum‹ of communications that determines societal boundaries, society still lends to a system its epithet and baptises it with a communicational talent that operates protectively against the disruption of such epithets. Even if society is simply a representation of the total selection of its subsystems (in other words, it is not society that delimits the horizon, but systems themselves), the systemic limitation is reinforced autopoietically in the sense of superimposition of the totality onto totality, thus totalising the cognitive experience within a set of (illusionary) secure exclusions. Even if there is no privileged point from which society can be observed, the totality of society with its capacity to include its exclusions is observed by autopoietic theory. The aspired autology of the theory, however, comes perilously close to a theological reinstatement of infallibility. Even in all-inclusiveness, there is a point from which the *impossibility* to observe the totality becomes observable, with all the ensuing fear of losing the illusion of all-inclusiveness. In order for the concept of society to avoid becoming paternalistic, the maternal protection of autopoietic society must allow its fear of the environment to resonate within. In its vaporous and rather desperate omnipotence, society rests on its boundaries that include and are determined by what the systems exclude, constantly including its exclusion while never including the absence of exclusion.

All this poses an important problem of miscorrespondence and unhelpful theoretical reduction between a society that is awakening to its ignorance and attempts to find ways of accommodating it, and an autopoietic society that ignores its ignorance. Why insist on a concept of society whose inevitable totalising still attempts to control an environment to which even in theory it has conceded intractability? When in *Beyond Barbarism* Luhmann ›recalls‹ the beginning of functional systems (empirically and theoretically) as »laid out to include the entirety of the population« (2008, 41), he demonstrates a certain nostalgia for a theory before exclusion, before inclusion of exclusion, before the geographies of favelas and the starkness of human bodies. And when he asserts that »the function systems themselves decide how far someone gets« (2008, 41), he seems to be positing a plural, effectively collective front of function systems that appear to operate through a consensus (however anathema this concept may be) that determines the grades of inclusion and exclusion. It is doubtful whether society, in its encompassing self-description as »one social system amongst many others« yet »at the same time inclusive of all others« (1997, 80; my translation), can retain the totalised aspiration of an ›all-encompassing‹ suprasystem in view of the barbaric ruptures within. This means that society as an autopoietic term may no longer be useful, considering that any alleged excursion outside is always followed and completed by the return to society as the consistently rather than contingently marked space. It does not constitute an adequate departure, either from a totalising form of filtering, or from an always already marked binarism that entertains doubts about its difference through a symbolic exercise in contingency. Society expresses the unity of difference, but not in the way Luhmann professes, namely the contingent co-existence of closure / openness; rather, societal difference can only be understood through a communicational unity. In other words, can society, the way Luhmann wants it, see whether there are any Barbarians outside its gates; or is it that by virtue of its all-inclusiveness no Barbarians can ever be seen? In order to see the Barbarians, one cannot be Hellenic (and this is the paradox, that only Hellenes saw Barbarians). If so, the only thing that one will see is the absence of Barbarians. In order for Barbarians to appear, one needs to suspend oneself and posit a space of non-inclusive exclusion within, a space of absence which can be filled by the incalculable contingency of the incommunicable.

Tim Murphy suggests that »instead of regarding ›society‹ as some encompassing system, in relation to which these others must be termed sub-systems, and merely reversing the old hierarchical scheme by switching into the driving seat the object rather than the subject, the ruled rather than the ruler, we need a cooler, more banal vision …«.[11] I could hardly agree more. But because a vision, however banal, risks always becoming a horizon, I want to focus here on the other side of whatever it is that thinks of itself able to contain exclusion, that is, on the environment of society, where the Barbarians are still communicating in a mode that remains invisible to society.

IV. On the Other Side

Where are the Barbarians of modern society to be located? If a system (and the suprasystem should be no exception) habitually thematises and constructs its environment, society has indeed moved beyond Barbarians by including their exclusion and by thematising their appearance as something to be treated within the ambits of society. But the difference between, on the one hand, the relentless incomprehensibility of ›barbar‹-ing noise and, on the other, societal communication, is again an exercise in identity building that returns to the starting point of society, and in the direction of a teleology that, although suspended, remains prioritised. This criticism is less unfair or indeed hasty than it would initially appear to a well-versed Luhmannian reader, who has habitually enjoyed Luhmann's regular references to ›old-european‹ theories of a world without an »outside« in order to differentiate and subsequently develop

11 Murphy 1997, 174, with different results to the ones here.

systems theory – a technique also employed in *Beyond Barbarism* by citing Koselleck, Dumont, Kant, Hegel and Husserl amongst others. Soon, however, Luhmann lapses into an observation of a society which is indeed without an outside (both the society and the observation), however strenuous the professing of difference maybe. Society's outside is an environment of non-communication, about which society may be able to communicate. But even when Luhmann deals with what he considers the most challenging ›environmental‹ problem of society, namely the ecological issue, he still resists doing anything more than »draw the barbarians into society«.[12] When the later Luhmann posits exclusion as the way in which the outside becomes finally present and on an equal (albeit necessarily negative) footing as the inside, he can only suggest an already inclusive exclusion whose contingency seems to be exhausting itself to a geographical ›total inclusion‹ and social fixity.

»To the surprise of the well-meaning …«: in this Danteian way Luhmann (2008, 44) introduces the revisiting of his own precedent in *Beyond Barbarism*. Although he would never identify with the ›well-meaning‹ (an odd disassociation in view of the theory's intended all-inclusiveness), Luhmann attempts to contain *his* surprise by ascertaining that exclusion still exists. Luhmann discovered his own *tristes tropiques* when he visited the favelas in Brazil. The story is almost mythical in its reiterability, not least because of the spectacular new vocabulary that followed the journey. Expressions such as »existences reduced to the bodily … attempting to get to the next day« in *Beyond Barbarism* (2008, 44) and »physical violence, sexuality, the elemental and impulsive satisfaction of necessities« and »the observation of bodies« in *Die Gesellschaft der Gesellschaft* (1997, 633) have narrowly although indelibly opened the text to the observation of the hitherto unobservable. I am not referring to human beings or indeed to the return of geography (despite, as Luhmann (1997, 632) says, that these phenomena can be seen »in some regions of this earthly globe«), but to the *acknowledgement* of an outside – what William Rasch (2000, 119) calls ›the Spasm of the Limits‹. This shot at a veritable reciprocal constitution, which has radical and possibly desirable consequences for the way autopoietic theory describes itself, has been drawn back very quickly through masterful gestures of yet more levels of societal decision- and distinction-making. Thus, in *Die Gesellschaft der Gesellschaft*, Luhmann carries on by positing care and self-help as emerging new systems. This may well be the case, and indeed there is an increasing bibliography moving in that direction (see for example la Cour 2004 and Scherr 1999). The problem, however, remains that the brazilian excursus was transparently patched up by revisiting the concept of exclusion and integrating it into a society and a theory that were not ready for such an integration.

---

12 See Luhmann 1989, and Philippopoulos-Mihalopoulos 2007 for a criticism.

Luhmann talks about religious and political regimes that »do not reflect on exclusion«, such as Calvinism in its connection to the apartheid. In these cases, the problem of exclusion was not hidden. It could still be formulated as an »original difference between just and condemned.« But now, modern society treats these problems as »problems that need therapy« (1997, 629f), namely as matters for internalised care. While this is an attempt to bring together theory and empirical observation, there is something that still eludes the matching up: conceptualising the problem as one of inclusive exclusion does not deal with the fact that society only nominally includes its exclusions (or to decontextualise it a little further, it includes the exclusion of its exclusions as a communicable event). The habitual assignment to a functionally excluded exclusion, namely an exclusion that alleviates from further reflection through an assignment to institutional care, reveals that there is a double side to it: society cares in order not to care. This teleological underbelly of care is not adequately represented in systems theory. Instead, by including all its exclusions, an autopoietic society closes itself off from the possibility of conceptualising the continuing lack of reflection (the exclusion of exclusion).[13]

Not reflecting on exclusion is not an isolated occurrence, but a symptom that repeats itself with variable intensity and visibility. At the same time, there can never be an absolute non-reflection on exclusion. To the extent that exclusion is reflected upon, it becomes internalised and a problem to be dealt with. If exclusion is theorised as ›not reflected upon‹, there can be only two solutions in terms of the theory: either to confine the non-reflection to a political or religious regime, as Luhmann does; or transcend the present limits of the theoretical construction in order to refer to precisely this absence of reference. The latter is suggested here. The absence of reference echoes circularly a reference to absence, and for this circularity self- and external reference are not adequate. At the same time, the counter-contingency of the two references has to remain in place. The system will still be thematising its environment on the basis of its crossing between self- and external reference. However, the very problems of crossing between the two, the impossibility of distinguishing between limits and limitations, and a suspicion that emerges, as Luhmann says, »if one adds up what one sees« come to occupy this shadowy space of the »margins of functional systems« to which Luhmann (1997, 630) refers in the context of exclusion. For the latter cannot be understood in any other meaningful way but as a reference to the absence of reference within the system.[14]

Just as the ›margins of systems‹ appear in Luhmann's text in a way that cannot be justified by the non-hierarchical inter- and intrasystemic plane, the distinc-

---

13 This is the reason for which Luhmannian society reaches its limits when it comes to issues of global poverty, environmental degradation, bare life and international law, invisibilised *homini sacer* and banalisation of exceptionality.

14 This is what Lyotard (1993), refers to when he talks about the hostage to which every singularity is submitted, the internal spectrality of the absent environment.

tion inclusion/exclusion, different from the previous human exclusion from society, can only with great difficulty be justified autopoietically. It appears more as a remnant of a time where the human was happily excluded from the theory. If inclusion/exclusion is a form of coupling between communication and perception, then the exact operations between psychic and social are still to be worked out, especially in the different ways in which exclusion affects the various systems. Verschraegen (2006) refers to primary and secondary exclusion, but such a construction posits issues of order, priority, hierarchy and even origin which risk either remaining unresolved, or simply clashing with basic autopoietic tenets of communicative closure. Without necessarily feeling averse to either eventuality, I would argue for a search for exclusion, not within inclusion as Luhmann would have it in his inclusive exclusion form, but within exclusion itself. This entails a systemic folding unto itself, a self-transcendence as it were, that would reveal to the system a space of ignorance within, in the ambits of the inclusive exclusion and simultaneously against it, transgressing it from within. Elsewhere (Philippopoulos-Mihalopoulos 2007), I referred to this systemic reference as the ›space of absence‹ within the system, a *memento vanitas* that irritates the system from within, constantly reminding it of its limitations. This acknowledgment of limitation breeds different forms of uncertainty to the ones previously produced by the system. While both are forms of self-generated uncertainty, the uncertainty produced from the reference to the absence of reference addresses directly the system's illusion of all-inclusiveness – something which Luhmann attaches to function systems – and allows for a more modest self-description of the system's abilities.

Whether this has any impact on the way, say, politics will conceptualise the excluded in the favelas is very doubtful. What may perhaps happen though is that autopoietic theory will manage to accommodate its limitations without perpetuating a unidirectional return to closure. If exclusion is conceptualised to be included in the system as absence of reference, the problem is not just of semantics but, significantly, of structure on the level of theory.[15] The two levels, therefore, of structure and theory converge and mirror each other in an attempt to reconfigure the way that theory in its turn reconfigures reality. A questioning of society along the lines advocated for earlier is a consequence and, not untypically, the simultaneous precondition for such a reference. The need for conceptualising society in the Luhmannian way becomes obsolete if a space of absence is included in the system. For then, what re-enters the system is precisely its difference with an environment not confined by a pre-filtering suprasystem that determines what is to be considered by the systemic code on the basis of the distinction between communication and non-communication. This is not meant to side with humanist criticisms of autopoiesis. On the con-

---

15 The two, *contra* Luhmann, have been shown to be connected and their difference irreducible to that of system/environment or systemic and communicable epistemological positions (see Stäheli 1996; 1997).

trary, it argues for an even greater internalisation of absence (of the human, the natural, the barbaric, or whatever other reference is found absent within) from within the system, and this can only take place via a return to the boundaries of each system. In this way, a system is self-described as both totalising (since every reference is framed in the difference between self and other) and at the same time fragmented and indeed traumatised by its self-inflicted trace of absence.

Unencumbered by the protective atmosphere of a supra-system, and in a self-referential whirlwind that remains incommunicable to any other system, the system returns as the only terrain on which absence is to be studied: an autopoiesis that demands viewing the phenomenon of the difference of society to its environment (in its altogether surprising and incidental apparition) from within the boundary of a system, indeed from a point of internalisation not only of systemic operations, but also of aporias: its impassable, unfoldable, unpostponable, uncivilisable paradoxes. In an autopoiesis that does not employ societal boundaries in order to carry on with its communications, communications are disrupted – as indeed they are – by an environment whose incommunicability guarantees its absence and, at the same time, prohibits its normative colonisation on behalf of the system. In other words, lifting the shield of autopoietic society from autopoiesis exposes the system to the draughts of an unmasticated environment, full of potential communications, but also fantasies, imperceptions, impossibilities, and other barbaric-sounding destabilising factors that demand a systemic reference different from the self-referential unity of self- and external reference. Since the gap between the two references grows exponentially, the system readjusts its self-description to unfiltered uncertainties, producing expectations that reveal its systemic limits and limitations to itself. Adequately exposed theoretical premises are necessary for the description of an inadequately compartmentalised environmental uncertainty.

Exclusion as absence does not result either in the absence of reflection, as in Luhmann's example of apartheid, nor in the illusion of therapy of the excluded, as in the case of inclusive exclusion. Conceptualising exclusion as absence opens a space within the theory to reflect precisely on the absence of a reference, an empty reflection that reveals a void within the system. Signalling the systemic limits within amounts to a self-description that includes systemic limitations. Working together with the shattering of the illusion of therapy, the empty reference disrupts the system's omnivalidity and suggests the possibility of a parallel system that cannot be reflected as an external reference on account of its incommunicability. At present, favelas appear in two ways: either as an empty yellow space on the map whose sprawling begins where neatly sketched streets end abruptly;[16] or as a land to be appropriated, a normativity to be normalised, minds to be educated etc. Non-reflection in the former,

16 as indeed it does in tourist maps of Rio de Janeiro.

opportunity for therapy in the latter. Exclusion as absence, however, would schematically appear on the other side of the map. Its location transcends the need for solution (in the sense of unfolding) and requires a parallel observation of an incomprehensibility, while retaining its incomprehensible traits:[17] an observation of the blind spot as it were, which leads nowhere but to an awareness of a suspicion of another system/society/life, which stands as the other side of the limit and at the same time a cognitive opportunity for the observing system. Cognising in symmetry, but only after and through the asymmetry of absence.

Pluralism is not adequate unless accompanied by an awareness of the uncolonisable difference. In that sense, the text can finally articulate its underlying double negation: exclusion *and* exclusion of exclusion. The simultaneous, form-like operation of both does not result in the positivisation of the former, nor does it entail a directionality of unfolding. Exclusion is to remain excluded (thus, to remain exclusion), but in a space of always already excluded difference within the system (exclusion of exclusion). Exclusion can indeed only be thought through exclusion, but also against exclusion, somewhat in spite of it, yet always within it. The form of exclusion and exclusion of exclusion is an instrumental self-limitation within the system, a way in which the question will recur in its full paradoxicality, a means of reawakening the suspicion of the fundamental paradox within the system while wrapping it with a halo of familiarity. An absent reference to absence (or an exclusion and an exclusion of exclusion) spans the problematic space of ethics within the system, never quite overstepping systemic limits in order to become a moralising threat (even if the impression that such a threat operates more on the level of systems theory than anything else cannot be easily dispelled). The totality of autopoietic society as a moral position is replaced by a systemic totality which exhausts itself to the *limitation* of the ethical position, with the ensuing difference that, now, the system can be described as finally allowing (or failing to resist) the internal production of uncertainty. The latter is only communicable to the extent that it may also not be – but this absence of communicability is communicable, and in its communication it produces the much repressed space of systemic doubt.

This space is the trapeze on which the system projects its self-description. And if self-description is the system's projection of unity within, then this unity now includes a reference to its fragmentation in a consistent exchange of positions between unity and fragmentation, continuum and rupture, marked and markable, telos and suspendable. The schema avoids being a societal prescription because it merely aims at a differently nuanced understanding of autopoiesis – hopefully one that reflects the complexity outside in a more faithful way. Returning to the boundaries of the system is one way of circumventing the

---

17 This is what Rasch (2000, 118), discussing Lyotard, calls a stalemate between the theoretical and the applied in view of the absence of Hegelian *Aufhebung*. Not a third term, a *lysis* or a *paralysis*, but »an attempt to make the ineluctable violence of enforced selectivity visible.«

limitations of communication as the sole point of entry for society, encouraging an autopoietic conceptualisation of precisely those spaces of absence within systems. It is only once this is in place that one can begin thinking on how to continue misunderstanding the Barbarians.

References

Åkestrøm Andersen, N. (2003): Discursive Analytical Strategies: Understanding Foucault, Koselleck, Laclau, Luhmann. Bristol: Policy Press.

Buzzati, D. (1940): Il Deserto dei Tartar. Milano: Arnoldo Mondadori.

Coetzee, J. M. (1982): Waiting for the Barbarians. London: Penguin.

Cornell, D. (1992): The Relevance of Time to the Relationship between the Philosophy of Limit and Systems Theory. Cardozo Law Review 13, 5, 1579-1603.

Dumont, L. (1966): Homo Hierarchicus: Essai sur le Système des Castes. Paris: Gallimard.

Kierkegård, S. (1985): Fear and Trembling, trans. A. Hannay. London: Penguin Classics.

Koselleck, R. (2004): Futures Past: On the Semantics of Historical Time. Columbia: University of Columbia Press.

la Cour, A. (2004): Frivilligt Socialt Arbejde som Paradoks. Social Kritik 16, 95, 38-51.

Luhmann, N. (1985): A Sociological Theory of Law, trans. E. King and M. Albrow. Boston: Routledge & Kegan Paul.

Luhmann, N. (1988): Closure and Openness: On Reality in the World of Law. Pp. 335-348 in: G. Teubner (ed.), Autopoietic Law: A New Approach to Law and Society. Berlin: de Gruyter.

Luhmann, N. (1989): Ecological Communication, trans. J. Bednarz, Jr. Cambridge: Polity Press.

Luhmann, N. (1990): Essays on Self-Reference. New York: Columbia University Press.

Luhmann, N. (1993): Risk: A Sociological Theory, trans. R. Barrett. New York: Aldine de Gruyter.

Luhmann, N. (1995): Social Systems, trans. J. Bednarz, Jr. & D. Baecker. Stanford, Cal.: Stanford University Press.

Luhmann, N. (1997): Die Gesellschaft der Gesellschaft. Frankfurt a.M.: Suhrkamp.

Luhmann, N. (1998): Observations on Modernity. Stanford, Cal.: Stanford University Press.

Luhmann, N. (1999): Grundrechte als Institution. 4th edition. Berlin: Dunker & Humblot.

Luhmann, N. (2002): The Modern Sciences and Phenomenology. Pp. 33-60 in: N. Luhmann, Theories of Distinction: Redescribing the Descriptions of Modernity, ed. and introduced by W. Rasch. Stanford, Cal.: Stanford University Press.

Luhmann, N. (2004): Law as a Social System, trans. K.A. Ziegert. Oxford: Oxford University Press.

Luhmann, N. (2008): Beyond Barbarism. Soziale Systeme 14, 38-46 (in this volume).

Lyotard, J. F. (1993): Political Writings, trans. B. Reading and K. Geiman. Minneapolis: University of Minnesota Press.

Maturana, H./Varela, F. (1972): Autopoiesis and Cognition: the Realization of the Living. Dordecht, Holland: Reidel Publishing.

Moeller, H. G. (2006): Luhmann Explained. Chicago: Open Court.

Murphy, W. T. (1997): The Oldest Social Science? Configurations of Law and Modernity. Oxford: Clarendon.

Neves, M. (2001): From the Autopoiesis to the Allopoiesis of Law. Journal of Law and Society 28, 2, 242-264.

Nobles, R./Schiff, D. (2006): A Sociological Jurisprudence. Oxford: Hart.

Philippopoulos-Mihalopoulos, A. (2003): Suspension of Suspension: Settling for the Improbable. Law and Literature 15, 3, 345-370.

Philippopoulos-Mihalopoulos, A. (2007): Absent Environments. London: Routledge-Cavendish.

Philippopoulos-Mihalopoulos, A. (2009): Niklas Luhmann: Law, Justice, Society. London: Routledge.

Rasch, W. (2000): Niklas Luhmann's Modernity: The Paradoxes of Differentiation. Stanford, Cal.: Stanford University Press.

Rasch, W. (2002): Introduction Pp. 1-30 in: N. Luhmann, Theories of Distinction: Redescribing the Descriptions of Modernity, ed. and introduced by W. Rasch. Stanford, Cal.: Stanford University Press.

Scherr, A. (1999): Transformations in Social Work: From Help towards Social Inclusion to the Management of Exclusion. European Journal of Social Work 2, 1, 15-25.

Spencer Brown, G. (1969): Laws of Form. London: George Allen and Unwin.

Stäheli, U. (1996): From Victimology towards Parasitology. Recherches Sociologiques 27, 2, 59-80.

Stäheli, U. (1997): Exorcizing the Popular Seriously: Luhmann's Concept of Semantics. International Review of Sociology 7, 1, 127-146.

Verschraegen , Gert (2006): Systems Theory and the Paradox of Human Rights. Pp. 101-125 in: Michael King / Chris Thornhill (eds.), Luhmann on Law and Politics. Critical Appraisals and Applications. Oxford / Portland: Hart.

Wagner, G. (1997): The End of Luhmann's System Theory. Philosophy of the Social Sciences 27, 387-409.

Dr. Andreas Philippopoulos-Mihalopoulos
The School of Law, The University of Westminster
4 Little Titchfield Street, London, W1W 7UW
andreaspm@wmin.ac.uk

Zusammenfassungen

William Rasch, Einleitung: Die Form des Problems

Indem Luhmann die Frage stellt, ob es in unserer Gesellschaft noch unverzichtbare Normen gibt, sucht er nicht nach einer normativen Antwort, sondern untersucht die »Form des Problems.« Diese Einleitung in den Band stellt Luhmanns Erörterung von Unentscheidbarkeit und die Aporien der Kommunikationsmedien der verschiedenen Funktionssysteme in den Zusammenhang mit der Form des Problems der modernen Gesellschaft, d. h. die Trennung von Vernunft und Moral. Innerhalb dieser Auslegung der Luhmannschen Sicht der Moderne gibt die Einleitung dann kurz die wesentlichen Argumente der Beiträge des Bandes wider.

Niklas Luhmann, Gibt es in unserer Gesellschaft noch unverzichtbare Normen?

In seiner Heidelberger Universitätsrede von 1992 führt der Autor uns ein heutzutage allzu bekanntes Folterungs-Szenario vor Augen, um die Funktion und angebliche Unverzichtbarkeit von Normen in der modernen Gesellschaft zu untersuchen. Sich auf die »Normativität von Normen« oder auf »Werte« zu verlassen, erweist sich im Ausnahmezustand als vergeblich, da sich alle Normen und Werten als unentscheidbar erweisen. Innerhalb des Rechtssystems bleibt die Geltung der Normen unbezweifelbar; aus der Sicht der Gesellschaft (z. B. der Soziologie) sind Normen dagegen Tatsachen, also diskutierbar. Der Autor stellt verschiedene Versionen des Szenarios dar; nicht, um eine normative Antwort auf die titelgebende Frage zu geben, sondern um die Unmöglichkeit der begründeten Erwartung aufzuzeigen, dass jede Rechtsnorm normativ unverzichtbar ist.

Niklas Luhmann, Jenseits von Barbarei

Der Autor behandelt die Frage nach dem Verhältnis von Barbarei und Moderne als ein Thema der Beziehungen zwischen Semantik und Gesellschaftsstruktur. Die altgriechische Unterscheidung von »Hellenen« und »Barbaren« repräsentiert das allgemeine, asymmetrische Differenzschema von »Inklusion« und »Exklusion«, wie es für stratifikatorisch differenzierte Gesellschaften kennzeichnend ist. Die moderne, funktional differenzierte Gesellschaft hebt diese Unterscheidung auf: Hier soll schließlich niemand mehr ausgeschlossen, vielmehr eine »All-Inklusion« vollzogen werden. Aber diese All-Inklusion erweist sich als eine bloße Selbstbeschreibung der modernen Funktionssysteme. In Wahrheit finden sehr wohl Exklusionen statt; in manchen Fällen werden bestimmte Personen sogar aus sämtlichen Funktionssystemen ausgeschlossen, während der systemische Inklusionsbereich, davon unberührt, stabil weiteroperiert. Daraus schließt der Autor, dass Inklusion/Exklusion als eine Art Supercodierung die Leitdifferenz der modernen Weltgesellschaft werden könnte.

Chris Thornhill, Normen als soziale Fakten. Die Perspektive der historischen Politikwissenschaft

Der Aufsatz befasst sich mit dem Begriff der Normen und mit dem Zusammenhang zwischen Normen, Gesellschaftsstruktur und Politik in den Werken Niklas Luhmanns. Dabei werden zwei Thesen vertreten: Erstens wird behauptet, dass in politischer Hinsicht Luhmanns Theorie der Gesellschaft einen eindeutig normativen – oder sozio-normativen – Gehalt hat. Die Theorie impliziert, dass Regierungssysteme, deren Verfassung der pluralistisch differenzierten Form der modernen Gesellschaft angemessen ist oder wenigestens den evolutionären Prozess der sozialen Differenzierung nicht gefährdet bzw. rückgängig macht, höhere Aussichten auf Legitimation (oder Selbstlegitimation) haben als Regierungsformen, die die Differenzierung der verschiedenen Funktionssysteme der Gesellschaft nicht beachten oder sogar in Frage stellen. Zweitens wird argumentiert, dass bei Luhmann die Frage der Normen oder der Werte nie explizit erhoben werden kann. Moderne Gesellschaften sind *polynormative* Gesellschaften: Normen sind höchst variabel in die Gesellschaftsstruktur eingebettet und können nicht einfach durch theoretische Fragestellungen aus dieser semantischen Struktur herausgelöst oder zur Debatte gestellt werden. In der modernen Gesellschaft hängt also die normative Funktion der Normen davon ab, dass sie durch ihr Schweigen die Differenzierung der Gesellschaft befördern und die eventuelle Konzentration der Gesellschaft auf normative oder politisch umstrittene Kontroversen verhindern. Luhmanns Frage, ob es unverzichtbare Werte gebe, kann also nicht entschieden und eigentlich gar nicht sinnvoll gestellt werden. Sie schreibt der Gesellschaft eine politisch zentrierte oder sogar exzeptionelle Gestalt zu, die sie tatsächlich nicht mehr annehmen kann.

John Paterson, Das Faktische der Werte

Basierend auf Luhmanns Bemerkungen hinsichtlich der Probleme, die für das Gesetz durch unverzichtbare Normen und insbesondere durch Konflikte zwischen zweien oder mehreren von ihnen entstehen, befasst sich dieser Artikel mit einigen Lösungsvorschlägen der Gesetzestheorie, bevor er sich mit verschiedenen neueren Theorien, die von den Gerichtshöfen selber stammen, beschäftigt. Da weder die Theorie noch die Praxis in der Lage zu sein scheinen, die von Luhmann aufgezeigten Probleme zu überwinden, werden Schlussfolgerungen gezogen, die darauf hinweisen, dass Luhmanns Analyse keineswegs Anlass zum Bedauern gibt, sondern vielmehr die praktischen Grenzen dessen aufzeigt, was in Bezug auf Werte erwartet werden kann. Darüber hinaus identifiziert seine Untersuchung den Punkt, an dem die mit dem Schutz der Werte Betrauten ihnen ihre volle Aufmerksamkeit schenken sollten.

Niels Werber, Ein Gewissenstest. Ohne unverzichtbare Normen: Niklas Luhmann Kampf gegen den Terror

In der Soziologie Niklas Luhmanns kommt der Ausnahmezustand nicht vor. Die großen Monographien gehen vom »normalen« Funktionieren der Kommunikation in der Weltgesellschaft aus; dies bedeutet, dass die Grenzen der Funktionssysteme und die Unterschiede zwischen Medien und Codes intakt sind: Politik ist Politik, Recht ist Recht, etc. Gilt dies aber auch im Fall von Terroranschlägen großen Ausmaßes? In seiner in Heidelberg gestellten Frage an Juristen, ob auch dann »unverzichtbare Normen« gälten, reißt Luhmann in die Normalität eine Lücke. Am Beispiel des Szenarios einer

»tickenden Bombe« werden die Aporien der Funktionscodes vorgeführt. Der Ausnahmefall ist normativ unentscheidbar, muss aber entschieden werden. Es geht um »hard cases« und »tragic choices«. Der Aufsatz führt das Entscheidungsdilemma an mehreren Szenarien für moralische, juristische, politische und massenmediale Kommunikationen vor Augen und zeigt, dass Luhmanns Plädoyer für ein »prinzipienloses Manövrieren« im Falle von Ausnahmefällen die Systemtheorie erstaunlich nahe an amoralische Theorien heranrückt, wie sie in den USA besonders seit »9-11« Konjunktur haben.

William E. Scheuerman, »Wider die normative Ton-Taubheit«

Luhmanns Aufsatz nimmt auf eine fast schon unheimliche Art und Weise die nach dem 11. 9. 2001 entstandene – und inzwischen in den USA weitverbreitete – These vorweg, dass selbst das grundlegende moralische Verbot von Folter keineswegs unantastbar ist. Obwohl Luhmanns Kritik auf den ersten Blick wie eine Beleidigung der traditionellen Formen moralischen Denkens erscheinen muss, basiert sie selbst implizit auf den traditionellen Formen schwacher (und vermutlich utilitaristischer) moralischer Argumentation. Luhmann behauptet, dass wir die Existenz unkontrollierbarer »tragischer Entscheidungen« einräumen müssen, aber gleichzeitig macht seine eigene, unübersehbare (und dennoch keineswegs beständige) Ablehnung des »alten europäischen« moralischen Rationalismus es ihm unmöglich, die Beschaffenheit dieser tragischen moralischen Situationen vollkommen zu begreifen.

Costas Douzinas, Folter und Systemtheorie

Niklas Luhmanns gegen die Rhetorik der Brigade der ›unverzichtbaren Werte‹ gerichteter Angriff ist wichtig und aktuell. Selbstverständlich haben gute Normen einen politischen Nutzen, aber sie besitzen keinerlei philosophischen Wert. Indem Werte durch Rechte ersetzt und Entscheidungen Anwälten überlassen werden, wird das Problem der Unbestimmtbarkeit und der Konflikte von Gesetzen und Rechten jedoch nicht behoben, sondern nur verschoben. Die (falsche) asketische Verpflichtung allein zur Beschreibung, verbunden mit der Akzeptanz der bestehenden Gesellschaftsordnung, macht die Systemtheorie zu einem wertlosen Werkzeug in einem Prozess der Verbesserung der Gesellschaft. Die Philosophie überbrückt die Kluft zwischen dem natürlich und sozial Gegebenen und dem ewigen Streben, ihr zu widerstehen und sie zu überwinden durch die Erforschung sowohl der dem Gesetz innewohnenden Gerechtigkeit und der Gerechtigkeit, die das Gesetz als Ganzes zur Verantwortung zieht.

Hans-Georg Moeller, »Menschenrechtsfundamentalismus«. Menschrechte im Spätwerk Luhmanns

Der Aufsatz behandelt zunächst die Frage, ob die Auseinandersetzung zwischen Luhmann und der ›linken‹ Gesellschaftstheorie primär ideologischer Natur war oder nicht. Es wird die These aufgestellt, dass Luhmann in dieser Debatte nicht primär an einem politischem Dialog interessiert war, sondern vielmehr daran, die theoretische Unzulänglichkeiten seiner Opponenten offenzulegen, um einen Paradigmenwechsel in der Gesellschaftstheorie herbeizuführen. Dieser Versuch der »Dekonstruktion« seiner intellektuellen Widersacher wird am Beispiel der Behandlung des Themas Menschenrechte in Luhmanns Spätschriften veranschaulicht. Dabei wird ersichtlich, wie Luhmann durch eine semantisch-historische und funktionale Analyse die Paradoxien dieses politisch so erfolgreichen Konzepts sichtbar macht und es allein als ein »wertfundamentalistisches« rhetorisches Konzept erscheinen lässt, mit dem die Utopie einer sozialen All-Inklusion aufrecht erhalten wird.

Andreas Philippopoulus-Mihalopoulus, Über Abwesenheit. Die Rückkehr der Gesellschaft zur Barbarei

Die Inklusion der Exklusion in die Autopoiesis des Systems ist ein weitreichender Schritt, der eine Überarbeitung des Konzepts der autopoietischen Gesellschaft erfordert. Basierend auf der Anerkennung der Unmöglichkeit von Kommunikation mit den Ausgeschlossenen, schlägt dieser Artikel eine Radikalisierung des Konzepts vor. Diese Anerkennung prägt die Gesellschaft von innen. Sie gründet auf der Luhmannschen Beschreibung des Barbarismus als einschließender Exklusion und wird als deren Exzess, als ein ›Raum der Abwesenheit‹, zusammengefasst. Innerhalb der Autopoiesis wird Abwesenheit eher als eine *aporetische* denn als eine paradoxale Struktur beschrieben, ein *memento vanitas*, der das System von innen reizt, indem er ihm ständig seine Grenzen vorhält.

About the authors

Costas Douzinas is Professor of Law, Director of the Birkbeck Institute for the Humanities and Pro-Vice Chancellor at Birkbeck College, University of London. Educated in Athens, London and Strasbourg, Costas has taught at the Universities of Middlesex, Lancaster, Prague, Athens, Griffith, Nanjing and Melbourne where he is a Professorial Fellow. He is a founding member of the Critical Legal Conference, the managing editor of *Law and Critique: The International Journal of Critical Legal Thought* and of the publishing house *Birkbeck Law Press*. Douzinas has written extensively in legal and political philosophy, human rights, aesthetics and critical theory. His books include *Postmodern Jurisprudence; Justice Miscarried; The Logos of the Nomos; The End of Human Rights; Law and the Image; Critical Jurisprudence; Nomos and Aesthetics; Human Rights and Empire; Adieu Derrida*. His work has been translated into ten languages.

Niklas Luhmann was Professor for Sociology at the Bielefeld University from 1968 to 1993. Throughout his academic career he worked on a nearly encyclopedical theory of modern society based on a social theory which conceptualizes sociality in systems theoretical terms. He published over 50 books on a wide array of themes. The most recent are: *Soziologische Aufklärung* (6 volumes, 1970-1995); *Gesellschaftsstruktur und Semantik* (4 volumes, 1980-1995); *Soziale Systeme* (1984; Social Systems, 1995); *Die Gesellschaft der Gesellschaft* (1997).

Hans-Georg Moeller is Professor at the Philosophy Department of University College Cork, Ireland. His publications on Daoism and Social Systems Theory include *The Philosophy of the Daodejing* (Columbia University Press), a translation of the *Daodejing, Daoism Explained*, and *Luhmann Explained* (all published by Open Court). His most recent book is *The Moral Fool. A Comparative Case for Amorality* (Columbia University Press, in press).

John Paterson is Reader in Law at the School of Law, University of Aberdeen, UK. Publications include: »Reflecting on reflexive law.« Pp. 13-35, in: Michael King/Chris Thornhill (eds.) (2006), *Luhmann on Politics and Law: Critical Appraisals and Applications*, Oxford: Hart (with Gunther Teubner); »Changing maps: empirical legal autopoesis.« Pp. 215-237 in Reza Banakar/Max Travers (eds.) (2006), *Socio-Legal Research Methods*, Oxford: Hart; »Trans-science, trans-law and proceduralisation.« *Social and Legal Studies* 12, 4 (2003), 523-543.

Andreas Philippopoulos-Mihalopoulos, LLB, LLM, Ph.D, is a Reader-in-Law at the University of Westminster, London. His research interests include critical legal theory, autopoiesis, geography, psychoanalysis, art, phenomenology, linguistics, and their critical instances of confluence. His edited collection *Law and the City* and his monograph *Absent Environments: Theorising Environmental Law and the City* are published by Routledge-Cavendish. He is currently working on a book on Niklas Luhmann's systems theory from a poststructuralist perspective as part of the Routledge Critical Legal Thinkers Series.

William Rasch is the author of *Niklas Luhmann's Modernity: The Paradoxes of Differentiation* and *Sovereignty and Its Discontents* (translated into German as *Konflikt als Beruf.*) He is the editor of a collection of Luhmann's essays translated into English (*Theories of Distinction*); co-editor of *Bombs Away: Representing the Air War over Europe and Japan* and *German Postwar Films: Life and Love in the Ruins*; and has edited or co-edited special issues of the journals *New German Critique, Cultural Critique*, and *South Atlantic Quarterly*. He teaches German Studies at Indiana University, Bloomington (USA).

Bill Scheuerman teaches political theory at Indiana University (Bloomington). His primary research and teaching interests are in modern political thought, German political thought, democratic theory, legal theory, and normative international theory. He is the author of *Between the normal and the exception: The Frankfurt School and the rule of law* (MIT, 1994); *Carl Schmitt: The end of law* (Rowman & Littlefield, 1999); *Liberal democracy and the social acceleration, of time* (Johns Hopkins, 2004); *Frankfurt School perspectives on globalization, democracy, and the law* (Routledge, 2008) and editor of a number of others. He has published in many professional journals, and he is co-director of an annual international conference for critical theorists held in Prague.

Chris Thornhill has been Professor of Political Theory at der University of Glasgow since 2006. He is the author of numerous studies on political theory, political sociology, political history of ideas, and the theory and history of constitutions.

Dr. Niels Werber is Professor of German and Media Studies. His most recent publications include *Die Geopolitik der Literatur. Eine Vermessung der medialen Weltraumordnung,* München 2007, and the edited volume *Niklas Luhmann. Schriften zu Kunst und Literatur,* with afterword and editorial notes, Frankfurt a.M. 2008.

Hinweise für unsere Autoren

Verfahren der Einsendung und Form des Manuskripts: Manuskript (in deutscher, englischer oder französischer Sprache) einseitig und anderthalbzeilig schreiben und in dreifacher Kopie *sowie* als Word- oder WordPerfect-Datei per E-Mail-Attachment einsenden. Ein Manuskript sollte nicht länger als 25 Seiten (ca. 65.000 Zeichen) sein. Die Gesamtzeichenzahl bitte auf dem Deckblatt vermerken.

Bitte unbedingt eine 10- bis 15zeilige *Zusammenfassung* des Beitrags in deutscher *und* englischer Sprache auf einem gesonderten Blatt beifügen. Weiterhin bitten wir um eine kurze Notiz zum Autor (ca. 10 Zeilen).

Die *Fußnoten* sind fortlaufend zu numerieren und sollten *nicht* für bibliographische Angaben, sondern nur für inhaltliche Anmerkungen genutzt werden.

Hervorhebungen in Kursivschrift.

Tabellen und Abbildungen bitte dem Manuskript gesondert beifügen. Im Manuskript müssen die Stellen angegeben werden, an denen Tabellen oder Abbildungen eingefügt werden sollen. Von den Abbildungen müssen reproduktionsfertige Vorlagen geliefert werden.

Literaturhinweise im Text: Nennung des Autorennamens, des Erscheinungsjahres und ggf. der Seitenzahl. Bei mehrfacher Zitierung der gleichen Quelle, Literaturhinweise in derselben Form wiederholen und keine Abkürzungen wie »a.a.O.«, »op.cit.«, »ebd.«, »ibid« etc. verwenden. Im einzelnen:

1. Wenn der Autorenname im Text vorkommt, Erscheinungsjahr in Klammern anfügen: »... Parsons (1960) ...«.
2. Wenn der Autorenname im Text nicht vorkommt, den Familiennamen des Autors und das Erscheinungsjahr in Klammern einfügen: »... (s. Arendt 1958) ...«.
3. Bei einem Buch mit mehreren Autoren die Familiennamen der Autoren durch »/« trennen: »... Maturana/Varela (1980) ...«.
4. Seitenangaben hinter dem Erscheinungsjahr nach einem Komma: »... Luhmann (1984, 242ff.) ...«.
5. Sofern mehrere Titel desselben Autors aus einem Jahr zitiert werden, der Jahreszahl zur Unterscheidung die Buchstaben a, b, c usw. hinzufügen: »... Esser (1994a, 12) ...«.
6. Bei Nennung mehrerer Titel eines Autors in einem Literaturhinweis, die Angaben durch Semikolon trennen und in eine gemeinsame Klammer einschließen: »... Esser (1994a, 12; 1994b, 124)...«. Ebenso bei mehreren aufeinanderfolgenden Literaturhinweisen: »... (Parsons 1960; Maturana/Varela 1980; Glanville 1988) ...«.

Literaturverzeichnis: Alle zitierten Titel alphabetisch nach Autorennamen und nach Erscheinungsjahr geordnet in einem gesonderten Anhang am Schluß des Manuskripts unter der Überschrift »Literatur« aufführen. Die Titel bitte vollständig, d.h. auch mit u.U. vorhandenen Untertiteln anführen. Den Vornamen des Autors ungekürzt angeben. Den Verlagsnamen in abgekürzter, aber noch verständlicher Form nennen. Beispiele:

1. Bücher: Parsons, Talcott (1972): Das System moderner Gesellschaften. München: Juventa.
   Zu beachten: Mehrere Autoren bzw. Herausgeber eines Titels werden durch »/« voneinander getrennt, die Reihenfolge »Nachname, Vorname« wird nicht durchbrochen: Müller, Hans-Peter/Schmid, Michael (Hrsg.) (1995): Sozialer Wandel. Modellbildung und theoretische Ansätze. Frankfurt a.M.: Suhrkamp.

2. Zeitschriftenbeiträge: Geser, Hans (1986): Elemente zu einer soziologischen Theorie des Unterlassens. Kölner Zeitschrift für Soziologie und Sozialpsychologie 38, 643-669.

3. Beiträge aus Sammelbänden: Derrida, Jacques (1979): Structure, Sign and Play in the Discourse of the Human Sciences. S. 247-265 in: Richard Macksey/Eugenio Denato (Hrsg.), The Languages of Criticism and the Sciences of Man: The Structuralist Controversy. Baltimore: The Johns Hopkins Press.
   Zu beachten: Die Nennung der Herausgeber erfolgt hier in der »natürlichen« Reihenfolge, d.h.: »Vorname Nachname«.

Korrekturen werden vom Verlag mit der Bitte um sorgfältige Prüfung und umgehende Rückgabe vorgelegt. Es wird nur eine Korrektur (Fahnenkorrektur) verschickt. Kosten für außergewöhnlich umfangreiche, verspätete oder vom Autor verschuldete Korrekturen müssen dem Verlag erstattet werden.

Entgegennahme und Verbleib der Manuskripte: Manuskripte nimmt die Redaktion entgegen. Eine Rückgabe an die Autoren ist nicht vorgesehen.

Redaktionsadresse
Johannes Schmidt
Soziale Systeme, Soziologisches Seminar, Universität Luzern
Kasernenplatz 3, Postfach 7455, CH-6000 Luzern 7
Tel. (++41) (0)41/228-7590, Fax (+41) (0)41/228-7377
E-Mail: soziale.systeme@unilu.ch

Revolutionary Aristotelianism

Ethics, Resistance and Utopia

edited by Kelvin Knight and Paul Blackledge

With contributions from
Alex Bavister-Gould, Ron Beadle, Paul Blackledge, Bill Bowring,
Timothy Chappell, Russell Keat, Kelvin Knight, Marian Kuna,
Christopher Lutz, Piotr Machura, Alasdair MacIntyre, Seiriol Morgan,
Cary J. Nederman, Thomas M. Osborne Jr., Carey Seal, Benedict Smith

Themenheft Analyse & Kritik Heft 1/2008

2008. 287 S., kt. € 35,–. ISBN 978-3-8282-0442-3

This special issue is composed of revisions of papers originally presented at a conference on Alasdair MacIntyre's Revolutionary Aristotelianism: Ethics, Resistance and Utopia, hosted by the Human Rights and Social Justice Research Institute at London Metropolitan University from 29th June to 1st July 2007. In publishing them, Analyse & Kritik demonstrates a continuing interest in MacIntyre's work which began with an important symposium on After Virtue in 1984, 6(1). Now republished in a third edition, After Virtue remains central to the understanding of his work in several of the papers below (Duckworth 2007; as some papers deal with MacIntyre's theoretical development, reference is also made to different editions). As in the earlier symposium, MacIntyre responds in a way that clarifies and extends his past arguments, his present position, and his relation to rival theories of moral, social and political practice. As the title of his response suggests, much more remains to be said on the subjects that are opened here.

 *Stuttgart*

Realitäten zur Ansicht
Die Gruppendiskussion als Ort der Datenproduktion
Von Stephan Wolff und Claudia Puchta

Qualitative Soziologie Band 8

2007. VI/255 S., kt. € 36,-. ISBN 978-3-8282-0407-2

Die Gruppendiskussion ist ein qualitatives Forschungsverfahren von rapide wachsender Beliebtheit. Es ist daher bemerkenswert, dass man über die kommunikative Infrastruktur dieser Gesprächsform empirisch kaum etwas weiß.

Was passiert eigentlich in Gruppendiskussionen? In der Literatur zu diesem Erhebungsverfahren herrscht die ‚Fiktion des transparenten Fensters': Man unterstellt, dass eine geschickt bestückte und gut moderierte Gruppendiskussion einen direkten Durchblick oder interpretativ erschließbaren Tiefblick auf die Meinungen und Erfahrungen ihrer Teilnehmer erlaubt. Dieser methodologische Anspruch lässt sich aber erst überprüfen, wenn man die Gruppendiskussion nicht nur als Instrument der Forschung einsetzt, sondern als soziologischen Gegenstand betrachtet. In diesem Sinne rekonstruiert die vorliegende Studie die interaktive (Ethno-)Methodologie von Gruppendiskussionen. Sie untersucht einen breiten Materialkorpus aus der Sozialforschung und der Marktforschung und zeigt, dass Gruppendiskussionen eine kunstvolle Praxis eigener Art darstellen. Moderatoren und Gruppenmitglieder arbeiten an genau jenem Fenster, das die Forschung unterstellt: Die Beteiligten stellen gemeinsam für die praktischen Zwecke der jeweiligen Situation Transparenz her, sie dosieren sie in ihrer Durchlässigkeit, sichern und demonstrieren ihre Belauschbarkeit, kurz: sie präsentieren Realitäten zur Ansicht.

 LUCIUS & LUCIUS   *Stuttgart*

Bei Fragen zur Produktsicherheit wenden Sie sich bitte an:
If you have any questions regarding product safety,
please contact:

Walter de Gruyter GmbH
Genthiner Straße 13
10785 Berlin
productsafety@degruyterbrill.com